SPREE
KILLERS

SPREE KILLERS

The enigma of mass murder

RODNEY CASTLEDEN

Futura

FUTURA

First published in Great Britain in 2011 by Futura

Copyright © Omnipress 2011

The moral right of the author has been asserted.

A CIP catalogue record for this book
is available from the British Library.

ISBN 978-0-7088-6694-8

Typeset in Great Britain by Omnipress Limited
Printed and bound in Great Britain

Futura
An imprint of
Little, Brown Book Group
100 Victoria Embankment
London EC4Y 0DY

An Hachette UK Company
www.hachette.co.uk

www.littlebrown.co.uk

The views expressed in this publication are those of the author.
The information and the interpretation of that information is
presented in good faith. Readers are advised that where ethical
issues are involved, and often highly controversial ethical issues
at that, they have a personal responsibility for making their own
assessments and their own ethical judgements.

CONTENTS

Introduction 9

PART ONE: ANCIENT SLAYINGS: THE LONG HISTORY OF SPREE KILLING

Neolithic Mass Killings (3500 BC) 20

Homer's Heroes (1250 BC) 26

Viking Berserkers (AD 900) 31

PART TWO: MASS MURDER BY THE STATE

'Tortured and Condemned – The Spanish
     Inquisition (1483–98) 40

'Not for Three Thousand Pound!' – Protestant
     Persecution (1550s) 53

'I Can't Do It' – Jack Ketch (1663-85) 63

'Such Heavy Usage' – Charles Sanson and the
     Guillotine 1788-95 69

'Terror is the Quickest Way' – The White and Red
     Terrors in Russia (1917-22) 78

'Incomprehensible to the Normal Mind' – the
     Holocaust (1933-45) 91

'Mr Karadzic Will Explain That to the World' –
     Srebrenica (1995) 107

PART THREE: WARTIME MASSACRES

'We shall never surrender' – the Blitz (1940-41) ... 120

'Worse Than Being on the Russian Front' –
   the Bombing of Dresden (1945) 133

'A Rain of Ruin From the Air' – Hiroshima and
   Nagasaki (1945) 143

'What The Hell is Going On?' – My Lai (1968).... 158

PART FOUR: BREAKING POINT KILLERS

'We Generally Kills Them Where We Go' –
   Alton Coleman (1984) 172

'I Wish I Had Stayed in Bed' – Hungerford
   Massacre (1987) 181

'No-one Gets Away From Me' – Port Arthur
   Massacre (1996) 191

'I Can't Wait to Join You' – The Ford Hood
   Shootings (2009) 204

'Everything Seemed Normal' – Appomattox
   Shootings (2010) 211

'One Day I'm Going to Get a Gun' – Derrick
   Bird (2010).. 219

'Did the Media Help to Pull the Trigger?' – Raoul
   Moat 2010 229

PART FIVE: SCHOOL MASSACRES

'No Cause to Suspect' – the Bath School Disaster
   (1927)... 244

'Intentions Towards the Boys' – Dunblane
      Massacre (1996) 252
'No-one Should Survive' – Columbine High
      School Massacre (1999) 257
'We Must Not Think Evil of This Man' – Amish
      School Shooting (2006) 268
'Well-prepared to Continue' – Virginia Tech
      Massacre (2007) 276
'For Fun – Because it's Fun!' – Winnenden School
      Shooting (2009) 288
'Let Kip Have the Guns' – The Kip Kinkel
      Shootings (1998) 295

PART SIX: WORKPLACE KILLINGS

An Armed Citizenry? – The 101 California Street
      Killings (1993) 302
'I Hope This Won't Ruin Your Trading Day' –
      Atlanta Day-trader Killings (1999).................... 310
Going Postal – The Postal Service Murders
      (1983-2006) 321
'I Can't Give You Excuses': the Huntsville
      Shootings (2010) 339
'Not Because of Name-Calling' – Hartford
      Distributors Killings (2010).............................. 348

PART SEVEN: MISSION MURDERS

'As Gruesome as You Can' – Charles Manson and
      Helter Skelter (1969).. 352

Pan Am Flight 103 – The Lockerbie Bombing
  (1988).. 383
9/11 (2001) 405
911 Days After 9/11 – the Madrid Train Bombings
  (2004)... 419
7/7 – The London Bombings (2005) 429
'Get the Gun!' – The Tucson Assassination
  Attempt (2011).. 440

INTRODUCTION

There is a clear distinction between mass murder (or spree killing) and serial killing. Both serial killers and mass murderers are multiple killers with lots of victims. The difference is that serial killers usually murder their victims one at a time. The murder is followed by a cooling-off period when the killer returns to functioning normally, maybe for weeks or months, before killing again. Then there is another cooling-off period. Mass murderers kill and kill again – and again – within a short time with no cooling-off period in between. The killing happens in one surge of action, one rage, often lasting just one day. A killing spree. There are some exceptions to this, but generally the distinction is clear: serial killers kill one victim at a time and mass murderers kill all their victims at once or in quick succession over a matter of hours, while the rage lasts.

The second half of this book deals mainly with the dangerous, lone, breaking-point killers. In England in 2010 there were two high-profile cases of men going berserk and shooting several people, Derrick Bird and Raoul Moat. These are people who are pushed over the edge of sanity by a variety of circumstances, perhaps the breakdown of family relationships, perhaps stress or unfair treatment at work, perhaps financial problems, and often a pile-up of several different sorts of problem. The stress generates rage and the rage generates violence. Pushed beyond breaking-point, the killer sometimes lashes out randomly at whoever happens to be to hand, perhaps a group of co-workers. Often the killing starts with a significant choice of target. The target may be family members, especially if the stress has been generated within the family. In these situations, the killer starts by killing selected members of the family in cold blood, and then, psyched up for killing, he goes outside and kills whoever he happens to meet, perhaps someone passing in the street, completely at random. The Derrick Bird killings were of just this type, targeted killings followed by random killings. And just as frequently there is a third stage – suicide. The rage burnt out and with the realisation dawning that he has gone too far, the killer shoots himself. This pattern is so common that it implies that it is the suicide that may be the real focus. First, *I can't go on like this, so I'll kill myself; then, why don't I take some other people with me? Why don't I punish the people*

who have made my life so intolerable, and kill them too?
So the suicide may in many of these cases be an integral and crucial part of the psychology of the action.

There are other kinds of mass murder, very different in scale and motivation. At the other end of the scale from Derrick Bird, the lone killer, is the Third Reich, where the state machine is geared to exterminating perceived enemy groups within the state. It is not just a particular family member who is perceived as making the killer's individual life a misery, it is an entire racial group within the state that is seen as threatening the state's communal stability and well-being. In the 1930s and 40s, Germany was gripped by a kind of collective insanity that led to the mass murder of millions of people. The Holocaust is unfortunately not a unique event in human history, but it is perhaps the most extreme of its kind – a genocide.

And there are many kinds of spree-killing madness at intermediate scales in between these two extremes.

Some of the lone breaking-point killers are unstable misfits who are going to go off the rails at some point, but many are, again like Derrick Bird, inconspicuous people who keep their problems to themselves for as long as they can. Many are male, generally conventional, accepting of received societal values, conformist, and they come from lower-middle-class backgrounds. It is rare for mass murderers to be rich. They are usually men who are aspiring, trying to make their way in the world, perhaps finding it something of a struggle, and not quite in control of the events around them. They are trying to achieve more than they can. They see their ambitions thwarted and seek to blame the people round them for keeping them down. They feel excluded from the social or economic group that they would like to join and develop an unreasoning hatred for the members of that group. Because they are outwardly so conventional, often rigidly so, it is an enormous shock to those who think they know them well when they go berserk and kill six people at work.

There are many different paths to mass murder. Some people are frustrated by their family circumstances. Christopher Speight is a particularly sad example of someone stressed beyond endurance by a developing situation over which he has no control, in his own home. He feels in the end that the only thing he can do is to shoot his way out of it. So family annihilation is one all-too-common type of mass murder.

There are also the military enthusiasts, the gun fanatics who can't resist trying their hand at taking a shot at moving targets. Often when they are handling their guns they fantasise, and in their minds they become commandoes, snipers, sharp-shooters or assassins. And this is where a country's laws about gun ownership play a vital role. In countries where gun ownership is tightly restricted and there are few guns in private hands, this type of crime is rare. In countries where there is a long tradition of private gun ownership, and the gun laws are permissive, there are many more cases of people going crazy with guns and committing mass murder.

A third type of mass murderer is the disgruntled worker, the man (or woman) who thinks he (or she) is being treated unfairly, passed over for promotion. Worst of all is the worker who feels he has been unfairly dismissed. There have been many cases of people who are so furious at being sacked that they go home for their gun and return at once to shoot their supervisor – and one or two co-workers at the same time.

A fourth type is the school shooting, where a student gets his own back on a community for excluding or undervaluing him. This is often the flip side of the buddy culture. The Columbine School

Massacre is a classic case. School cultures that place too much emphasis on team games, on belonging to groups, on being socially successful, on having lots of friends, run a significant risk of creating angry, bitter and frustrated outsiders. The onus is on teachers to cut across peer-group pressure, which can slide so easily into bullying and oppression; instead they have to encourage individuality to flourish.

When this book was being planned, an initial thought was that 9/11 was too exceptional an event to include, that the scale of it went beyond mass murder. But further thought suggested that the murder of three thousand people by Al Qaeda terrorists, however exceptional in scale and style, was a mass murder. So it has been included, along with related events, the Madrid and London bombings of 2004 and 2005. These terrorist acts represent a very particular type of crime against humanity but, having said that, it is clear that there are large differences in the scale of the crimes described in this book. Some mass murders are the murder of a whole family, although that may be 'only' three or four people. Other mass murders are on the scale of Srebrenica or the Katyn Forest Massacre, when thousands of people were systematically destroyed, or the Holocaust, where millions died. Mass murder stretches across a much wider spectrum than at first appears possible.

Today mass murder is regarded as the ultimate horror. Someone goes berserk and kills a number of other people apparently completely at random. We feel vulnerable because there is no possibility of knowing that we are going to be targeted, and no possibility of defending ourselves. We are not safe anywhere, as the spree killing can take place at school or college, workplace, supermarket, or out in the street. We are at the mercy of the mass killer. Fortunately mass killings do not happen very often. But attitudes towards mass killing have not always been exactly as they are today.

It is particularly worthwhile to explore the nature of mass murder, because it keeps on happening. A reason for looking closely at mass murders is that we need to understand why they happen. There is a possibility that we are doing something to one another that makes certain individuals behave in this way, that as a society we malfunction. What are we doing that turns some people into frustrated and aggressive outsiders? Could we change the way we interact with one another to stop this from happening? Or is it the case that inside everyone, even the most ordinary, well-adjusted and well-balanced person, there is a streak of destructiveness that seeks to find gratification? Like the apparently normal middle-aged woman who threw a harmless little cat into a bin and left it there for fifteen hours?

The alternative is that a percentage of every population is psychopathic and that we are just not very good at identifying individuals who belong to this group. This is an idea that emerged in my book *Serial Killers*. Psychopaths are often very clever at covering up their 'illness'; often they can be superficially sociable, outgoing people, and they are therefore able to deceive the people they work with and even their own families into believing that they are normal and safe; they are able to win the confidence of their victims in the same way.

Are mass murderers psychopaths of the same kind as serial killers? Or are they a special type of pyschopath?

We certainly need to understand them better – not in order to forgive them, and not in order to mitigate the awfulness of their crime, but for a purely pragmatic reason. We need, if we can, to rescue more potential mass murderers before they commit their crime, and in effect save ourselves. If we can identify the people around us who are developing in a direction that may lead them eventually to commit mass murder, we may be able to avert these terrible tragedies. Mass murderers have co-workers, family members and neighbours, and if they can recognise the signs, the symptoms of the mental illness, they may be able to prevent the ultimate tragedy: the random, pointless slaughter of innocent people.

The terrible school killings and the workplace rage killings have the texture of modern crimes, as if they are manifestations of some sickness of twentieth and twenty-first century urban living. Yet when we look back into history, we will see that mass murders, on every scale, have always happened. They are part of the common fabric of human life, part of the shadow side of human behaviour. Examining a sample of these past mass murders may give an insight into the mechanisms involved. Most of all we need to be able to find ways of dealing with spree killers and the unfortunate men and women who are potential spree killers.

Because of its subject matter, this has been a challenging book to write and it may be a challenging book to read. Together, as writer and reader, we are travelling to a dark place, and there is no point in pretending otherwise. But I have found some inspiring incidents along the way – people who, confronted with extreme danger, show extraordinary courage and selflessness, and some who literally sacrifice themselves so that others can live. I think of two little girls asking a deranged gunman to kill them first, in the hope that other, younger girls held hostage might have a chance to escape. This is really the peak: human beings can't behave much better than this. And when it comes to the mass murderers, you may find as I do that you will pity many of them, hate what they do and grieve for their victims, but understand something of the torment that leads them to do what they do. They are often tortured and damaged people – but they are no less dangerous for that.

PART ONE

ANCIENT SLAYINGS

THE LONG HISTORY OF SPREE KILLING

NEOLITHIC MASS KILLINGS
(3500 BC)

Many of us like to think of the ancient past as a peaceful idyll, a time when people lived in harmony with nature and one another – but there is increasing archaeological evidence that there was a significant level of violence. There is also some documentary evidence for this violence. Even in the otherwise idyllic account the Bible gives of the birth of Jesus, we get a glimpse of something much darker and more barbaric in King Herod's mass murder: the slaying of all the male children under the age of two in the region of Bethlehem.

In Britain in the neolithic period, people lived mainly in small scattered farmsteads, but here and there were some large enclosures that were early and perhaps premature experiments in town life. Some enclosures, like Stonehenge and Avebury, were purely ceremonial. Others had houses built inside, like Durrington Walls, not far from Stonehenge, and I suggested in my 1993 book *The Making of Stonehenge* that Durrington Walls was a very early British experiment in town living, four-and-a-half thousand years ago; the archaeologist Mike Parker Pearson has suggested it again recently. And town-living seems to be the breeding-ground for mass murder.

On Crickley Hill, a spur of the Cotswold escarpment in Gloucestershire, commanding a panoramic view across the Severn valley, stood a neolithic enclosure.

At Crickley Hill in 3000 BC, two deep boundary ditches were dug across the neck of the spur, with a stone wall on the inner side of each ditch. A rampart was built faced with drystone walling on its outer face and a timber stockade on the back, the whole structure topped with a wooden fence. This was a defensive structure. Within, there were houses and roadways, so the site had become a fortified village. This structure makes Crickley Hill a fascinating site, because there are very few neolithic sites in Britain that show this level of interest in defence – and defence implies agression from another quarter. The defensive wall at Crickley Hill was pierced by two entrance gaps, closed by gates. There was evidence of burning and a scatter of more than two hundred arrow-heads revealing that the settlement was attacked by aggressors outside the gates. They attacked the gates and set fire to them. The scatter of arrow-heads inside the village shows that the attackers chased the inhabitants along the streets, firing more arrows at them.

Here was a raid that may be the earliest mass murder in Britain – at least that we know about.

At Crickley Hill, there was no sign of the victims killed in this attack, but a similar attack on another neolithic enclosure on Hambledon Hill left archaeological evidence of some of those who lost their lives. Hambledon Hill in Dorset is a site that has been fortified and defended repeatedly, first in the neolithic, then in the iron age, and later still in an episode of the English Civil War, when the Clubmen (a local rebel group) made it their base; Oliver Cromwell led an attack on it in 1645.

The southern summit of Hambledon Hill is ringed by a large neolithic enclosure built in 3500 BC. Its outer earthworks are large in scale, implying that defence was a major motive. The main enclosure and the smaller enclosure beside it, the Stepleton enclosure, were both set within a large web of earthworks. In 1981, archaeologists explored the Stepleton enclosure. They found that after several rebuildings it was destroyed in a single catastrophic armed attack. There were several intact skeletons (which is unusual in British neolithic burial practice), one with a leaf-shaped arrow-head in its rib-cage.

A curiosity of this excavation is that it produced a single grape pip, which provides surprising evidence that grapes were part of the English diet five thousand years ago. The past is full of surprises.

The palisade of the Stepleton enclosure was set on fire. Presumably some of the inhabitants were killed in this attack. One youth ran for his life, carrying a baby with him. He was killed as he fled, perhaps brought down by an arrow or a slingshot, and as he fell he crushed the baby to death.

The same period of prehistory, but a continent away ... The site of the ancient city of Nagar in Syria is marked by a towering mound forty metres high, an artificial hill made of the disintegrated mudbricks from a succession of cities built on the same site. This type of artificial mound is called a tell, and this particular one is known as Tell Brak. This was one of the earliest attempts at a city in the world, with houses, large buildings, temples and workshops, and people lived there for over three thousand years. Today we take cities for granted, and in the West nearly everybody lives in a town or city. But six thousand years ago it was an experiment and this experiment in a new way of living produced tensions and stresses that can scarcely be imagined.

A short distance away from Tell Brak is Tell

Majnuna, a kind of satellite site. When it was excavated in 2006 an extraordinary discovery was made: the remains of over a hundred healthy young people from their late teens to mid-twenties. Hands and feet were missing, many of the skeletons had their skulls detached and the limb bones were gathered into piles. This would have been a very unusual ceremonial burial, and it seems we are looking at a prehistoric massacre. The hundred young people were brutally killed, butchered, and left to decompose. Then there was a huge feast, with drinking and the consumption of mutton and beef, and the remains of this feast were thrown on top of the decaying corpses. The bodies were finally buried long after death.

The archaeologists working on the site know they have only examined a sample of the bodies, and that the final body count may run into hundreds. The massacre may represent an attack by outsiders, possibly people from another city. Or it may be connected with the social conflicts within the settlement, brought on by the process of urbanisation itself. It is no coincidence that the massacre happened at a time when the nearby city of Brak was growing at an unprecedented rate. And this was all happening in 3500 BC.

Archaeology only gives occasional glimpses of such killings, but they certainly happened, and we can be sure that they happened again and again throughout prehistory, from 3500 BC through the late neolithic, bronze age and iron age.

HOMER'S HEROES
(1250 BC)

The great Greek epic poem, the *Iliad*, was written down for the first time around 700 BC, from versions that had been handed down from memory across several generations. It seems extraordinary that bards were able to memorise 15,000 lines of poetry, but it is a feat that is achievable. In both Ireland and eastern Europe as recently as the last century, bards were able to recite very long poems from memory. The *Iliad* was a story about an episode in the Trojan War, which happened in 1250 BC, so at least parts of the story (some historical, some fictitious) were remembered across a span of five hundred years before they were written down.

The resulting poem is a strange hybrid, with elements that date from the time when it was written down and other elements that date from earlier times, some even from the time of the Trojan War itself.

The *Iliad* is famous for describing a style of warfare that is quite alien to us, but which seems to have been characteristic of the bronze age. Julius

Caesar saw vestiges of this ancient way of fighting when he encountered the 'barbarians' of northern Europe – the Gauls and Britons. One feature of this old way of fighting was the war cry. The Celts were known for making a terrible noise to intimidate their enemies immediately before a battle. Their heroes or champions also rode in chariots to the front line to offer insults to the enemy and there were challenges to single combat before the general melee of the battle commenced.

The battles in the *Iliad* often have these same elements. Achilles and the other heroes have their characteristic war-cries that they give before going into battle. Homer does not tell us what these war-cries were, but presumably they were some kind of wordless yelling that could not have been written down anyway. And of course the aristocratic heroes famously rode against one another on their chariots, freely insulted and provoked their opponents, and fought one-to-one duels. Homer dwells on these exploits of the heroes, and often the surging masses of the armies behind them is ignored in the narrative.

During the battles, the warrior-heroes in the *Iliad* were sometimes described as having their aristeia. This was a special moment for them during the battle when they became, for a time, invincible and god-like – killing and killing anyone who came against them. It was during the aristeia that they attained their heroic peak of mass slaying on the battlefield. Homer thought the aristeia was the hallmark of the great warrior-hero. This kind of mass murder, on the field of battle, was regarded as defining the hero, rendering him worthy of unqualified respect and admiration.

But gratuitous killing off the battlefield was strongly frowned upon. A classic example of this comes from a lost poem. This was the ancient prequel to the *Iliad*, which in my re-creation of the poem I call *The Apple of Discord*. Although the poem itself disappeared about 1,500 years ago, detailed summaries were made before the last few copies were lost, so we know exactly what the poem was about.

When the Greeks arrived in their ships to begin the siege of Priam's city, Achilles rode out onto the Plain of Troy and saw in the distance two people on horseback, riding out of the city of Troy, southwards towards the next town, Thymbra. Urged by Athena, the story tells us, Achilles sped off to intercept them. One of the two figures in the distance was a youth called Troilus, the other was Polyxena, his sister. They were Trojans, and they were children of King Priam. They stopped to collect water from a fountain-shrine, and there Troilus was ambushed by Achilles. While Achilles was fully armed, Troilus was completely unarmed and taken by surprise. Troilus ran out, mounted his horse and tried to escape, but Achilles, often described by Homer as swift or fleet-footed, or fast runner, overtook Troilus' horse and pulled Troilus off by his long hair. The youth ran into a temple, the Temple of Thymbrian Apollo, hoping for the safety of sanctuary, but Achilles followed him in and butchered him, literally cutting him to pieces.

The people of Troy, from King Priam downwards, were shocked and horrified at this pointless and cruel murder. Achilles' slaying of Troilus was gratuitous and unheroic. The two were not matched in battle skills, and Troilus was caught unarmed and unprepared. Nor was it just the Trojans who disapproved: the Greeks disapproved of Achilles' action too. Achilles was in temporary disgrace. Killing had to have an appropriate context.

Much later, came another story featured in two more lost poems that came after the Iliad, one called *The Ethiopian* or *The Coming of Memnon*, the other called the *Little Iliad*. This was the strange story of the Greek hero Ajax slaughtering a harmless flock of sheep. After his Achilles' death in battle a quarrel broke out between Odysseus and Ajax about which of them should have the dead hero's armour. It was special, not just because it had belonged to Achilles, but because it had been made by the god Hephaistos. When it was decided that Odysseus should have the armour, Ajax was bitterly disappointed and humiliated – so much so that he lost his reason. In a fit of mad rage, Ajax went berserk and killed a flock of sheep. Ajax's mass slaughter of sheep was thought disgraceful in much the same way as Achilles' murder of Troilus. Ajax himself saw this as soon as he regained his sanity and in his shame he committed suicide in an attempt to retrieve some honour. The dramatist Sophocles took this episode and wrote a drama about it.

We can see from these examples that binge-killing, spree-killing, has a very long history, reaching right back four and five thousand years.

VIKING BERSERKERS
(AD 900)

Berserkers are the Norse warriors described in Old Norse literature as fighting in a nearly uncontrollable trance-like fury. Probably the warriors worked themselves up into a rage before going into battle, and some have suggested that they consumed narcotic substances to help them do this. The condition is said to have begun with shivering, chattering of the teeth and chill in the body: then the face swelled and changed in colour. The warriors became hot-headed, then raged, howling like wild animals, and cut down everything they met without discriminating between friend or foe. They killed anyone in sight, unable to distinguish between friend and foe. After the berserker phase came to an end, the warriors were overtaken by lassitude and exhaustion, which could last for several days.

According to tradition the berserkers wore a shirt or coat made from a bearskin or wolfskin. One early reference in a ninth century poem in honour of Harald Fairhair describes them as 'men clad in wolf skins':

I'll ask of the berserkers, you tasters of blood,
Those intrepid heroes, how are they treated,
Those who wade out into battle?
Wolf-skinned they are called. In battle,
They bear bloody shields.
Red with blood are their spears when they fight,
The prince in his wisdom puts trust in such men
Who hack through every shield.

King Harald Fairhair used berserkers as shock troops. In the thirteenth century, Snorri Sturluson wrote about them in a saga:

Odin's men rushed forward without armour, were as mad as dogs or wolves, bit their shields, and were as strong as bears or wild oxen, and killed people at a blow.'

In the frenzy of battle, a berserker was believed to be transformed, shape-shifted into a wolf or bear. Of one berserker it was said, 'He slew more with his forepaws than any five of the King's champions. Blades and weapons glanced off him, and he brought down both men and horses in King Hjorvard's forces, and everything which came in his path he crushed to death with his teeth, so that panic and terror swept through King Hjorvard's army…'

The concept of immunity in battle may flow from a kind of anaesthetic effect of the berserker rage. The warrior may actually have stopped noticing blows and wounds while he was in this heightened state. A warrior who continued fighting while sustaining mortal wounds would have been a terrifying opponent.

The berserker is associated with the god Odin. Adam of Bremen, in describing the All-father says, in Latin, *Woden – id est furor* or 'Woden – that means fury.' The name Odin derives from an Old Norse word that means 'rage' or 'fury', bringing to mind the berserker's madness. Odin was a shape-shifter. The berserker, too, was often said to change into the form of a beast, or at least take on the ferocious qualities of the wolf or bear.

It is likely that the berserker was a member of the cult of Odin. The practices of such a cult would have been a secret of the group's initiates, although the Byzantine emperor Constantine VII refers in his *Book of Ceremonies* to a Gothic Dance performed by members of his Varangian guard, who took part wearing animal skins and masks: this may have been connected with berserker rites. This type of costumed dance is also seen in figures from Swedish helmet plates and scabbard ornaments, which depict human figures with the heads of bears or wolves, dressed in animal skins but having human hands and feet. These figures often carry spears or swords, and are depicted as running or dancing. One plate from Torslunda, Sweden, may show the figure of Odin dancing with a berserker.

Other ritual practices attributed to berserkers may represent the initiation of the young warrior into a band of berserkers. Such bands, often numbering twelve warriors, are mentioned in the sagas.

The physical appearance of the berserker was calculated to be terrifying. There are parallels between the berserkers and the tribe called the Harii described in the *Germania of Tacitus*. The tribesmen used not only 'natural ferocity' but dyed their bodies to cause panic and terror in their enemies. This is similar to the berserker combining his fearsome reputation with animal skin dress to suggest the terrifying metamorphosis of the shape changer. Ulf, a retired berserker, is mentioned in this light in Egil's *Saga Skallagrimsonar*.

But every day, as it drew towards evening, he would grow so ill-tempered that no-one could speak to him, and it wasn't long before he would go to bed. There was talk about his being a shape-changer, and people called him Kveld-Ulf ('Evening Wolf').

In the sagas, berserkers are often described as fantastically ugly, often being mistaken for trolls, as were Skallagrim and his kinsmen in Egil's *Saga Skallagrimsonar*. Egil himself is described as being 'black-haired and as ugly as his father', and at a feast in the court of the English king Athelstan, Egil is said to have made such terrible faces that Athelstan was forced to give him a gold ring to make him stop:

His eyes were black and his eyebrows joined in the middle. He refused to touch a drink even though people were serving him, and did nothing but pull his eyebrows up and down, now this one, now the other.

There may be some clues to the mindset of modern mass murderers in the Norse berserkers. During the berserker 'bout', the berserker seems to have lost all human reason; he was in a condition in which he could not distinguish between friend and enemy, and which was accompanied by bestial screaming. In *Arrow-Odd's Saga*, Odd remarks upon hearing a group of berserkers, 'Sometimes I seem to hear a bull bellowing or a dog howling, and sometimes it's like people screaming.' And the aftermath of the berserker bout was characterised by complete physical debility. Egil's *Saga Skallagrimssonar* says:

> *What people say about shape-changers or those who go into berserk fits is this: that as long as they're in the frenzy they're so strong that nothing is too much for them, but as soon as they are out of it they become much weaker than normal. That's how it was with Kveldulf; as soon as the frenzy left him he felt so worn out by the battle he'd been fighting, and grew so weak as a result of it all that he had to take to his bed.*

A common technique that was used by saga heroes to overcome berserkers was to wait, and catch them after their madness had left them, as Hjalmar and Arrow-Odd do in *Herverar Saga*, and slay the berserkers while they lay in their enfeebled state after their fury had ended.

As superb warriors, the berserkers were admired. Both King Harald and King Halfdan employed berserker shock-troops. Aside from their military value, the berserker's ties to Odin would have been welcome in a royal army, since Odin had a particular association with rulership. Odin was venerated in Anglo-Saxon England as the ancestor of chieftains, and throughout the North as god of kings and protector of their royal power. But their usefulness was limited. A particular problem was their tendency to turn indiscriminately upon their friends while the madness was upon them. This went squarely against the heroic ethic, which demanded fidelity to friends. An eleventh-century monument raised in Soderby in Uppland, Sweden in memory of a brother reads: 'And Sassur killed him – he betrayed his comrade.'

Not surprisingly, because of this capacity for treachery, the berserkers became stock villains in the sagas, portrayed as murderous, stupid brutes. They were seen as a predatory group of brawlers and killers who repeatedly disrupted the peace of the Viking community. The berserker is in fact the persona that we often call 'Viking', the type of warrior who harries and pillages the neighborhood, spilling great quantities of blood, devastating homes, and butchering men and women indiscriminately – the ultimate spree killer.

PART TWO

MASS MURDER BY THE STATE

'Tortured and Condemned'
THE SPANISH INQUISITION (1483-98)

The Spanish Inquisition had its beginnings when a mischief-making Dominican friar persuaded Queen Isabella, during her stay in Seville in 1477–8, that some Andalusians posing as Christians were secret Jews, or *conversos*. A formal investigation led to a report by the Archbishop of Seville and another Dominican friar, Tomás de Torquemada, and their report corroborated the rumour. A kind of witch-hunt was launched. The monarchs, Ferdinand and Isabella, set up the Inquisition to uncover and punish the crypto-Jews. They tried to get papal approval for this, but Pope Sixtus IV was very reluctant to give it. He issued a bull – a formal order – to stop the Inquisition, but Ferdinand was able to apply pressure. He threatened to withdraw military support at a moment when the Turks were threatening Rome. Sixtus IV gave in and in November 1478 published a bull allowing the establishment of the Inquisition in the Kingdom of Castile; it also allowed the monarchs the authority to name the inquisitors. The first two inquisitors were Miguel de Morillo and Juan de San Martin.

Heretics were duly found and put to death, in public executions. The first of these was held in Seville on 6 February 1481, when six people were burned to death. After that the Inquisition developed rapidly. By 1492 there were tribunals (committees sitting in judgement) in eight towns in Castile. Pope Sixtus IV was still very unhappy with this systematic persecution and issued a new bull that banned any extension of the Inquisition into Aragon. He was very explicit about his objections too; he hated the Inquisition because it was cruel and unjust.

Many true and faithful Christians, because of the testimony of enemies, rivals, slaves and other low people – and still less appropriate – without tests of any kind, have been locked up in secular prisons, tortured and condemned like relapsed heretics, deprived of their goods and properties, and given over to the secular arm to be executed, at great danger to their souls, giving a pernicious example and causing scandal to many.

But Ferdinand went on undeterred, applying pressure on the Pope to issue another new bull, in late 1483, naming Torquemada Inquisitor-General of Aragon, Valencia and Catalonia. Torquemada, whose name has become indelibly and infamously identified witrh the Spanish Inquisition ever since, quickly set up procedures. A court was to be announced with a thirty-day period for confessions and the gathering of accusations by neighbours. The sort of evidence that he was looking for was the absence of smoke from the chimney on Saturdays, which was taken as sign that the family might be secretly honouring the Jewish Sabbath. The court was to use physical torture to extract confessions from those accused. The crypto-Jews were allowed to confess and do penance; those who lapsed were burned at the stake. Jews had been allowed to gain acceptance in Spain by converting to Christianity, and there was a suspicion that some, perhaps many, of the 'converts' had not genuinely converted at all. The aim of the Inquisition was to identify those who had not properly converted and make them give up Jewish practices.

A new pope, Innocent VIII, tried in 1484 to allow victims of the Inquisition a measure of justice by enabling them to appeal to Rome. Ferdinand countered this by decreeing death and confiscation of property for those who tried to avail themselves of this procedure without his consent. So by this stage the Inquisition had become unassailable, the dominant authority across all the kingdoms under the Spanish monarchy. There was rebellion. The towns of Aragon resisted the Inquisition, but the murder of one of the inquisitors, Pedro Arbues, in Zaragoza had the effect of swinging public opinion in the Inquisition's favour.

Torquemada was active between 1483 and 1498, but the activity of the Inquisition continued over a longer period; it was still very active until 1530.

How many people were killed by the Inquisition? Estimates vary. One historian has estimated that 8,800 people were burnt and 9,634 were punished in other ways. Other historians put the figures lower. About 2,000 were executed, based on the auto da fe documentation. One researcher claims that between 92 and 99 per cent of those judged were of Jewish origin, though it is difficult to know how reliable this statistic might be. In any case, what was being judged was whether they had genuinely converted to Christianity, rather than what they had been before. In 1498 the pope was trying to gain acceptance for his view that the New Christians should be accepted and treated with leniency, an approach that was far more progressive and liberal than the approach of those in control in Spain.

The Spanish authorities then took the line that the converts were being subverted and seduced by contact with Jews, and that to bring the converts into the Christian fold the remaining Jews must be expelled. This was the rationale for the Alhambra Decree of January 1492. How many Jews were forced to leave Spain at this time is not known, though historians believe the number was very high, certainly over 40,000 and perhaps as many as 800,000. The Jews who were forced to leave Castile went mainly to Portugal, but they were expelled from there too five years later. The Jews who left Aragon went mainly to Italy. Of the tens of thousands of Jews who accepted baptism in order to stay in Spain, it was suspected that many were not making a sincere change of faith; this put renewed impetus and energy into the Inquisition, to find out which of the converts were insincere.

This persecution of Jews or *conversos* went on until 1530, but after that the Inquisition trials had a different focus – most, though not all, of the accused after that date were backsliding, heretical Christians. The last person to be tried for being a crypto-Jew was Manuel Santiago Vivar, and he was tried in Cordoba as late as 1818.

The Inquisition had other targets besides Jews. It was concerned to examine Moriscos, who were Muslim converts to Christianity, and similarly suspected of practising Islam in secret. Generally this group was not treated so severely, because the commercial activities of the Spanish nobility depnded to a great extent on the Moriscos. Even so, there was an eventual expulsion of the Moriscos too, in 1609. As is usual in these cases, the persecuted minority had to leave without taking with them any money, bullion or jewels; their property was confiscated.

Contrary to popular belief, the Inquisition did not have Protestants as its major target. There were very few trials involving Protestants. There were some trials of those the Inquisition labelled 'Lutheran', but the accused were mystics known as the Alumbrados. These were long trials, and in the end none of the Alumbrados were executed. Some followers of Erasmus were regarded with suspicion too. The first trials of genuine Lutherans took place around 1560, and about a hundred of them were executed. This virtually brought Spanish Protestantism to an end. Many of the later trials of so-called Protestants were really trials of misbehaviour that contained no real issue of faith, such as disrespect to church images, or eating meat on the wrong days. But those found guilty were burnt anyway.

Witchcraft was another target for the Inquisition, though the witch-hunt was far less severe than it was in England, perhaps because there were enough alternative imaginary enemies to deal with. Oddly, the Inquisition took an enlightened view of witchcraft allegations, seeing them as no more than groundless superstition. Other offences dealt with by the Inquisition included blasphemy, bigamy, bestiality and sodomy.

The Inquisition had no budget, so it relied on confiscation from its victims for its funding – a self-evident motive for corruption and miscarriage of justice. It comes as no surprise that many of those prosecuted were rich. A converso pleaded with the king to change this practice. The inquisitors' expenses should not come from the properties of the condemned; as it was, 'if they do not burn, they do not eat'.

The documents relating to the Spanish Inquisition are remarkably complete, and the trials and procedures were recorded in great detail. The interrogators were not allowed to draw blood or cause permanent damage, but this still left open a wide range of torture techniques to obtain confessions, and these were applied to people of any and every age, including children. One technique, the *garrucha*, consisted of suspending the victim from the ceiling by the wrists, tied behind the back.

Sometimes weights were tied to the ankles, with a series of lifts and drops, during which the arms and legs were sometimes dislocated. The *toca* consisted of stuffing a gag into the victim's mouth and spilling water from a jar onto it so that the victim had the sensation of drowning. This is identifiable as an early version of waterboarding, and it would find approval in many parts of the world today. The *poltro*, the rack, was the form of torture used most frequently. Confessions obtained by torture were legitimised by a disingenuous note to the effect that the subject had freely confessed to the offences – after the torture had ended. In this way all confessions acquired through torture could be made to seem valid.

The outcome of a trial could be acquittal, though this rarely happened. The trial could be suspended. Then the accused went free, but remained under suspicion and could be recalled for a resumption of the trial. This was a way of letting someone go without admitting that they had been wrongly accused. Alternatively, the accused was held in prison long-term until the trial resumed. The accused could be penanced or reconciled, which meant being required to own up to and renounce their crimes in public, and accept a punishment, which might be a fine or a sentence to the galleys. The most extreme punishment was misleadingly called *relaxation*. This meant surrendering the accused to the secular authority for burning at the stake. The Church in this way carefully ensured that it did no actual murder, not even judicial murder. That was always done by someone else. If the condemned repented, they were shown mercy by being garrotted before they were burned; if not, they were burned alive.

In the early days of the Inquisition, before 1530, nearly half the trials ended with the death penalty being imposed. After that date, the courts were more lenient.

The notorious *auto da fe* ceremony, which could be public or private, involved either a formal solemn return to the Church or a punishment as an unrepentant heretic. Over the course of time the *auto da fe* became elaborated into a baroque public spectacle, generally held on holidays. The last public *auto da fe* took place in 1691. Executions never happened at an auto da fe; they were held separately, later, though for those undergoing the experience this would have seemed a technicality. *Autos da fe* happened as early as 1242, in Paris, but the ceremony was not conducted in Spain until 1481. The six Spanish men and women subjected to this ritual were afterwards executed.

If executing people as heretics seems barbarous, it comes as a shock to discover that the last execution in Spain for heresy happened as late as 1826 – the victim was a schoolteacher called Cayetano Ripoll.

The man whose name is most closely associated with the Spanish Inquisition is Tomás de Torquemada, who was born in Valladolid in Castile-Leon. In his early life he served as a monk and cook at the Dominican monastery in Valladolid, but somehow rose to become advisor to King Ferdinand and Queen Isabella. He had been Isabella's confessor, and it was she who had him appointed Inquisitor-General in 1483. He was the Grand Inquisitor of Spain from 1483 until his death in 1498. We see him now as the epitome of mad fanaticism and implacability. It is possible that his fanaticism was driven partly by his own Jewish background. Torquemada's ancestor Alvar Fernandez de Torquemada married a first-generation Jewish *conversa*. Torquemada's grandmother was also a *conversa*.

Under his direction, the Spanish Inquisition grew from a single tribunal operating at Seville to a network of over twenty tribunals. He was one of the principal supporters of the Alhambra Decree, ordering the mass expulsion of Jews from Spain.

Torquemada had enormous power. The pope tried

repeatedly to rein in the power of the Inquisition, but Ferdinand in effect banned anyone accused by the Inquisition of appealing to Rome. Every Christian male in Spain over the age of fourteen and every female over the age of twelve was answerable to the Inquisition and therefore to Torquemada. Anyone who spoke against the Inquisition could fall under suspicion. Both St Teresa of Avila and St John of the Cross came under suspicion in this way.

Torquemada fanatically promoted the burning of non-Catholic literature, especially the Talmud; after the defeat of the Moors in 1492, he advocated burning Arabic books as well. He was an extremist, but few dared oppose him. Pope Sixtus dared, and his outspoken words (quoted earlier) show clearly how worried liberal-minded people were at the direction the Inquisition was taking.

Because the Inquisition had no jurisdiction over the Jews, Torquemada was uneasy about their continuing presence in Spain. It was he who urged Ferdinand and Isabella to compel all the Jews in Spain either to convert to Christianity or to leave Spain. In an attempt to frustrate this plan, the Jews agreed to pay the Spanish government 30,000 ducats if they were left unmolested. Tradition has it that, when Ferdinand was about to give in to this offer, Torquemada appeared, bearing a crucifix and shouting, 'Judas Iscariot sold Christ for thirty pieces of silver; Your Highness is about to sell him for 30,000 ducts. Here He is; take Him and sell Him.' He left the cross on the table and left. Largely through Torquemada's insistence, the Jews were expelled from Spain in 1492.

Some of Torquemada's contemporaries thought highly of him. He was 'the hammer of heretics, the light of Spain, the saviour of his country, the honour of his order.' But others agreed with Pope Sixtus, that what he was doing was pernicious and scandalous. He was widely and intensely hated. At one time public hatred for him had grown to such a pitch that he could only travel safely with a huge retinue of fifty mounted bodyguards and 250 armed men.

In the fourteen years Torquemada served as Inquisitor-General, he caused thousands of men, women and children to be tortured and executed. One historian has computed that during the period 1483-1498, Torquemada's term of office, 8,800 people suffered death by fire; 9,654 people suffered in other ways. But these figures have been challenged by other historians, and there is a convergence on a figure nearer 2,000 burnings. It is still an alarming and disturbing number of needless killings.

Tomás de Torquemada died of natural causes in Avila in 1498. The personal hatred did not stop with his death. In 1832, Torquemada's tomb was ransacked, and his bones were seized and burnt. It was a kind of late and futile revenge on one of the cruellest of mass murderers.

'NOT FOR THREE THOUSAND POUND!'
PROTESTANT PERSECUTION (1550S)

After the death of Henry VIII's Protestant son, Edward VI, there was an unsuccessful attempt at a coup by Northumberland on behalf of Lady Jane Grey. When this failed, Mary Tudor, Henry VIII's elder daughter, became queen. She was no Protestant but a committed Catholic and she was determined to restore England to Catholicism. Many in the upper classes had made huge gains from the sell-off of Church properties during the Dissolution of the monasteries, and there was little enthusiasm for a return to Catholicism.

When she became queen of England in 1553, Mary apparently had no idea that a return to Catholicism would be the great struggle it proved to be. She believed that people longed for a return to the old religion, and she had no intention of instigating persecution. Protestant clergy were replaced by Catholic clergy. Prominent Protestants like Cranmer, Latimer and Ridley were imprisoned.

Much of the Protestant legislation of her brother was repealed, including the Prayer Books and the marriage of the clergy. Those who refused to attend Catholic acts of worship were to be punished. The Act of Supremacy, putting the monarch at the head of the church in England, was annulled; in 1554 the country was restored to allegiance to the Pope. Mary hoped to take England back to the state it had been in before the Dissolution. The monasteries, convents and friaries were to be restored, though this was going to be much more difficult, because the monastic estates had been broken up and sold off during the years of change. Work began on restoring statues and paintings in churches, and re-creating the great crucifixes that had been taken away.

There was resistance to all this change, and in 1555 the persecution of Protestants started. Those who would go along with the return to Catholic worship were to be left alone, but those who refused to conform would be tried, pressed to conform and, if all else failed, executed for heresy. Queen Mary became increasingly unpopular. The persecutions and her controversial marriage to the head of an enemy state – Philip II of Spain – alienated the support of the common people. As far as the persecutions were concerned, Mary herself appeared to be the fanatical driving force. She believed that the more of her subjects she burnt for heresy, the more favour she would be shown by God. She wanted a child, and when she failed to become pregnant, she saw this as a sign that she was being too tolerant of Protestantism. Her advisors saw that this policy of intolerance and persecution was extremely damaging politically, but Mary was adamant.

In four calendar years, 1555-1558, she caused three hundred people to be burnt to death. These executions took place in Suffolk, Essex, London, Kent and Sussex. Some high-profile clergymen were burnt at the stake for heresy, notably Cranmer, Latimer and Ridley, but there were also very ordinary people who were burnt to death, and this gratuitous focus on the powerless made her deeply unpopular.

During these times, her half-sister, the Princess Elizabeth, Queen Ann Boleyn's daughter, became more and more popular. As she watched Mary's reign unfolding, Elizabeth must have been watching, listening, thinking, learning how, and how not, to govern England.

Lines of poetry were later dedicated to the queen-in-waiting:

When these with violence were burnt to death,
We prayed to God for our Elizabeth.

Burning people to death for heresy was a customary punishment in England. But Mary's definition of heresy was odd; heresy was a religious belief other than her own. Heresy was by tradition a minority belief. As it happened, during Mary's reign Protestantism was the majority faith in England, so the Queen was in effect putting most of her subjects outside the law.

Sussex produced its share of rebels. In the summers of 1555, 1556 and 1557, seventeen Protestant martyrs were burnt in the street in Lewes. Four were burnt in the village of Mayfield in the autumn of 1556 and two more in Lewes. None of these unfortunate people were very high-profile. The most prominent of them was Richard Woodman, a wealthy yeoman farmer and ironmaster who lived at Warbleton. He employed a hundred people, which in itself made him a significant local public figure. He was a staunch Protestant. He publicly condemned George Fayrebank, the curate at Warbleton, 'for turning head to tail'; Fayrebank had been a Protestant under Edward VI but turned Catholic under Queen Mary. Fayrebank had Woodman arrested. In order to understand the impact Woodman's tragic downfall had in Sussex, we need to look at the drawn-out sequence of events that led to his execution. In 1553 he was taken before local magistrates, who sent him to the King's Bench, where he remained in prison for over a year. Woodman was brought before the Bishop of Chichester. The bishop told Woodman he was sorry to see him a prisoner, as he had heard that he was a man greatly esteemed in the country where he lived. He and several other clerics tried to persuade him to convert, but Woodman refused.

He was questioned by Bishop Bonner at his palace close to St Paul's. The bishop often kept suspected heretics in his coalhouse. Bonner was not a gentle questioner. He beat one man's face black and blue. But he could also be charming and hospitable; he used the 'nice and nasty' method of questioning.

In December 1555 Bishop Bonner unexpectedly released Woodman and four other prisoners. Woodman went about angering prominent Sussex Catholics with his opinions, and his re-arrest was ordered. When officers came to arrest him in Warbleton, he asked to see the warrant. They had not brought it, so he refused to go with them. While one went to fetch the warrant, Woodman managed to get away. For six weeks he hid in a wood, where his supporters supplied him with food.

After the hue and cry died down, Woodman crossed the Channel. But he became homesick in

France and returned home to Warbleton, where he was betrayed by his brother. The house was surrounded, but when the sheriff's men went in Woodman was not there. They were sure Woodman must still be somewhere inside and they had been told of secret hiding places. They got very close to the secret chamber where Woodman was hiding and pressed his wife to tell them where the door was. In a panic she called out to her husband to get away while he could. His only way out was by breaking out through the roof. He leapt down into the road and ran off, but the officers caught him.

There were more interrogations, thirty-two in all. Again and again he was asked to give up his religion. 'Not for three thousand pound!' he said. While imprisoned, Richard Woodman wrote a detailed account of his experiences, including all the questions put to him and the answers he gave. He named the churchmen who had 'consented to the shedding of my blood'. All this publicised his case, ensured that everyone in Sussex would know what he had gone through. He really was 'the Iron Man' of Warbleton. Two weeks after being sentenced, Woodman was taken to Lewes with nine others. They were chained to stakes outside the Star Inn on 22 June 1557, and burnt in one great fire. The mass murder in the street outside the Star in Lewes was a traumatic event for the whole community, and it has never been forgotten. Anyone who has witnessed the Lewes Bonfire 'celebration' on 5 November will be in no doubt that the Protestant martyrs of Sussex are still remembered, and that the crimes against humanity committed by Queen Mary have been neither forgotten nor forgiven.

Queen Mary herself died in 1558, to be succeeded by the Protestant Elizabeth.

The Protestant persecutions were over. There were some executions of Catholics, but these were plotters, conspirators who intended to overthrow Elizabeth and replace her with her Catholic Scottish cousin, another Mary. In the early years of Elizabeth's reign, a commemorative book about the Protestant martyrs was published. With the change in head of state, it was safe to publish a book eulogising the Protestants who had lost their lives under Mary. What would have happened to Foxe if Elizabeth had been assassinated and replaced by the Scottish queen one can only imagine. It was called *Acts and Monuments* but became known as *Foxe's Book of Martyrs*. It was an affirmation of the Protestant Reformation in England. It went through several editions and became the official version of the events of the persecutions in the reign of Bloody Mary; its third part, the most important part in terms of influence, contained detailed accounts of the sufferings of the Marian martyrs, full of touching personal detail. Foxe's book contains a sequence of images of martyrs at the moment of their death, drawn shortly afterwards and published in 1563. One has the victim saying, 'Lord help me, and forgive them'. There were mistakes in it and Foxe had the sense to remove them, but he also documented and defended the rest. The 1570 edition became a work that was accepted by the Church of England as a sacred book in its own right. A convocation of Canterbury meeting in 1571 ordered that a copy of the *Bishop's Bible* and 'that full history entitled *Monuments of Martyrs*' should be installed in every cathedral church and that church officials should place copies in their houses for the use of servants and visitors.

The book went a long way towards establishing a long-lived national repudiation of the Roman Catholic Church, and provided an historical justification for the establishment of the Church of England. Foxe began his *Book of Martyrs* in 1552, during the reign of the Protestant King Edward VI, when the traumatic events of the reign of Mary's reign were still in the future. In 1554, from the safety of foreign exile, Foxe published the first part of his book, which had as its focus the persecution of the English Lollards in the fifteenth century. As news of contemporary persecutions crossed to the Continent, Foxe started to collect material for an unplanned final part to his book. This was published in Basle, in Latin, immediately after Mary's death. Later, he would expand this and publish it in English; it was this 1563 version that had such enormous influence. Foxe himself became England's first literary celebrity, though he made no money from his book. Catholic writers tried to write ripostes and refutations. Robert Parson, a Jesuit, wrote a *Treatise of Three Conversions of England* in 1604. Thomas Harding, another Catholic writer, described *Acts and Monuments*, 'that huge dunghill of your stinking martyrs' as being 'full of a thousand lies'. But comment like this is counter-productive. How many readers can you expect to win to your cause with a phrase such as 'your stinking martyrs'?

The mass murders ordered by Mary Tudor had the opposite effect of the one she intended. They were supposed to be a deterrent. She intended to make an example of the Protestants she punished, an example that others would not want to imitate.

In fact, the killing of the Protestant martyrs destroyed her cause, pushing Catholicism out of the mainstream of English politics for over four hundred years. Queen Mary had badly miscalculated.

'I Can't Do It'
JACK KETCH (1663-85)

Jack Ketch was probably the best known and also the most incompetent English executioner in history. He was to become a black joke, almost a cartoon figure in the seventeenth century, and the model for the Hangman in Punch and Judy.

Usually, people were hanged singly, but execution was raised to an industrial scale at the beginning at the seventeenth century. One of Jack Ketch's predecessors, Derrick, was a celebrated figure who, in about 1600, invented a huge gantry, and this could hang as many as twenty-three people at once. This new type of gallows naturally became known as a 'derrick', after its inventor. And the word quickly passed into general usage as a nickname for any contrivance for moving heavy weights about; so by the middle of the seventeenth century the hangman's surname was applied, in jest, to any kind of hoist, such as a crane on a ship for lifting cargo on board. After Derrick, Gregory Brandon became the public executioner, then his son Richard Brandon inherited the post. It was Richard Brandon who beheaded Charles I. 'Squire' Dun followed Richard Brandon.

Then came Jack Ketch, the notorious bungling Jack Ketch, though that was not his name. His real name was Richard Jacquet, but his name, ironically, was beheaded. The surname became his whole name, and that became so well known that it was used as a nickname for his successors for nearly two hundred years. He was appointed public hangman in about 1663, in the reign of Charles II.

By 1672, Jack Ketch was a well-known public figure. It was in that year that a broadside was published entitled *The Plotters Ballad, being Jack Ketch's incomparable Receipt for the Cure of Traytorous Recusants and Wholesome Physick for a Popish Contagion.* These were certainly not Ketch's own words, but words put into his mouth by the anonymous author. It was quite common for 'Confessions' to be circulated at public executions; these too were fake; although they purported to be by the condemned man or woman they were not.

Ketch had a reputation for being a very incompetent executioner. He not only killed a lot of people: he caused them undue suffering. The high-profile execution of Lord William Russell on 21 July 1683 was carried out in a very clumsy way.

A pamphlet has survived, which in this case may genuinely represent Ketch's words. In this pamphlet he makes his *Apologie*, claiming that the prisoner was to blame for not lying down properly. Lord William, he said, 'did not dispose himself as was most suitable'. Ketch also claimed he was interrupted while taking aim, which amounts to owning up to poor concentration.

It has even been suggested that Ketch's extraordinary performances were due to more than just a simple lack of dexterity. He may have been a sadist rather than a bungler, taking pleasure from inflicting pain, from teasing out what should have been a quick death into a protracted and elaborate torture. Lord William Russell's execution was a terrible event. Russell suffered horrifically under blow after blow, each excruciating but not in itself lethal. Even among the bloodthirsty crowds that habitually attended beheadings, the agonising display created outrage.

One of Ketch's most notorious executions came two years after the Russell execution: the beheading of James, Duke of Monmouth, the illegitimate son of Charles II. Monmouth had led an unsuccessful rebellion against his uncle, King James II, and was consequently condemned to death for treason in 1685. He was unfortunate to have Jack Ketch as his executioner. On climbing the scaffold, Monmouth picked up the axe and ran his fingers along the blade, nervously asking Ketch if he thought it was sharp enough for the job. He handed Ketch six guineas, promising him six more if he did a clean job: 'Pray do not serve me as you did my Lord Russell. I have heard you struck him four or five times; If you strike me twice, I cannot promise you not to stir.'

Perhaps overwhelmed at the prospect of killing the son of Charles II, or perhaps rattled by the memory of the Russell execution, Ketch had an attack of nerves and his first blow only grazed the back of the duke's head. Monmouth, who had refused the blindfold, struggled to his feet and looked reproachfully at Ketch, which unnerved the executioner even more. He tried two more blows and still failed to sever the duke's head, leaving Monmouth screaming, writhing and moaning. The crowd was not enjoying this. Ketch threw the axe down with a curse and said, 'I can't do it'. At this the Sheriff of Middlesex, who was in charge of the execution, told Ketch he would have him killed if he did not finish his job; 'Take up the axe, man.' It took two more blows to kill the duke, but they still failed to sever the head. Ketch had to draw his butcher's knife from its sheath to cut the final sinews. The duke had been right, and Ketch had not honed his axe properly. The crowd, yelling in furious protest throughout this display, was so angry that Ketch had to be escorted away under guard.

There were many tracts aimed against Ketch. One was called *The Tyburn Ghost: or, Strange Downfal of the Gallows: a most true relation how the famous Triple Tree, near Paddington, was pluckt up by the roots and demolisht by certain evil Spirits, with Jack Ketch's Lamentation for the loss of his Shop, 1678*. The triple tree of the title was a triangular horizontal timber frame standing on three supporting posts. Each beam could carry several people at once.

Tyburn had been a place of execution since the twelfth century at least. It was the place where Roger Mortimer, who ordered the murder of Edward II, was hanged without trial in 1330. In 1537, Henry VIII chose Tyburn as the place where the ringleaders of the Pilgrimage of Grace were to be executed. In 1571, the Tyburn Triple Tree was built close to where Marble Arch now stands, and in the middle of the roadway. Its first victim was Dr John Story, a Catholic who refused to acknowledge Elizabeth I as queen. It was a major West London landmark and a deliberate deterrent, a warning to travellers of the grim force of the law. The Tyburn

Tree was was sometimes called 'the three-legged mare' or 'the three-legged stool'. The structure made it possible to kill twenty-four people at a time, eight on each beam – well-organised mass murder. On 23 June 1649 twenty-four prisoners were hanged simultaneously.

Ketch died in 1686. A hundred years or so later, Ketch had become a character in Punch and Judy shows. As the executioner was nobody's friend, it delighted audiences to see Punch in the end succeeding in hanging the hangman. It was what the real Jack Ketch deserved for the unnecessary suffering he inficted. But the crowds loved to be shocked by this random cruelty: it was all part of the show.

At Newgate in 1820, when the Cato Street conspirator Thistlewood and his companions were executed for treason, the sentences were carried out and the executioner held up the heads one by one to show the the crowd. He dropped the last one and, in the spirit of the occasion the crowd yelled, 'Oh, butter-fingers!' It was an execution in the Jack Ketch tradition.

'Such Heavy Usage'

CHARLES SANSON AND THE GUILLOTINE (1788–95)

Charles Henri Sanson was born in 1739. He was the public executioner in Paris from 1788, the year before the French Revolution broke out, until 1795, when it was all over. Sanson's great-grandfather, Charles Sanson, had received the office of executioner des hautes oeuvres de Paris in 1688, and this office became hereditary, passing from father to son. It was ironic that Sanson should be responsible for beheading Louis XVI, mainly for being an hereditary head of state, when he himself held office by hereditary right, but no doubt these small ironies were unnoticeable in the *melée* of the French Revolution.

Executing was very much a family tradition, and Sanson's brothers followed the same grisly trade in other towns.

In the final days of 1789, Gorsas in the Courier de Paris accused Sanson of harbouring a royalist press in his house. Sanson was brought to trial but acquitted, and Gorsas withdrew his accusation.

Sanson is closely asociated with the hundreds of

executions carried out in the Place de la Révolution, using the guillotine. The guillotine was at the time of the Terror not only a brand-new machine, but newly invented. Monsieur Guillotin's beheading machine was approved in principle in December 1789, partly on the grounds of humanity – it would behead quickly and reliably with one stroke – it would also treat all men equally. The same death for all. Sanson himself wanted to see the guillotine introduced. He delivered a well-argued memorandum to the French Assembly, explaining that the multiple executions which were then becoming common were too demanding for the traditional methods. It was difficult for him to maintain the tools of his trade under such heavy usage. Poor lighting at the places of execution often caused him to miss the nape of the neck with his sword. Swords were expensive, and could shatter during use.

The guillotine was built, Sanson carried out successful experiments on bales of straw and several dead bodies, and he first used it for a 'live' beheading in the Place de Grève for the execution of the highwayman Pelletier on 25 April 1792. Oddly enough, while the machine was in the experimental stage it was referred to as the Louisette. The King, who was so soon to die on the machine himself, was the one who helpfully suggested the sloping blade as more efficient; the diagonal blade became a permanent feature of the guillotine. From 28 April 1792, in other words once it was in use, it became known as la Guillotine after its main advocate and designer.

Some highly romanticised stories about Sanson were circulated, but they are probably fictitious. They seem to originate in the apocryphal *Memoirs* published in France in 1829, 1830 and 1863: these were almost certainly not based on writings by Charles Henri Sanson. The real man is hard to reach. We know that he had status and was able to maintain a substantial household. As a public executioner, he needed to, as he was a social outcast. He was a cultured man who enjoyed playing the violin and cello, and listening to the music of Gluck. At the same time his hobbies are said to have included dissecting the corpses of his victims. He was clearly a man apart, not allowed to lead the normal life of a French citizen.

We can tell that he was a meticulously conscientious and coolly practical man, quite the opposite of Jack Ketch. He for example drew his own plans and elevations for the construction of the guillotine that stood in the Place de la Révolution, the machine that was to become for ever the symbol of the terror and ferocity of the Revolution. One of his sons, Gabriel, slipped and fell off the scaffold while assisting his father by displaying a victim's head to the crowd, cracked his own skull and died. Sanson's cool and practical response to this was to fit a rail round the scaffold to make sure that it did not happen again.

Later, Marie Tussaud managed to acquire the guillotine to put on display in her waxworks exhibition in London, and there it stood until the disastrous fire of the 1920s. Most of the guillotine was destroyed in the fire – most, that is, except the crucial blade, complete with its massive weight bolted onto it and the horizontal catch for releasing the blade. But Sanson's scale drawings survived and a facsimile was built from these.

Probably the most momentous execution that Sanson had to carry out was that of Louis XVI on 21 January 1793. All the shops and places of business were closed to mark the solemnity of the day. The streets were lined with soldiers just in case there was an attempt to rescue the King. The King was taken in a carriage with his confessor, the Abbé Edgeworth, to the Place de la Révolution (now Place de la Concorde). The King mounted the scaffold and then broke away from his guards and began to address the crowd. An order was given begin a drum roll; the sound of the drums drowned his voice. Sanson and his assistants took a firm hold of the King, strapped him to the plank, and tilted his body forward. The neck-piece was adjusted to hold his head in position and the knife released immediately. The confessor shouted, 'Son of St Louis, ascend to Heaven!' Sanson lifted the head from the basket and held it up for the crowd to see. The body was unstrapped from the plank, rolled into a basket and the remains were taken to the cemetery of the Madeleine. There young Marie Tussaud was waiting; she was forced by the authorities to take a death mask.

Following the execution of Louis XVI, Sanson courageously published a statement in the *Thermomètre politique*, on 13 February 1793. He was concerned about some false statements that were being circulated about the King's behaviour when confronted with death. He wanted people to know the truth of the situation. The King had not been a coward: quite the reverse. Sanson was astonished by the King's cool and firm demeanour and convinced that this had been due to the King's religious faith. The truth was that Sanson was a royalist, though he could not admit it. He had not wanted to carry out the King's execution at all.

In the autumn, it was the Queen of France's turn. This time, Charles Sanson decided he could not take the leading role: he let his son Henri do that, and he acted instead as his son's assistant. Marie Antoinette was sentenced to death by the Revolutionary Tribunal at 4 am on 16 October. Marie Antoinette was allowed to return to the Conciergerie prison for a few hours' sleep. She rose at 10am, put on a plain white dress, Sanson arrived to cut her hair short and to tie her hands behind her back. A much-hated figure – purely because she was foreign, it seems – she was made to ride to the guillotine in a tumbril, an ordinary cart, which swayed and jolted and exposed her to all the insults of the crowd. She travelled with her priest and Sanson for company. The cart stopped beneath the guillotine, red and forbidding against the sky. The Queen moved quickly up the steps to get the business over with and accidentally trod on Henri Sanson's foot. She humbly begged his pardon. He grasped her firmly and strapped her onto the plank. There was a brief pause while the neckboard was adjusted. There was a click as the lever released the blade, which rushed down onto her neck. The head and body were thrown onto a waiting handcart and wheeled to the Madeleine where, once again, Marie Tussaud was forced to take a death mask of a face that she was fond of. The face at least was serene in death. The head and body were thrown, along with sixty other bodies, into a pit and covered with quicklime.

The victims of the Reign of Terror came to Sanson by the score, day after day. He can never have imagined when taking on the task in 1788 what he would be faced with and without any reliable memoirs we can only guess what was in his mind. Hundreds of ordinary French people were to be beheaded, many because someone had denounced them and for no other reason. Then the organisers of the Revolution began condemning one another to death.

Jacques Rene Hébert, who had bitterly attacked Marie Antoinette, was sent to the guillotine for trying to bring the the National Convention and the Paris Commune into conflict; Robespierre condemned him. Jean Paul Marat's assassin, Charlotte Corday, was executed by Sanson, too.

Robespierre, the driving force behind the Terror, was himself executed by Sanson – on 28 July 1794. Jean Baptiste Carrier, himself responsible for sending hundreds to be beheaded by Sanson, was in his turn guillotined by him. Sanson was the legal executioner of all of these people, a score at a time and sometimes as fast as one a minute (his top speed); he was the hands-on killer of an astonishing number of victims, a number that has been calculated at three thousand.

In 1795, he abdicated his office in favour of his son Henri, who had been his assistant for some time. Sanson was fifty-six and had had enough of killing. Henri later explained that he and his father had acted like robots through the Revolution, because the sheer volume of work left them no time for reflection about what they were doing. It was only when the Revolution ended that the reality of what they had done came home to them, and then they wavered. Henri Sanson nevertheless continued as executioner of Paris until his death in 1840; his son Clement Henri Sanson was the last of the Sanson dynasty to hold the office. There is no record of circumstances of the death of Charles Henri Sanson, the man who killed a king and a tyrant, and so many others whose deaths are minutely recorded. But we do know that he died in 1806 and his grave, a sober stone slab with his name on it, can be found in the Montmartre cemetery.

Sanson killed 3,000 people, but the French

Revolution was responsible for a total of perhaps ten times that number of deaths by execution. After it was all over, in 1796, the journalist Louis-Marie Prudhomme compiled a *Dictionary of individuals condemned to die in the Revolution*. Prudhomme listed details of 13,000 executions – fewer than half the total, but still they filled six volumes. In the end Sanson was not the real mass murderer – it was France itself.

'TERROR IS THE QUICKEST WAY'
THE WHITE AND RED TERRORS IN RUSSIA (1917–22)

White Terror is a phrase used to describe the violence used by reactionary (often monarchist) groups as part of a counter-revolution. In the twentieth century White Terror has been used of movements in several countries to oust Communism. The names White Terror and Red Terror have their origins in the French Revolution. White was the colour of the flag of the Bourbon monarchs. Red was the colour of the flag flown by the revolutionaries and republicans.

The White Armies and other opponents of the early Soviet government carried out acts of mass violence against the civilian population. They tortured and shot people they suspected of being allied with the Bolsheviks. As the White Armies captured each town, a massacre of suspected opponents followed. The White Terror began on 28 October 1917. On that day, Moscow cadets captured revolutionary soldiers, ordered them on a pretext to line up, then opened fire on them with machine guns, killing more than three hundred people.

The Red Terror was a campaign of mass arrests and mass executions instigated by the Bolshevik government in the wake of the Russian Revolution. Russian histories used to present the Red Terror as a short episode, officially announced by Yakov Sverdlov on 1 September 1918 and ending a month later, but now the Terror is seen as going on through the entire Russian Civil War, from 1918 through to 1922. The Terror was announced in the Bolshevik newspaper in the following, alarmingly maniacal, terms:

We will turn our hearts into steel, which we will temper in the fire of suffering and the blood of fighters for freedom. We will make our hearts cruel, hard, and immovable, so that no mercy will enter them, and so that they will not quiver at the sight of a sea of enemy blood. We will let loose the flood gates of that sea … For the blood of Lenin and Uritsky, Zinoviev and Volodarski, let there be floods of the blood of the bourgeois – more blood, as much as possible.

Lenin, the Communist leader, similarly declared in mid-September 1918;

To overcome our enemies we must have our own socialist militarism. We must carry along with us ninety million out of the hundred million of Soviet Russia's population. As for the rest, we have nothing to say to them. They must be annihilated.

The mass repression was officially instigated as a retribution for the assassination of Moisei Uritsky, the chief of the Petrograd Cheka, and the attempted assassination of Lenin by Fanni Kaplan on 30 August. Lenin was recovering from his injuries as he gave instructions for the purge; 'It is necessary, secretly and urgently, to prepare the terror.' But well before the assassination and the assassination attempt he was sending telegrams about launching 'mass terror' in Nizhny Novgorod as a response to a potential civil rebellion there. Elsewhere it was considered as a way of crushing landowners in order to requisition grain for soldiers. The tone of Lenin's message is chilling and alarming.

Comrades! The kulak uprising in your five districts must be crushed without pity … You must make an example of these people. (1) Hang (I mean hang publicly, so that people see it) at least 100 kulaks, rich bastards, and known bloodsuckers. (2) Publish their names. (3) Seize all their grain. (4) Single out the hostages as per my instructions in yesterday's telegram.

*Do all this so that for miles around people see it all,
understand it, tremble, and tell themselves that we
are killing the bloodthirsty kulaks and that we will
continue to do so. Yours, Lenin. PS. Find tougher
people.*

The Bolsheviks were purging opposition in order
to hold on to power. The mass repression was
conducted completely outside the law by the secret
police, the Cheka, together with participation
by the Bolshevik military intellligence, the GRU.
The Bolsheviks claimed that the Red Terror was
necessary because of the White Terror; the aim
was to overwhelm the counter-revolutionary
forces, who must be regarded as enemies of the
people. Some Russian communists openly argued
for the extermination of entire social groups, the
former ruling classes. Lenin revelled in the Terror.
He had apparently been thinking about it for a
decade. When the King of Portugal, Carlos I, was
assassinated in 1908, Lenin commented, 'We regret
that in what happened to the king of Portugal there
is still clearly visible the element of conspiratorial, ie
impotent, terror – one that essentially fails to achieve
its purpose and falls short of that genuine, popular,
truly regenerative terror for which the Great French

Revolution became famous.' So, what Lenin wanted for Russia was a Reign of Terror like the bloodbath that formed the climax of the French Revolution. If Lenin had studied the course of the French Reign of Terror closely, he would have seen that it ran out of control and consumed and destroyed its leaders. Launching a Red Terror was an extremely risky and dangerous thing to do. But it is what Lenin did.

Lenin called for revolutionary dictatorship, as described in his 1917 work *The State and Revolution*, a dictatorship of the workers and peasants, symbol-ised by the hammer and sickle. People were marked out as enemies of the people by their social status, regardless of what they had done. The chief of the Ukrainian Cheka, Martin Latsis, explained in a newspaper:

> *Do not look in the file of incriminating evidence to see*
> *whether or not the accused rose up against the Soviets*
> *with arms or words. Ask him instead to which class*
> *he belongs, what is his background, his education, his*
> *profession. These are the questions that will determine*
> *the fate of the accused. That is the meaning and essence*
> *of the Red Terror.*

Immediately following the assassination of Uritsky, five hundred 'representatives of the overthrown classes' were executed. The newspaper *Izvestiya* carried a piece on 3 September called *Appeal to the Working Class*, which explicitly warned that anyone who dared to spread the slightest rumour against the Soviet regime would be arrested immediately and sent to a concentration camp. Huge numbers of people were rounded up and summarily executed. In Petrograd 800 enemies were shot and another six thousand imprisoned. In the first two months of the Terror at least 10,000 people were killed.

The newspapers boasted of the numbers. In Kharkov up to 3,000 people were executed in early 1919, in Rostov, 1,000 in January 1920, in Kiev over 3,000 between February and August 1919. Similar numbers of people were killed in towns all over the Soviet Union, even in the small towns.

At the end of 1920 came one of the largest massacres in the Civil War. With Lenin's approval, Bela Kun executed 50,000 White (counter-revolutionary) prisoners of war and civilian. This followed the defeat of General Wrangel's White forces. The victims were either shot or hanged, even though they had been promised an amnesty if they surrendered.

The Red Terror took place within a political situation that was extremely chaotic. In March 1919, all the military detachments of the Cheka were combined to make a single force, the Army for the Internal Defence of the Republic. This amounted to a force 200,000 strong in 1921. Lenin needed these troops in order to police the labour camps, run the concentration camps, organise requisitions of food, suppress peasant rebellions and workers' riots. It was also needed to suppress mutinies in the Red Army, where desertion was rife. The Bolshevik hold on power was fragile – and correspondingly desperate and brutal.

One of the Bolshevik government's main organisers for the Red Terror was Army Commissar Yan Berzin. He had taken part in the October Revolution, then worked in the administration of the Cheka. Berzin initiated a system for taking and shooting hostages to pre-empt desertions and other acts of disloyalty. Berzin played a big part in suppressing the Russian sailors' mutiny at Kronstadt in March 1921. He was particularly effective in chasing, capturing and killing runaway sailors.

It is estimated that over three million conscripts to the Red Army deserted in 1919 and 1920. About 500,000 deserters were arrested in 1919 and 750,000 in 1920, by Cheka troops. Thousands of deserters were killed, and their families taken hostage. Taking and executing hostages was a standard practice of the Cheka Internal Troops and the Red Army. This punishment of families was done according to Lenin's specific instructions; 'After the expiry of the seven-day deadline for deserters to turn themselves in, punishment must be increased for these incorrigible traitors to the cause of the people. Families and anyone found to be assisting them in any way whatsoever are to be considered as hostages and treated accordingly.' A typical procedure was to take the deserters' families hostage and every so often shoot one person from each family; soon the deserters would come out of hiding, perhaps in nearby woods, and give themselves up. Then a representative number of the surrendered deserters would be shot as an example. In the suppression of one rebellion alone, the Tambov rebellion, 100,000 rebels and their families were imprisoned or deported and 15,000 executed.

This campaign marked the beginning of the Gulag (concentration camp) system. As many as 70,000 people were imprisoned in camps by September 1921. Living conditions in the camps were poor and they had high mortality rates, just as a result of starvation and disease; but there were deliberate mass killings in the camps as well. At the Kholmogory camp, the Cheka took to killing their prisoners systematically by tying them up and throwing them into the River Dvina. Occasionally, if a town was about to be taken by an approaching White force, entire prisons were emptied of their inmates by mass executions.

Striking industrial workers were treated with similar harshness. In March 1919, Cheka troops attacked the Putilov factory. Over 900 workers on strike there were arrested and during the next few days two hundred of them were executed, without trial. At around the same time there were strikes in several industrial towns. They were all suppressed in the same ruthless way by the Cheka. In the town of Astrakhan, the strikers were put onto barges and then thrown into the River Volga with stones tied round their necks – hundreds of them. The continuing strikes worried Lenin and he urged his troops to be even more draconian in their suppression of dissent. His concern about the strikes in the Ural region led him to send a telegram to the local Cheka chief; 'I am surprised that you are taking the matter so lightly, and are not immediately executing large numbers of strikers for the crime of sabotage.'

Cheka interrogators were alleged to use torture, and extreme torture methods at that. At Odessa, the

Cheka troops lashed White officers to planks and fed them slowly into furnaces or tanks of boiling water. At Kharkov, they went in for flaying, peeling the skin of victims' hands to produce gloves. At Voronezh they rolled people around, naked, inside barrels studded with nails. At Ekaterinoslav, people were crucified or stoned to death. At Kremenchug, they were impaled or buried alive. At Orel, in the winter, victims had water poured over them in the street until they turned into ice statues. There was no end to the cruelty the Cheka were ready to inflict on their victims. It was common practice for the Cheka to take a husband hostage and wait for the wife to come to them, to offer her body to save her husband's life.

The executions sometimes took place in the cellars or courtyards of prisons, sometimes at isolated spots on the edges of towns. The condemned were stripped of their belongings and clothes, which were shared among the executioners. Then they were either shot individually with a revolver or machine-gunned in batches. Those executed in prisons were usually shot in the back of the neck as they entered the execution cellar; the cellar filled with blood and corpses. Those taken to the edge of town by lorry were sometimes made to dig their own graves before being shot.

During one of the genocide episodes, the so-called Decossackisation, the massacres grew to a previously unheard-of scale. The Communist leaders tried to justify these ethnic massacres by including them in the propaganda of the class struggle, though in fact they were nothing to do with class. The clergy too were treated to completely unjustifiable cruelty. In 1918 alone, about 3,000 priests, monks and nuns were murdered, often in indescribably barbaric ways.

The Bolsheviks mounted this Red Terror largely because they lacked popular support. Although they had support among the workers and soldiers, and in the revolutionary soviets, they achieved only a fifth of the popular vote in the elections for the Constituent Assembly that were held straight after the October Revolution. The resulting insecurity of the Bolsheviks may go some way towards explaining, though certainly not justifying, the blood-letting. There was also an element of violence implicit in Marxism. It was a Marxist belief that human lives are expendable in the cause of building Communism. The revolutionary generation had to conquer the world, but it also had to perish in the process. When Stalin was reading Marx, he came across the passage, 'There is only one way to shorten and ease the convulsions of the old society and the bloody birth pangs of the new – revolutionary terror.' This remark registered with Stalin, and he noted in the margin, 'Terror is the quickest way to new society.' Later he would act on this memo.

Violence was also implicit in the nature of the Russian Revolution. Some Bolsheviks were unhappy about the Terror. Kamenev, Bukharin and Olminsky warned that the violence Lenin was using to seize power would lead to the Bolsheviks being forced to rely on it; it would be the only way to silence critics and 'subjugate a society they could not control by other means.' The idea that the Red Terror was a spontaneous eruption of the class war is entirely unconvincing. The documentary evidence points to Lenin himself organising, instructing and promoting the Terror over quite a long period, continually urging local Chekas to escalate the violence. It was what we now call terrorism, though of an unusual kind. Today, we tend to see terrorists as frustrated minority groups who have no chance of gaining power by normal political routes, and who have to fall back on violent mass killings because they have no other route. In the Red Terror it was the government officials who were the terrorists, and the terrorist leader was the head of state, waging a barbaric, cruel and totally repellent war on his own people.

The Bolshevik terror was systematic and organised, and it had been thought through before the civil war broke out. It was also brutally simple, in that it targeted entire social classes. The Cheka and the Troops for the Internal Defence of the Republic were a powerful agent of repression, supported and encouraged at the highest level in the Bolshevik regime. For these reasons, the Red Terror was more 'successful', if such a word can acceptably be used about mass murder, than the White Terror. The White Terror of the counter-revolutionaries was not organised systematically. Mainly it was the work of units that were out of control and taking situations into their own hands. What the White Terror consisted of was mainly reprisals that were not officially authorised by a military command. It was only the Ukrainian anarchist Nestor Makhno and some Cossack forces who were able to employ terror on a scale similar to the Red Terror.

'INCOMPREHENSIBLE TO THE NORMAL MIND'
THE HOLOCAUST (1933-45)

When the Nazi régime came to power in Germany in 1933, it began a campaign to eradicate various groups, notably the Jews, but also several other groups regarded as in some way a threat to the Nazi state. Gypsies, homosexuals, Communists and Jehovah's Witnesses were among the groups singled out for persecution. During the 1930s and early 1940s this campaign of persecution and extermination became progressively more brutal, cruel and extreme, resulting in the mass murder of about six million Jews.

The word Holocaust is of Greek origin and it means a particular kind of animal sacrifice in which the animal is completely consumed by fire, sacrifice by total destruction. The term was first used in relation to the persecution of Jews by English chroniclers in the 1190s. The episode, which is the largest-scale genocide in modern times, is also known by Jews as *The Shoah*, the calamity or catastrophe, in

Hebrew. In 1934, Chaim Weizmann told the Zionist Action Committee that the rise to power of Adolf Hitler was in itself an unforeseen catastrophe, and in itself the equivalent of a world war. This proved to be truly prophetic. His word, *Katastrophe*, was translated by the Hebrew press as *Shoah*.

It is estimated that in 1933 there were more than nine million Jews in Europe, most of them living either in Germany or in countries that Nazi Germany would shortly overrun, occupy and control. During the Second World War, most European Jews lived under the threat of persecution and murder. The Final Solution system developed by the Nazis succeeded in eradicating two-thirds of the Jews in Europe. Between two and three million Soviet prisoners of war were either murdered or allowed to die of starvation or neglect. 200,000 Gypsies were exterminated too, and over 200,000 physically and mentally disabled people fell victim to the Nazis' Euthanasia Programme. Altogether, the Holocaust claimed between twelve and seventeen million victims – mass murder on a massive scale.

The Nazis' programme of persecution began on 1 April 1933. At 10 am that day, members of the Sturmabteilung moved into position all over Germany. They stood outside Jewish-owned shops and other businesses to deter customers. Stormtroopers put up signs to warn people off: 'Germans! Defend yourselves! Don't buy from Jews!' It was the first step. Eventually Jewish-owned shops were vandalised and handed over to non-Jews.

Early in the 1930s the Nazis started setting up concentration camps. These were ostensibly to detain political and ideological opponents of the Nazi regime, but soon they were filled with ethnic minority groups who were the object of racial hatred. They also changed from being detention centres to death camps. To facilitate the supervision and later deportation of Jews, the Germans and their collaborators in occupied countries created ghettos, a system of rail transport in freight trucks, transit camps, forced-labour camps and extermination camps.

As Allied forces moved across Europe at the close of the Second World War, they discovered the concentration camps one by one, at first not believing what they saw. The prisoners were liberated at camp after camp. But the retreating Germans tried to prevent this from happening by moving prisoners with them, either by train or in forced marches called death marches. These only ceased on 7 May 1945, when Germany surrendered.

In the aftermath of the Holocaust, many survivors

were housed in displaced persons camps run by the Allies. Between 1948 and 1951, almost 700,000 Jews emigrated to the newly created state of Israel. The devastation to European Jewish communities, especially in Eastern Europe, was almost total, and it is inevitable that the Holocaust hangs over succeeding generations of Jews as an overwhelmingly traumatic event, an event that can never be forgotten or put aside.

The system the Nazis arrived at was not fully envisaged at the outset, or at least not explicitly. There were plans to deport the Jews right out of Europe, perhaps to Madagascar, which was Heydrich's favourite territorial solution, but the logistics of these plans were difficult because of the large numbers of people involved. The Final Solution, which was mass murder in extermination camps, was arrived at in stages. Even that involved a huge amount of administration, and created work for every limb of Germany's bureaucracy, to the extent that Nazi Germany has been described as 'a genocidal state'.

There is some evidence that Adolf Hitler himself was personally committed to exterminating the Jews long before he came to power. A journalist, Joseph Hell, alleged that Hitler confided in him in 1922:

*Once I am really in power, my first and foremost
task will be the annihilation of the Jews. As soon as I
have the power to do so, I will have gallows built in
rows – at the Marienplatz in Munich, for example – as
many as traffic allows. Then the Jews will be hanged
indiscriminately, and they will remain hanging until
they stink; they will hang there as long as the principles
of hygiene permit. As soon as they have been untied, the
next batch will be strung up, and so on down the line,
until the last Jew in Munich has been exterminated.
Other cities will follow suit, precisely in this fashion,
until all Germany has been completely cleansed of Jews.*

It is difficult to know how much credence can be
put in Hell's allegation, but Hitler was capable of
realising a horrific fate for millions of Jews, so he
must have been capable of imagining and planning it
too. The curiously Hitlerian eye for tidy detail arues
for authenticity; he wants lots of gallows – 'as many
as traffic allows' – and he has an eye for hygiene.

There are different opinions about how much
the civilian population of Germany knew about
the Nazi government's conspiracy against the Jews.
Most historians take the view that the civilian
population did not know about the atrocities that
were being committed. This is quite possible. The

post-war generations are familiar enough with the stories, photographs and films of the concentration camps. We know now what happened. But those stories and images came as a great shock when they first came to light; it would not, I think, have been possible to guess that that was what was happening at the time. The ordinary people living in adjacent towns and villages knew that there were camps, but assumed they were just internment camps or prison camps. They would have had no reason to suppose that persecution, torture and mass murder were under way inside.

The anti-semitism of the Nazis was virulent, and based on an irrational fantasy that the Jews were conspiring to take over the world, but even that did not really betray what was happening. Anti-semitism was very deeply rooted and very widespread at all levels of European society in the nineteenth century. Richard Wagner talked and wrote anti-semitically, but he did not mistreat his friends and fellow-musicians who were Jewish. Anti-semitism was common in Britain as well as Germany, and it surfaces fairly frequently in the writings of early twentieth century authors. Anti-Jewish prejudice was socially acceptable, in a way that it no longer is. That is largely, ironically, a result of the Holocaust;

it is as if the horrors of the Nazi Holocaust purged the poison of anti-semitism from European society.

Some people guessed that something was very wrong. I know a Jewish woman who was a young girl growing up in Germany in the 1930s. Her parents noticed that various friends – whole families – were disappearing without trace. They guessed what was happening and took steps to emigrate to England while they could, in about 1935. But that took an imaginative leap.

One peculiar and distinctive feature of the concentration camps was their use for medical experiments. The most notorious experimenter was Dr Josef Mengele, who worked at Auschwitz. His experiments involved putting people in pressure chambers, freezing them, trying to changing children's eye colour by injecting them, amputations and a variety of cruel and unnecessary surgical procedures. The full extent of his experiments will never be known; he sent a lorry-load of records to another doctor, who destroyed them. The unfortunate people Mengele experimented on either died during his experiments, or they were killed and dissected afterwards. He was particularly fond of working with Gypsy children. He gave them sweets and toys, and he would take them to the gas chambers himself. They called him 'Onkel Mengele'. Vera Alexander was a Jewish prisoner at Auschwitz who looked after fifty sets of Romany twins.

I remember one set of twins in particular, Guido and Ina, aged about four. One day, Mengele took them away. When they returned, they were in a terrible state: they had been sewn together, back to back, like Siamese twins. Their wounds were infected, oozing pus. They screamed day and night. Then their parents – I remember the mother's name was Stella – managed to get some morphine and they killed the children in order to end their suffering.

This horrible story is an indication of the sort of pointless, gratuitous cruelty that was an everyday part of life, and mass murder, in the concentration camps. And one such story is enough.

One of the first concentration camps to be set up was Dachau, which opened in March 1933. At first the camps were intended only as detention and torture centres for political prisoners, often converted basements or warehouses. Later they were developed into full-blown, custom-built camps on sites outside cities run, after the middle of 1934, exclusively by the SS. Those sent to concentration camps were divided into those who could be 'educated' into becoming National Comrades (and so eventually released) and the 'biologically depraved' who could not be released and were either killed or 'annihilated through labour'.

The mass killing of Jews did not start until 1941. At that moment the Madagascar Plan was shelved; the German Foreign Office was offered the official explanation that, owing to the war with the Soviet Union, Jews were to be sent to the east. The German extermination programme was full of strange euphemisms like this. The only resettlement plan to take was by a 1933 agreement between the Nazi government and the Zionist Federation of Germany; this resulted in the transfer of about 60,000 German Jews to Palestine. The mass killing programme became a preferred option after September 1939, with the German invasion of Poland, where there was a very large Jewish population. Initially, Reinhard Heydrich advocated concentrating all the Polish Jews in ghettos (Jewish quarters) in the major cities. There, they could be put to work for the German war effort, and they would also be easily located so that 'future measures could be accomplished more easily'. This was another Nazi euphemism; 'future measures' meant extermination.

The Final Solution, discussed at the Wannsee Conference in 1942, envisaged the destruction of all the Jews in Europe, including the 330,000 Jews in Britain. This was fanciful, as Hitler had given up his idea of invading Britain after the failure of the Battle of Britain and the Blitz. But the doctrine was still, somehow, to rid the entire continent of Jews.

By 1942, the Nazis had set up six large extermination camps. These were different from the earlier concentration camps in that their only purpose was to kill the people sent there. The way prisoners were transported to the camps was itself horrific. They were packed into rail freight rolling stock, without sanitation or heating, and many died during the journey. Huge numbers might be transported at once. The deportations from the Warsaw ghetto went on for eight weeks beginning in July 1942, and in that time 300,000 people were transported to the Treblinka extermination camp.

The numbers murdered at the big death camps in the east are unimaginably high: 65,000 at Maly Trostinets, 60-97,000 at Jasenovac, 250,000 at Sobibor, 320,000 at Chelmno, 360,000 at Majdanek, 600,000 at Belzec, 870,000 at Treblinka, 1,400,000 at Auschwitz. Concentration camps such as Dachau and Belsen had high death rates, but they were not primarily for mass extermination; they were intended as prisons and labour camps.

Some camp inmates were worked to death in labour camps. They might die from malnutrition, disease, or from random execution carried out on a whim. Work was in shifts lasting twelve or fourteen hours, and the roll calls before and after the shifts might themselves go on for hours.

Some of the mass murders were ad hoc shootings of groups of people outside their villages or towns. But shooting was seen as messy and inefficient by the Nazi élite. In August 1941, Heinrich Himmler travelled to Minsk, where he watched a hundred Jews being shot in a ditch outside the town. An SS officer who was also present noted the incident in his diary. 'Himmler's face was green. He took out his handkerchief and wiped his cheek where a piece of brain had squirted up on to it. Then he vomited.' It was incidents like this that led to the focus on organised, factory-scale killing under very controlled conditions in death camps. Experiments with gas had been going on since 1939. Initially, experimental vans were fitted with gas cylinders and a sealed rear compartment. They were filled with mentally ill patients from various mental hospitals, who were then gassed inside the vans.

Vans designed to kill a hundred people at a time, and using the vans' exhaust fumes, were used at the Sachsenhausen and Chelmo concentration camps. They were monitored and after a month of use it was reported that 'ninety seven thousand have been processed using three vans, without any defects showing up in the machines.' But even this was not enough. A factory-scale method was needed.

In the end an SS officer, Christian Wirth, invented the gas chamber. When the prisoners arrived by train at the extermination camps, sometimes they were all sent straight to the gas chambers. But usually there was a camp doctor on duty, and he selected a small percentage deemed strong enough to work in the slave labour camps. Most were led straight from the platform to a reception area, where all their belongings and clothes were seized by Nazi officials. Then they were herded naked into the gas chambers. There were signs outside saying 'baths' and 'sauna' and they were told they were to have a shower. Sometimes they were given soap and a towel to make this pretence more convincing. They were told to remember where they had left their belongings for the same reason. They were told to hurry up because there was coffee waiting for them inside the camp. Many of the victims nevertheless suspected what was going to happen, and entered the chamber in a state of terror. At Auschwitz there were two chambers, one holding 800 people, the other 1,200. When the chamber was full, the doors were bolted shut and pellets of Zyklon-B were dropped in through vents in the walls. Death followed within twenty minutes. Rudolf Hoess, the commandant at Auschwitz, and a mass murderer on a grand scale, believed that a third of the prisoners died immediately. The other two-thirds could be heard shouting and screaming as they fought for their lives.

The hydrogen cyanide gas was then pumped out and the bodies removed, which took up to four hours. Gold teeth were removed with pliers. The floor of the gas chamber was cleaned and the walls were whitewashed. This work was all done by units of Jewish prisoners. To begin with, the bodies were buried in deep pits and covered with lime, but late in 1942 Himmler ordered them to be dug up and burned; the evidence of the Final Solution had to be destroyed.

Rudolf Hoess gave his testimony at the Nuremberg Trial: in the spring of 1943, he boasted, Auschwitz had new gas chambers to cope with the numbers.

Another improvement we made over Treblinka was that we built our gas chambers to accommodate 2,000 people at once, whereas at Treblinka their ten gas chambers only accommodated 200 people each. The way we selected our victims was as follows: we had two SS doctors on duty at Auschwitz to examine the incoming transports of prisoners. The prisoners would be marched past one of the doctors, who would make snap decisions as they walked by. Those who were fit for work were sent into the camp. Others were sent immediately to the extermination plants. Children of tender years were invariably exterminated, since by reason of their youth they were unable to work. Still another improvement we made over Treblinka was that at Treblinka the victims almost always knew that they were to be exterminated and at Auschwitz we endeavoured to fool the victims into thinking that they were to go through a delousing process. Of course, frequently they realised our true intentions and we sometimes had riots and difficulties due to that fact. Very frequently women would hide their children under the clothes but of course when we found them we would send the children in to be exterminated. We were required to carry out these exterminations in secrecy but of course the foul and nauseating stench from the continuous burning of bodies permeated the entire area and all of the people living in the surrounding communities knew that exterminations were going on at Auschwitz.'

The infamous Crematorium II gas chamber at Auschwitz-Birkenau has been dismantled, though its foundations survive. It is said that more people died in that room than in any other room on earth – 500,000 people.

The first big death camp to be discovered by the outside world was Majdanek, which was stumbled upon by the advancing Soviet army on 23 July 1944. Auschwitz was liberated by the Soviets on 27 January 1945, Buchenwald by the Americans on 11 April, Belsen by the British on 15 April, Dachau by the Americans on 29 April, Ravensbruck by the Soviets on the same day. Treblinka, Sobibor and Belzec were never liberated, but destroyed by the Nazis in 1943 – to avoid discovery. The very fact that these camps were destroyed shows that the Nazis knew that what they were doing was wrong.

The American colonel who went into Dachau said, 'There our troops found sights, sounds, and stenches horrible beyond belief, cruelties so enormous as to be incomprehensible to the normal mind.' Richard Dimbleby of the BBC described what he saw when he went into Belsen:

*Here over an acre of ground lay dead and dying people.
You could not see which was which ... The living
lay with their heads against the corpses and around
them moved the awful, ghostly procession of emaciated,
aimless people, with nothing to do and with no hope of
life, unable to move out of your way, unable to look at
the terrible sights around them. . . Babies had been born
here, tiny wizened things that could not live. A mother,
driven mad, screamed at a British sentry to give her
milk for her child, and thrust the tiny mite into his
arms. He opened the bundle and found the baby had
been dead for days. This day at Belsen was the most
horrible of my life.*

'MR KARADZIĆ WILL EXPLAIN THAT TO THE WORLD'

THE SREBRENICA MASSACRE (1995)

The Srebrenica massacre, which was one of the worst mass murders of modern times, certainly the worst in Europe since the Second World War, was the organised killing of over 8,000 Bosniak men and boys in and near the town of Srebrenica in Bosnia and Herzegovina. The massacre took place in July 1995, and was carried out by units of the VRS (Army of Republika Srpska), commanded by General Ratko Mladić. There was also participation in the killings by the Scorpions, a paramilitary unit from Serbia.

Two years earlier, the United Nations had declared the besieged enclave of Srebrenica in northeastern Bosnian a 'safe area' and placed it under UN protection. This protection, four hundred lightly-armed Dutch peace-keepers, turned out to be totally inadequate to ensure the safety of the refugees who arrived there, and incapable of preventing the town's capture by Mladić and the VRS. The inadequacy of the UN force and huge errors of judgement at a high level within the UN were in large measure responsible for the scale of the massacre that followed, though the greater responsibility obviously lies with the perpetrators of the massacre, Mladi and his army. The actions of the VRS were motivated by an intense religious and racial hatred, and the massacre was a determined attempt to wipe out the Muslim population of Bosnia and Herzegovina. These actions have subsequently been repeatedly denounced by the international community, for instance by the International Court of Justice in 2007, as atrocities and acts of genocide. Ratko Mladi has similarly been denounced for responsibility for the killings, though he still remains at liberty.

Those responsible for the massacre went to considerable lengths to conceal the extent of their crimes by exhuming bodies from mass graves and reburying them elsewhere at secondary grave sites. But the mass graves have been found and DNA analysis of body parts has allowed 6,557 of the genocide victims to be identified. A list of missing persons contains 8,373 names, so a fair proportion of the victims has now been accounted for. 4,500 of the victims have been buried (again) at the Memorial Centre at Potocari.

The run-up to the massacre began in October 1991, when the Republic of Bosnia and Herzegovina declared itself independent from Yugoslavia. The republic was recognised by the European Union. Then a struggle for control of the new territory erupted among three groups: the Bosniaks, the Bosnian Serbs and the Bosnian Croats. The mainly Bosniak area, the area round Srebrenica, was strategically important; without it there could be no territorial integrity within the Serbs' new political entity of Republika Srpska. The Serbs then began the ethnic cleansing of Bosniaks from Bosniak ethnic territories. Once Serb forces gained control of a town or village, they ransacked or burnt Muslim houses, and Muslim villagers were rounded up, sometimes beaten and killed. Men and women were separated, and the men often detained in prison. Bosniaks who were able to fled to Srebrenica. There were casual ethnic killings in several towns and 296 villages are known to have been destroyed by Serbs in the Srebrenica area – during this 1992 phase. More than 3,000 Bosniaks were systematically killed and 70,000 Bosniaks forcibly removed from their homes.

The onslaught continued into 1993, with Serb military assaults on Srebrenica town and the villages round it. The pattern was unvarying. Serb soldiers surrounded the village, told the villagers to surrender their weapons, then fired indiscriminately into the village. They then entered the village, expelled or killed the inhabitants and destroyed their houses. Srebrenica was shelled from all sides, daily. The Srebrenica enclave shrank from 900 to 150 square kilometres, becoming more and more vulnerable as the Serbs pressed in. As the enclave shrank, more and more refugees from outlying villages fled to the town for safety. Before long, there were 60,000 people in Srebrenica town.

As the siege situation became more dangerous, the commander of the UN Protection Force, General Morillon, visited crowded Srebrenica and told the frightened population that the town was under the UN's protection; he would never abandon them. It now sounds a hollow promise, though in the spring of 1993 several thousand Bosniak refugees were evacuated by the UNHCR. The Bosnian government in Sarajevo objected to this as, in their view, it contributed to the ethnic cleansing of Bosniak territory.

In April 1993 the UN Security Council, without any sense of irony, passed a resolution declaring Srebrenica and the area round it a 'safe area'. In the wake of this resolution a group of UNPROFOR troops arrived in Srebrenica, now surrounded by up to 2,000 well-armed Serb troops. The 'safe area' status was violated from the outset by both sides. UN forces were obstructed when they tried to return to Srebrenica, and Bosnian government troops used the safe area as a cover for counter-attack. The UN tried to expand the safe area so that the town would be less vulnerable to mortar attack, but the Serbs refused to draw back.

What was happening has been described as slow-motion genocide. By early 1995, few supplies were getting through to the weakening enclave. Even the UN forces were running low on food, medicine and fuel. UN soldiers who left the area on leave were prevented from returning, so the number fell from 600 to 400 men. By contrast, Serb forces increased, ready to move in and take Srebrenica. The president of Republika Srpska, Radovan Karadzic, ignored UN pressure, indeed global pressure, by giving the army, the VRS, the fatal directive, which was to create an unbearable situation of total insecurity with no hope of further survival or life for the inhabitants of Srebrenica. The result was catastrophic. By July, eight people had died of starvation in Srebrenica. On a direct order from Karadzic, the Serb troops entered the town, 'cleansing' the houses as they did so.

One of the Dutch armoured vehicles was fired on by the Serbs and withdrew. A Bosniak man, angry at the withdrawal, threw a hand grenade at the vehicle killing a Dutch soldier. The Dutch troops were powerless to act. They fired warning shots over the advancing Serbs' heads, but did not fire at them. NATO planes flew in, attempting to bomb VRS artillery positions that overlooked the town, but they had to abort their mission because of poor visibility. Then the Serb army threatened to seize and kill Dutch troops and French pilots who had been taken hostage if the NATO air strikes continued, so they were stopped. The Serbs also threatened to shell the UN compound outside the town and surrounding areas where up to 30,000 civilians were seeking refuge.

On 11 July General Mladić, General Zivanović and General Krstić took a triumphant stroll through the streets of Srebrenica, filmed by Serbian journalists. Chillingly, Lieutenant-Colonel Karremans of the UN force was filmed drinking a toast with General Mladić, as the fate of the civilian population was 'negotiated'. But Mladić already knew what was to happen. He warned Karadzić that the removal of whole populations from one area to another could not be done without killing. 'People are not little stones, or keys in someone's pocket, that can be moved from one place to another just like that. We cannot precisely arrange for only Serbs to stay in one part of the country while removing others painlessly. I do not know how Mr Krajisnik and Mr Karadzić will explain that to the world. That is genocide.' And genocide is exactly what Mladić delivered.

By 11 July 1995, up to 25,000 Bosniak refugees were in the village of Potocari, where they hoped for protection from the UN. Most were women, but about one thousand men were there too. Conditions were poor, there was very little food or water, and the people were very frightened. The UN's response was to pass a resolution condemning the humanitarian situation in Potocari.

On 12 July, Serb soldiers mingled in the chaotic crowd, murdering men at random. A pile of perhaps twenty-five bodies was seen behind one of the hangar-like buildings at Potocari. Another witness saw Serb soldiers executing, he thought, over a hundred Muslim men behind a zinc factory, then load their bodies onto a truck. But the witness evidence is conflicting, as other witnesses reported only sporadic killings; men and boys were picked out of the crowd two or three at a time and taken away. Stories spread that women were being raped. Many women were to suffer not only rape but repeated rape. The fear engendered was so intense that several people hanged themselves.

The Serb troops separated the male refugees at Potocari and moved them to different places. The women and children were loaded onto buses and moved out, but boys of fourteen and fifteen were taken off with the men – for execution. By this stage the Dutch troops were in no doubt that the men were being executed. One Dutch soldier saw two soldiers take a man behind a building; he heard a gunshot and then he saw the two soldiers return alone. There was a gunshot from somewhere every two or three minutes. The killing went on through the night, under arc lights, and bulldozers pushed the bodies into mass graves.

The Dutch soldiers were still there. They saw the rapes, they saw the shootings, they saw the atrocities committed even against children, but they behaved as if there was nothing happening at all. It is easy to imagine that they went into a state of shock; there was after all absolutely nothing they could do to prevent any of this from happening. In most cases, their minds seem simply to have switched off. But there is one telling photograph that was taken that day of a Dutch soldier completely overwhelmed by emotion, his face contorted, tears streaming.

Most of the women were deported by bus out of the enclave, never to see their husbands and sons again. Meanwhile some of the Bosniak men took to the woods, formed a column and tried to break out into Bosnian government-held territory round Tuzla. They thought that would give them a better chance of surviving than staying in the enclave. It meant crossing 55 kilometres of rugged hill country, and they had virtually no food. Many of them were exhausted before they started. They were shelled. They were ambushed. Some believed they were attacked by some chemical agent that caused hallucinations. In despair, several of them committed suicide; those who surrendered were often killed on the spot and the rest were corralled together for mass execution later. But about a third of the men made it to Bosnian government territory on 16 July or later. Journalists in Tuzla described the arrival of 'an army of ghosts': men in rags, gaunt with hunger, exhausted, some being carried on makeshift stretchers. Many of them were still visibly terrified, some of them hallucinating as a result of prolonged intense stress. The survivors expressed deep bitterness at the UN's failure to protect them in the 'safe area'.

Near Sandici, the Serb troops forced a Bosniak man to call other Bosniak men down from the wooded hillside. Perhaps 250 men, including the witness's brother, did as he said and went down to the road. The witness himself stayed in the trees and watched to see what would happen. The men were made to line up in seven long ranks with their hands behind their heads. Then they were cut down by machine gun fire.

There was never any doubt in the world outside former Yugoslavia that the massacre was the work of Serb forces, but it took until 2004 for Serb officials to acknowledge the truth. It was Serb security forces that had planned and carried out these monstrous killings of innocent civilians. A Serb commission's report acknowledges that the mass murder of Muslim men and boys was planned. The whole operation to contain, capture and execute Muslim men was comprehensively organised. The mass executions were carefully orchestrated, starting on 13 July 1995 just north of Srebrenica. The executions followed a set pattern. The men were taken first to empty schools or warehouses. Then they were made to board trucks or buses and taken to execution sites, usually in isolated locations. Resistance was minimised in various ways, by removing the victims' shoes, tying their wrists together behind their backs, blindfolding. Then they were shot.

When General Krstić was put on trial, the prosecution's military adviser, Richard Butler, pointed out that by executing its Bosniak prisoners the Serb Army deprived itself of a bargaining counter. Butler said that with the Potocari refugees taken into custody as prisoners of war the Serb Army could have gained far more political concessions from a subsequent negotiation. The mass murder had no military justification whatever. It was therefore impossible to explain the killings as any kind of act of war. It was and still is only possible to see them as a crime against humanity. Perhaps the explanation is the simple cold-blooded one offered by General Mladić himself to one of the groups of prisoners about to be killed: 'Well, your government does not want you, and I have to take care of you.'

The mass graves were found relatively easily. There were witnesses, survivors who managed somehow to escape execution, and they knew where the graves were. These accounts were verified from air photos taken by American spy planes, which confirmed that the land had been disturbed on particular and significant dates, coinciding with the executions. Two mass graves were uncovered in the summer of 2000. Not only were hundreds of bodies recovered in this way, but the method used in the mass murders was confirmed; what the survivors had said was true.

After the war ended in November, both Radovan Karadzić and Ratko Mladić were indicted by the International Criminal Trial for their alleged direct responsibility for the atrocities committed in July 1995. In the aftermath, several states examined their own roles in this human catastrophe. The French and the Dutch considered that they had failed in their involvement and to an extent contributed to the disaster. In 2003 a Srebrenica Genocide Memorial was opened by President Clinton, who said, 'We must pay tribute to the innocent lives, many of them children who were snuffed out in what must be called genocidal madness.'

In 2004, the Serbs confirmed the names of 8,731 people who were either dead or missing from Srebrenica and must be assumed to have died in the massacre in that one terrible week, between 10 and 19 July 1995. The president, Dragan Čavić acknowledged on television that Serb troops had killed several thousand civilians in violation of international law; Srebrenica had been a dark chapter in Serb history.

PART THREE

WARTIME MASSACRES

'WE SHALL NEVER SURRENDER'
THE BLITZ (1940-41)

Between September 1940 and May 1941, Germany waged a sustained bombing campaign against British cities. This traumatic episode in the Second World War took place some time after Britain had declared war on Germany, but was otherwise unprovoked. What makes these deliberate and determined attacks into acts of mass murder rather than acts of war is that the Germans deliberately and knowingly attacked civilian populations.

The Blitz started with the bombing of London, for seventy-six nights in a row. Twenty-six other towns and cities, including Coventry, Birmingham, Portsmouth and Glasgow, shared the bombing, but of the 43,000 deaths inflicted half were in London. More than a million houses were destroyed in London alone. The Germans' main targets were industrial cities, but other places suffered too; Brighton and Eastbourne were hit, even though they had no industry. Birmingham was a particular target because of the factories there making tanks and Spitfires. Coventry was badly hit because of its munitions factories. Some towns were for various reasons respected: Blackpool was scarcely bombed at all. It was rumoured that Hitler planned to use Blackpool as a resort for his troops after he had conquered England, but it seems more likely that, with its distinctive three piers, the town was considered a useful landmark to help German aircraft navigators to find Manchester, Liverpool and Barrow.

The overall aim of the Blitz was to reduce civilian morale in Britain and induce the British government to surrender. Because this was not achieved, the Blitz did little to help the planned German invasion of England, Operation Sealion. With the failure of the Blitz and the failure of the Battle of Britain too, the invasion looked impracticable. By May 1941, Hitler's attention had swung away from Operation Sealion towards Operation Barbarossa, the invasion of Russia. It was a doubly fortunate decision; it meant that Britain was not invaded, and it also meant that Germany would lose the war. Although the Germans never again reached the same intensity of bombing against British towns and cities, they did carry out smaller-scale attacks right through the war. This took the British civilian death toll from bombing up to 51,500. In 1944, the development of pilotless flying bombs, the V-1s or doodle-bugs, enabled the Germans for a short time to attack London from the European mainland. Towards the end of the war, the more powerful V-2 rockets were developed. These V weapons killed a total of 9,000 people in London and the south-east.

The Germans launched their major air attack on Britain, the Battle of Britain, in July 1940. The Luftwaffe directly confronted the Royal Air Force, and the idea was to knock out the RAF and gain control in the air as a prelude to invasion by sea and land. The Luftwaffe at the same time attacked factories manufacturing aircraft, so that planes lost in combat could not be replaced, but this was a failure. British efficiency in producing both planes and parts was far ahead of the estimates of German intelligence. It was far harder to replace pilots at the rate at which they were lost. The British authorities had to fall back on Polish and Czech pilots and pilots from other German-occupied countries.

The first German plane to be shot down was brought down over Edinburgh after a failed raid on the Forth Rail Bridge. The Germans bombed Edinburgh's docks and suburbs, including a whisky factory, which went on burning for days.

Churchill was told about a new German system

for bombing through clouds by using radio beam guidance. It was called *Knickebein*. The British discovered that they were able to parry this new technology by 'bending the beams', and successfully made German bombers miss their targets. In August 1940, German aircraft strayed into residental areas in east London, dropping bombs on Islington, Bethnal Green and Hackney, and there has been speculation that this may have been a negative result of British beam-bending. Whether it was that or a simple German navigational mistake, the resulting bombing of civilian housing led directly to a token retaliatory bombing raid on Berlin the next night. Hitler was furious and ordered day and night disruptive attacks on British cities, including – explicitly – attacks 'on the population'. That led to a focus on the cities, which was a relief to the RAF airfields, which had been under concentrated attack.

Before the Blitz started, the British authorities were apprehensive about the numbers of casualties that would be likely to result from this kind of bombing. A Ministry of Health report in early 1939 (before the war itself had begun) anticipated that bombardment from the air would lead to the deaths of 600,000 people in the first six months; probably twice that number would be injured.

This fortunately turned out to be wrong, mainly because the Germans had fewer bombers than the British thought but also because the bombs were less lethal; in other words fewer people were killed by each bomb. One positive outcome of this rather pessimistic report was that it led directly to a plan for the evacuation of children to foster homes in rural areas. About 650,000 children were evacuated.

The first intentional raids on London were mounted on 7 September 1940, beginning in the late afternoon. The target was the Port of London. It was, for Londoners, a very frightening experience. A fleet of 364 bombers escorted by 515 fighter planes attacked the London Docklands. Later that night another 133 bombers attacked. Many of the bombs intended for the docks fell on nearby residential areas, where 436 civilians were killed and 1,666 were injured. The streets packed with terraced houses backed right onto the docks and warehouses, so it was inevitable that there would be civilian casualties. But Hitler had made it clear that he wanted 'the population' to suffer. The British press published poignant photographs of 'Children made homeless by the random bombs of the Nazi night raiders, waiting outside the wreckage of what was their home.'

London was not in any sense prepared for this. The Cabinet War Rooms had been installed in a secret underground bunker beneath the Treasury, and this was to house the government during the war. But these War Rooms were not buried very deep and they were vulnerable to a direct hit: they were not really bomb-proof. There were anti-aircraft guns, but too few of them to deal with raids on the scale to which London was going to be subjected: only ninety-two. But General Pile, who was in charge of Anti-Aircraft Command, was quick to act and by 11 September, less than a week after the initial attack, he had twice as many guns in place.

In this initial phase, the bombing was intense, with between 100 and 200 bombers attacking London nearly every night for two solid months. On 15 October came the heaviest attack os the war so far, a six-hour raid by 400 bombers. During this raid, the RAF succeeded in shooting down only one German bomber. From the German point of view this bombing campaign was a huge success. They unloaded 13,000 tons of high explosive and over a million incendiary bombs on the enemy capital – and lost very few planes in the process.

Then, from November 1940 on to February 1941, the Luftwaffe mounted bombing raids on other British industrial cities and ports. Coventry Birmingham, Clydebank, Cardiff, Swansea, Plymouth, Avonmouth and Portsmouth all came under attack. But the bombing of London continued relentlessly as well. The worst raid came on the evening of 29 December: the raid on the City of London. This was an attack with high-explosive bombs and incendiaries, and it generated a firestorm that became known as the Second Fire of London. A photograph of the fire, with the dome of St Paul's Cathedral standing proud and unscathed among clouds of smoke, has become the definitive historic image of the Blitz and one of the defining images of the British experience of the Second World War.

In February 1941, Doenitz persuaded Hitler to agree to attack the ports of Britain in support of the German Fleet's supremacy in the North Atlantic. There followed a series of bombing raids on ports. But by this point it had become clear that Germany had still not gained air superiority over Britain, and Germany needed the Royal Air Force seriously disabled before it could risk sending large numbers of troops across the Channel in canal barges, which is how Operation Sealion was intended to happen. Unlike Poland, Britain had no land frontiers across which fleets of tanks and troop carriers could roll, so the sea crossing was the only possibility. Under attack by the RAF, that would suffer huge losses.

So now the bombing was no longer a logistical preamble to invasion landings on the Kent and Sussex coast. The British sensed that Hitler was trying to terrorise the civilian population and thereby get its government to surrender. By now British defences were improving with ground-based radar. This was used to guide fighters to their targets at night. The Bristol Beaufighter was fitted with airborne radar, which helped it against enemy night bombers. The legend was deliberately promoted that British pilots could see in the dark thanks to eating carrots – a piece of pseudo-folkloric nonsense to distract the Germans from the fact that the British now had significant new technology on their side.

The Blitz came to an end in May 1941 as Hitler turned his attention to the East. German air power was needed there. The last raid was a big one. It came on 10 May, when 515 bombers damaged or destroyed many major public buildings in London – the Houses of Parliament, the British Museum, St James's Palace. And this last raid caused more casualties than any of the earlier raids: 1,364 people were killed and as many again were seriously injured. Then it went quiet for more than a year.

There were more blitzes. There were the Baedeker blitzes, named after the German tourist guide books. In retaliation for the bombing of Lubeck, Hitler ordered the bombing of some tourist centres in Britain. The historic centre of Canterbury was demolished by bombs, though mercifully (and by chance) not the cathedral itself. In June 1944, the first V-1 flying bomb attack was carried out on London. These flying bombs were launched in France, crossed the Channel, crossed Sussex or Kent without the aid of a pilot, and then, when the engine cut out, fell on London. A total of more than 9,000 V-1 bombs fell on Britain, mostly on or near London. The 2,500 that reached London killed over 6,000 people and injured nearly 18,000. It was possible to intercept and bring down V-1s, and by various means over 4,000 of them were destroyed, some by the Royal Air Force, some by the Army's Anti-Aircraft Command, some by the Royal Navy, some by barrage balloons.

Right at the end of the Second World War came a more sophisticated weapon, the V-2. This was a rocket, the precursor of the space age rockets of the post-war period. The first V-2 rocket was fired at London on 8 September 1944, and in all 1,115 V-2s were fired, killing 2,754 civilians in London. The

V-2 weapons were regarded as far more sinister and evil than the bombs dropped by planes, or even the V-1s. The V-1s were treated as slightly comic, and given the nickname 'doodle-bugs'. You could hear them coming, and going overhead, because of the engine noise. When you could no longer hear the engine noise, you knew they were falling, so you had to dive for cover. There was some warning, so you had a sporting chance of escape. But with the new V-2s there was no warning whatever, no sound of an approaching engine.

The effect of the Blitz on the civilian population was not the effect that Hitler had hoped for. It tended to improve morale rather than destroy it, making people more determined that Britain would not surrender.

Churchill made several speeches in this vein. One, made in June 1941 after the London Blitz had ended, prepared Londoners for more and addressed the cruel enemy.

You have committed every crime under the sun. Where you have been the least resisted there you have been the most brutal. It was you who began the indiscriminate bombing. We will have no truce or parley with you, or the grisly gang who work your wicked will. You do your worst – and we will do our best."

We live in a terrible epoch of the human story, but
we believe there is a broad and sure justice running
through its theme. It is time that the enemy should be
made to suffer in their own homelands something of the
torment they have let loose upon their neighbours and
upon the world. We believe it to be in our power to keep
this process going, on a steadily rising tide, month after
month, year after year, until they are torn to pieces by
their own people.

It is for this reason that I must ask you to be
prepared for vehement counter-action by the enemy.
Our methods of dealing with them have steadily
improved. They no longer relish their trips to our shores.
I do not know why they do not come, but it is certainly
not because they have begun to love us more. It may
be because they are saving up, but even if that be so,
the very fact that they have to save up should give us
confidence by revealing the truth of our steady advance
from an almost unarmed position to superiority. But all
engaged in our defence forces must prepare themselves
for further heavy assaults. Your organisation, your
vigilance, your devotion to duty, your zeal for the cause
must be raised to the highest intensity …

We shall never turn from our purpose, however
sombre the road, however grievous the cost, because we

know that out of this time of trial and tribulation will
be born a new freedom and glory for all mankind.

Civilians who were for reasons of age or health unable or unwilling to join the armed forces became members of other organisations instead. There were the Air Raid Precaution Service, the Auxiliary Fire Service, the Home Guard. Some public bomb shelters were created, but not enough. The reason was that if people were provided with deep central shelters a 'shelter mentality' would develop; people would spend too much time underground. Instead people were encouraged to build small domestic shelters in their back gardens. These Anderson shelters provided very little protection from bomb blast, and probably saved few lives. For a time, attempts were made to stop people from using the London Underground as a shelter, but had to be given up. In the end about eighty Tube stations were used to house nearly 180,000 people.

The British attitude was strikingly different from the German attitude. For all that the Nazi régime was callous and brutal, it made a concerted and organised effort to shelter its civilian population in the closing stages of the war when Germany came under Allied attack. In the 1960s I stumbled by chance on a huge undergound shelter on the Rhine, created to house the entire population of a village when the Allied came through from the west. It was an artifical cave system dug out of a steep rocky hillside; the entrance was disguised by a ruined barn. The locals were not pleased that a British tourist had found it, either.

Even so, the British casualty rate was remarkably low – only ten percent of the estimate made in early 1939 – and this implies that successful planning had reduced the losses. Evacuation of children had helped, certainly. But nearly 60,000 civilians died, and many of the survivors, often severed from their families, suffered emotionally and psychologically long after the war was over.

'WORSE THAN BEING ON THE RUSSIAN FRONT'
THE BOMBING OF DRESDEN (1945)

The bombing of the city of Dresden in February 1945 was one of the most controversial actions by Britain in the Second World War. Dresden was a city that had been untouched by bombing up to that moment in the war, a moment when the war was nearly over. The Allied bombing created a firestorm that killed many thousands of civilians. It was in some ways a strange incident. The Allies were advancing towards Berlin from the west, and the Russians were rapidly advancing from the east, and it was clear that the war would soon be over. So why was this brutal bombing considered necessary?

Dresden was the cultural centre of northern Germany, a beautiful city, full of museums and historic buildings, such as Frauenkirche Cathedral and the Zwinger Palace. It was known as 'Florence on the Elbe'. Throughout the Second World War, the Allies had spared this beautiful city; other cities were subjected to bombing raids, but not

Dresden. By early 1945, Dresden was filling up with refugees, people fleeing west from the Russians as they advanced into Germany from the east. Nazi propaganda had successfully frightened people into expecting the worst from the Russian Red Army. It is not certain how many people were packed into Dresden. The town's official population was 350,000, but to this must be added an unknown number of refugees.

The carpet bombing of Dresden took place across three days, 13-15 February 1945. In that short time perhaps 25,000 people were killed.

Why did the British single out Dresden for this unusual treatment? Arthur Harris, the head of Bomber Command, took the view that any city connected in any way with the Nazi war effort was a fair target; it could be that it was targeted just because it had so far escaped bombing. Much has been made of the fact that Dresden was a beautiful city and a great cultural centre; but it was also an industrial city, producing arms for the German war effort. It was also an important railhead for sending German troops to the Eastern Front. On the other hand the communciations nodes and the industrial areas were not targeted in the bombing raids. Was this just poor aiming? Or was it that the bombing had another motive? The focus of the bombing, the centre of the target area, was the sports stadium near the Altmarkt. This may have been easy to identify from the navigational point of view, but it can scarcely be represented as an industrial target of any kind.

On 25 January, the Joint Intelligence Committee discussed the information that dozens of divisions that had been deployed in the west were being moved to reinforce the Eastern Front. It would be good, it was decided, if these troop movements could be intercepted, blocked. This was the rationale behind the intensive bombing of Chemnitz, Leipzig and Dresden. Arthur 'Bomber' Harris, who was in charge of Bomber Command, was known to be in favour of area or carpet bombing. He was the one who proposed simultaneous attacks on Chemnitz, Leipzig and Dresden. Churchill then took soundings from others and found there was support for hampering German troop movements from west to east.

Wreaking havoc on German cities was the essence of British strategy. In May 1942 the British Cabinet formally agreed that RAF Bomber Command was to destroy fifty-eight of Germany's biggest cities. So it was British policy to destroy German cities.

The Russians were allies of the British and Americans, but it was clear to Churchill and Roosevelt that Stalin was going to be a major problem when the war ended. As the Red Army advanced into an exhausted and defeated Germany, it had no measure of what a military force of equal or even greater strength might be able to do. Dresden was bombed as a display of western military power, just to prove to Stalin what the western Allies were capable of doing. It was a way of warning Stalin not to think that Britain and America were weak; they were capable of naked aggression too.

An internal RAF memo dated January 1945, the month before the bombing raids, sheds a significant amount of light on the bombing. It opens by describing Dresden as the seventh largest city in Germany, not much smaller than Manchester. In other words, the city is a big, important, significant German target. It goes on:

> *The intentions of the attack are to hit the enemy where he will feel it most, behind an already partially collapsed front, to prevent the use of the city in the way of further advance, and incidentally to show the Russians when they arrive what Bomber Command can do.*

Allied air superiority meant that a large proportion of the bombers got through to Dresden. There were 1,300 bombers in all – a huge number. The RAF led their attack with Lancasters. The US Air Force used their B-17 Flying Fortresses. The attack was organised in three waves. 3,300 tons of bombs were dropped, many of them incendiary bombs. The fires were so many and so intense that a firestorm developed. Dresden roared like a furnace, with temperatures rising to 1,500 degrees Celsius. The tarred road surfaces melted and people had their feet burned as they ran to get away from the flames. At various points round the city were water reservoirs to assist fire-fighting. These tanks were smooth-sided, three metres deep and had no internal ladders, so many people jumping into them to escape the fires were drowned. Few people in the city centre survived. Fifteen square miles in the centre of the city were destroyed in the firestorm.

When they first heard about the attack on Dresden, some German leaders, especially Goebbels, wanted to use it as a pretext for abandoning the Geneva Conventions on the Western Front. They did not go this far, but they did exploit it for propaganda purposes ('Dresden – Massacre of Refugees'). Some of this propaganda was very effective. In early

March, *Das Reich*, a weekly founded by Goebbels himself, ran a long article describing the terrible architectural and cultural losses caused by the Dresden bombing. This had an influence in neutral countries and caused some British MPs to waver. For the first time, the public in the Allied countries seriously questioned the military actions that were being used to defeat the Nazis. Multiplying the actual death toll by ten, making it 200,000, clinched the emotional power of the German argument.

It is said that Goebbels wept with rage for twenty minutes when he heard about the disaster. Then he launched into an attack on Goering, who was responsible for the Luftwaffe:

If I had the power, I would drag this cowardly good-for-nothing, this Reich marshal, before a court. How much guilt does this parasite not bear for all this, which we owe to his indolence and love of his own comforts?

A survivor who had served on the Eastern Front, Rudolph Eichner, described what the Dresden bombing was like:

There were no warning sirens. We were completely taken by surprise and rushed back down to the cellars

*of the hospital. But these quickly became hopelessly
overcrowded with people who could no longer find
shelter in their own burning buildings. The crush was
unbearable; we were so tightly packed together you
could not fall over. Apart from the fire risk, it was
becoming increasingly impossible to breathe in the cellar
because the air was being pulled out by the increasing
strength of the blaze. We could not stand up. We were
on all fours, crawling. The wind was full of sparks and
carrying bits of blazing furniture, debris and burning
bits of bodies. There were charred bodies everywhere.
The experience of the bombing was far worse than
being on the Russian front, where I was a front-line
machine gunner.*

Another survivor, Lothar Metzger, describes the
panic and the trauma of the bombing:

*It is not possible to describe. Explosion after explosion.
It was beyond belief, worse than the blackest nightmare.
So many people were horribly burnt and injured. It
became more and more difficult to breathe. It was
dark and all of us tried to leave this cellar with
inconceivable panic. Dead and dying people were
trampled upon, luggage was left or snatched up out
of our hands by rescuers. The basket with our twins*

covered with wet cloths was snatched up out of my mother's hands and we were pushed upstairs by the people behind us. We saw the burning street, the falling ruins and the terrible firestorm. My mother covered us with wet blankets and coats she found in a water tub.

We saw terrible things: cremated adults shrunk to the size of small children, pieces of arms and legs, dead people, whole families burnt to death. Burning people ran to and fro, burnt coaches filled with civilian refugees, dead rescuers and soldiers, many were calling and looking for their children and families, and fire everywhere, everywhere fire, and all the time the hot wind of the firestorm threw people back into the burning houses they were trying to escape from. I cannot forget these terrible details. I can never forget them.

The thousands of fires set alight in the burning city could be seen over sixty miles away, at ground level, and 500 miles away from the air because of the smoke column rising to 15,000 feet. When the bombing was over, SS guards were drafted in from a nearby camp. They burnt the bodies in Dresden's Old Market Square, the Altmarkt. There were so many corpses that it took two weeks to dispose of them all. A huge area of the city was totally destroyed, so that when the Red Army arrived and took it over Dresden had all but ceased to exist. A Dresden police report listed the damage. The old town and inner eastern suburbs had been consumed in a single fire that had destroyed 12,000 dwellings, 24 banks, 31 stores, 640 shops, 64 warehouses, 2 market halls, 31 hotels, 26 pubs, 63 administrative buildings, 3 theatres, 18 cinemas, 11 churches, 19 hosiptals, 39 schools, 19 post offices. 200 factories were damaged. The RAF assessed that 78,000 dwellings had been destroyed and nearly a quarter of the industrial buildings.

At the end of the Second World War it was a shell of a city. The Russians remained there in the 1950s, the period of the Cold War, but because they were putting their efforts into rebuilding Russian cities Dresden was just left. The bombing of Hamburg in 1943 was on a grander scale, killing twice as many civilians (50,000) and practically destroying the entire city. So, the bombing of Dresden was by no means the worst that the US Army Air Force and the Royal Air Force could do. But the raids still stand as emblematic of civilian suffering – caused by Allied bombing. They continue to cause controversy. Was the bombing of Dresden a legitimate act of war? Or was it a war crime, a mass murder?

Churchill had backed it totally, but when the

British public were revolted by what they heard he tried to distance himself from it. One of the things that particularly repelled people was the fact that Germany was all but defeated, certainly in retreat. At an earlier stage in the war, perhaps in 1940, an action like this might have been acceptable, but not now. Churchill changed his mind about area bombing:

We must see to it that our attacks do no more harm to ourselves in the long run than they do to the enemy's war effort.

Following German reunification, great efforts have been made to reconstruct some of the old landmarks, the masterpieces of architecture destroyed in the raids. Gradually, Dresden has been rebuilt. The Semperoper, the Dresden state opera house, was rebuilt in 1985. It was reopened exactly forty years after the bombing, with the same opera that was last performed just before its destruction, Der Freischutz. The Zwinger Palace was rebuilt. Still in ruins in 1991, Dresden's magnificent cathedral, the Frauenkirche, has finally been rebuilt, completed in 2008. In a gesture of reconciliation, Queen Elizabeth II hosted a concert in Berlin in 2004 to raise money for its reconstruction.

'A RAIN OF RUIN FROM THE AIR'

HIROSHIMA AND NAGASAKI (1945)

Right at the end of the Second World War, the United States dropped atomic bombs on two Japanese cities. These deliberate and calculated destructions, of Hiroshima on 6 August and Nagasaki on 9 August 1945, were considered necessary by the Americans to bring the war to an end, but there has been debate ever since (as with Dresden) as to whether they were legitimate acts of war or war crimes.

The attacks did not come entirely out of the blue, in that the Americans had waged a campaign of strategic fire-bombing of sixty-seven Japanese cities over the previous six months. In the Potsdam Declaration, the US, UK and Republic of China had demanded Japan's surrender, but Japan had ignored the ultimatum. It was because of this refusal to surrender that President Truman issued the order to drop a nuclear weapon on the city of Hiroshima, and then another on Nagasaki. These two events represent the only deployments of nuclear weapons in wartime.

The initial, acute effects of the bombings killed perhaps 100,000-150,000 people in Hiroshima and about half that number in Nagasaki. About half of the deaths occurred at the moment of the bombing, the other half over the course of the next four months. Of those who died on the day of the explosions, an estimated sixty per cent died of burns, thirty per cent from falling debris, ten percent from other causes. During the months that followed, large numbers of people died from the effect of burns, radiation sickness and various injuries. In both cities, most of those who died were civilians.

In the strategic sense, the two atom bomb detonations were successful. Six days after the Nagasaki bombing, on 15 August, Japan formally surrendered to the Allied Powers, bringing the War in the Pacific to an end. Germany had signed its instrument of surrender on 7 May, so the War in Europe was already over. The bombs therefore can be seen as bringing the Second World War to its final close.

The project to create the first atomic weapon, the Manhattan Project, was a joint American, Canadian and British project, directed overall by General Leslie Groves with Robert Oppenheimer directing the scientific research. The early research had started in

1939, mainly out of fear that German scientists might develop a nuclear weapon first. The first nuclear bomb was tested at Trinity site near Alamogordo in New Mexico on 16 July 1945. By then Germany had surrendered, so it was not necessary to deploy the new weapon against Germany; but Japan had still refused to surrender.

Many Japanese cities had come under attack by the Americans, so why Hiroshima and Nagasaki? A target committee was set up, laying out criteria. The target needed to be a significantly large urban area, more than three miles in diameter; the target needed to be big enough to 'benefit' from substantial blast damage. Any small target such as a military installation would need to be embedded in a significant urban area, so that the bomb damage would not be wasted. The target needed to be in southern Japan, so as to be within range for bombers coming in from the south-south-east.

On 11 May, the Target Committee, chaired by Robert Oppenheimer, recommended Kyoto, Niigata, Hiroshima, Yokohama and the arsenal at Kokura as potential targets for the nuclear bomb. The chosen targets had been so far untouched by night bombing raids, and they were left off so that after the nuclear bombing an accurate assessment of the capabilities of the new bomb. Hiroshima was a worthwhile target because it had a major army depot; it was also an important port and industrial centre. The fact that there were hills close by was considered another advantage: the hills would have the effect of concentrating and increasing blast damage. The presence of rivers (which form natural fire-breaks) had meant that Hiroshima was a poor target for incendiary bombing. The scale of devastation possible in a medium-sized city like Hiroshima was such that it would have a major traumatising effect on the Japanese people. It was important that the bomb explosion should be as spectacular as possible in order to achieve maximum psychological effect. Kyoto, another favoured target, had the advantage of being a major military industry centre; it was also a major intellectual centre and this was considered to raise the level of appreciation of the weapon. The existence there of the Emperor's palace meant that this site was going to be better known than the others, but otherwise it had a lower strategic value. It is said that Kyoto was saved from destruction for sentimental reasons by Henry Stimson, the US Secretary for War at the time, who had known and admired Kyoto ever since he spent his honeymoon there some decades before.

The Potsdam Declaration of 26 July presented Japan with terms of surrender. Included in it was a clear ultimatum. Unless Japan surrendered, the Allies would attack Japan and this would lead to 'the inevitable and complete destruction of the Japanese armed forces and just as inevitably the utter devastation of the Japanese homeland'. No mention was made a nuclear bomb, but the intention to lay waste the Japanese mainland was clear enough. On 28 July, Japanese newspapers reported that the Japanese government rejected the Declaration and this was confirmed at a press conference that day by the prime minister, Kanataro Suzuki; his government intended to ignore it. The emperor, Hirohito, said nothing to contradict this.

Truman thought very carefully about using the nuclear bomb against Japan, and he may have hoped that the Japanese government would agree to surrender under the terms of the Potsdam Declaration. But in the end he decided to order the bombings as a way of bringing the war to a speedy end. A thought that may have been in Truman's mind is the knowledge that if the Japanese were forced to retreat inch by inch across Japan, they would almost certainly kill all their prisoners of war. The prisoners of war had been gathered from prisons and camps all over the Pacific region to use as a human shield on the Japanese mainland. The best chance of saving the lives of these prisoners of war was to bring the war to a sudden end.

President Truman must also have known that this way of dealing with the Japanese would be popular in America. During the course of the Second World War an exceptional level of anti-Japanese rhetoric was common at all levels in American society. British embassy officials noted that talk of annihilation and extermination was generally tolerated, and that the Japanese were caricatured as a subhuman species, little better than vermin (in the language of the embassy officials). Truman must have known that news of an atomic bomb totally destroying a Japanese city would be greeted with enthusiasm in an America conditioned by several years of this kind of violent talking and thinking. In this respect, we may recall recent comments about the Tucson shooting, to the effect that violent language leads to violent deeds. News of the atom bombs was welcomed in America; in fact a minority of Americans wanted more atom bombs dropped on Japan. A 1944 opinion poll asking what should be done with Japan produced what now looks like a deeply disturbing response. Thirteen percent of

Americans were in favour of exterminating ALL Japanese: men, women and children. If people can get themselves into that state of mind, it is small wonder that atrocities like mass murders occur.

Hiroshima was an important industrial city with military camps nearby and the HQ of the Second General Army defending all of southern Japan. It was a communications and storage centre, an assembly point for troops. And it had been left deliberately untouched by American bombing, allowing a very precise measure of the effectiveness of the nuclear bomb. Its population was about 350,000.

The day for the bombing of Hiroshima, 6 August, was chosen for its weather. The skies had been cloudy until then, and the clear sky on that day gave a better chance of hitting the target accurately. The B-29 bomber Enola Gay was deployed to carry the atomic bomb Little Boy. Accompanied by two other B-29s, Colonel Paul Tibbets took off from the North Field airbase on the island of Tinian in the Pacific and began the six-hour flight to Japan. The escort planes had their assigned roles; one carried instruments, the other was to take photographs. The three planes made their way separately to Iwo Jima, where they met and flew together to Japan. Captain William Parsons armed the bomb during the journey; it was thought safer to have the bomb unarmed during take-off to reduced the risk. Second Lieutenant Morris Jeppson removed the safety devices thirty minutes before Enola Gay (the name of Paul Tibbets' mother) reached Hiroshima.

The Japanese early warning radar spotted the American aircraft approaching southern Japan about an hour before the bombing. Many south Japanese cities were alerted, including Hiroshima. At 8 am the radar operator at Hiroshima could see that the number of planes was very small, maybe only three, and the air raid alert was lifted: it did not look like a bombing raid. A radio broadcast warning was given, that if bombers were sighted it would be advisable to take cover in the air raid shelters. But there was no sense of emergency. At 7.30 am the first B-29 had flown over. Its job was to observe the weather conditions at Hiroshima, and it reported back that conditions were fine (for bombing). People on the ground assumed from this fly-over that the planes were just reconnaissance planes. The first B-29 turned back out to sea, so in Hiroshima the 'all clear' was sounded. It was far from all clear. Enola Gay arrived over Hiroshima at 8.15 and the bomb was released at 31,000 feet (9,470 metres). It took forty-three seconds to fall to the detonation height, 1,900 feet above the ground. Enola Gay was eleven miles away before it felt the shock waves from the explosion.

The target was the Aioi Bridge, but a cross-wind caused the bomb to detonate nearly 800 feet away, over the Shima Surgical Clinic. The blast was equivalent to thirteen kilotons of TNT. There was total destruction over a distance of about a mile, with fires breaking out across 4½ square miles. About two-thirds of the buildings in the city were destroyed and one-third of the population were killed instantly. Nearly all of the doctors and nurses in the city were killed or injured; most of them were in the target area.

The Tokyo control operator of the Japanese Broadcasting Corporation was aware that the Hiroshima station had gone off the air. From some small railway stops within ten miles of the city came confused reports of a terrible explosion in Hiroshima. The military tried to call the Army Control Station in Hiroshima. The total silence was baffling. There had been no big enemy raid. There were no large stores of explosives in Hiroshima. A young officer of the Japanese General Staff was told to fly straight away to Hiroshima to survey the damage and report back; at HQ there was a feeling that the big explosion was just a rumour. The staff officer was about 100 miles from Hiroshima when he and his pilot saw a huge pillar of smoke from the bomb. Their plane reached Hiroshima, or rather the site of Hiroshima, and circled it. There was a great smoking scar on the landscape, covered by a pall of smoke. They landed south of the city, reported to Tokyo what they had seen and began to organise relief. Newspapers in America reported what the Japanese radio was saying about the event: 'Practically all living things, human and animal, were literally scorched to death.'

In the months that followed, more and more people caught in the blast were to die, from burns and from radiation sickness. The death rate was worsened by the shortage of medical resources. Some sources say that as many as 200,000 people had died, from radiation-induced cancer and other long-term effects of the bombing. Nor did the effects end in 1950. Many people who survived the bombing were to die much later, but still prematurely, from cancer and leukaemia related to the radiation.

Some of the buildings in Hiroshima were very strongly constructed, not to make them nuclear bomb-proof but to make them earthquake-proof. The frames of some of them remained standing, even at the hypocentre of the bomb zone, the point vertically beneath the exploding bomb. People who were in the cellars of these buildings survived the bombing, even close to the hypocentre. The Prefectural Industrial Promotional Hall survived; it is now commonly called the Genbaku or A-bomb Dome. This building, designed by Jan Letzel, is now the Hiroshima Peace Memorial and a UNESCO World Heritage site.

Following the bombing of Hiroshima, President Truman announced that a new weapon had been used. He made the Japanese a promise:

If they do not now accept our terms, they may expect a rain of ruin from the air, the like of which has never been seen on this earth. Behind this air attack will follow sea and land forces in such numbers and power as they have not yet seen and with the fighting skill of which they are already well aware.

But still the Japanese government did not respond to Potsdam. Apparently it was considering the conditions under which it would be prepared to surrender. Japanese officials hoped to preserve the national polity, allow Imperial Headquarters to be responsible for disarmament and demobilisation; they did not want the Home Islands, the Japanese mainland, occupied, and the punishment of war criminals was to be delegated to the Japanese government. But the Japanese government was in a poor position to make such demands, with the prospect of one city after another turned into a smoking ruin.

Colonel Tibbets was made responsible for choosing the timing of the second bomb. Initially, 11 August was chosen for the bombing of Kokura or Nagasaki, but it was moved forward by two days to avoid a forecast spell of bad weather.

Nagasaki had been a great seaport and had enormous wartime strategic value because of its wide-range of industries. Unlike Hiroshima, most of the buildings were of old-style Japanese construction, with wooden frames and tiled roofs. Even the smaller industrial buildings were built in this way, not at all designed to withstand explosions. There had been some conventional bombing here, and the children had been evacuated to rural areas for safety.

The B-29 bomber Bockscar took off on the morning of 9 August 1945, carrying the second atomic bomb, this one nicknamed Fat Man. The crew were led by Major Charles Sweeney. The plan was almost exactly the same as for Hiroshima, with two scout planes travelling ahead to report on weather.

One reported both targets clear of cloud. The third plane failed to rendezvous so, after circling for forty minutes, Sweeney went on without it. By the time Sweeney reached Kokura, there was quite a lot of cloud, which meant that, according to orders, visual aiming would be impossible. Sweeney made three passes over the city and, with fuel running low, he aborted the Kokura attack and headed for Nagasaki. Sweeney knew he would now have insufficient fuel to take him back to Iwo Jima and would have to divert to Okinawa.

Sweeney decided that if Nagasaki too was under cloud cover he would get rid of the bomb by dropping it over the sea. But he was advised by Commander Ashworth that if necessary he could use a radar approach. As at Hiroshima, an air raid alert was given in Nagasaki at 7.50 am and an 'all clear' at 8.30. Nothing had been learnt from Hiroshima. At 11 am the support plane dropped instruments on parachutes. It was a strange idea, but with the instruments was a letter addressed to a Japanese nuclear physicist, Professor Ryokichi Sagane. He had studied with three of the scientists who had produced the atomic bomb, and the letter urged him to warn the Japanese about the dangers of the new weapons. But within the hour, the people of

Japan would need no words – they would know the awful truth about the new weapon. The authorities found the message, but did not pass it on to Sagane until a month later.

At 11.01 am, there was a break in the clouds and the bomb was released over Nagasaki's industrial valley. It exploded 1,540 feet above the ground, nearly two miles from the target. As a result, the blast was confined to the Urakami valley; a large part of the city was protected from the blast by a hill ridge. The explosion generated temperatures up to 3,900 degrees Celsius and 600 mph winds. The Mitsubishi-Urakami Ordnance Works was destroyed in the explosion; this was the factory that manufactured the torpedoes used at Pearl Harbor. 50,000 to 75,000 people died in Nagasaki. Some unfortunate survivors from the Hiroshima bombing had taken refuge in Nagasaki, only to be caught by the second nuclear bomb.

The Americans were prepared to drop nuclear bombs on more Japanese cities. A third bomb might be dropped in the third week in August; three more would follow in September; three more in October. The War Department was in a quandary. If the Japanese refused to surrender, should the Americans go on dropping them at a rate of one every week or

two, or save them up and rain them down upon the
Japanese all at once – for maximum shock value?
Meanwhile, because there was no word from the
Japanese government after the second bombing,
Colonel Tibbets was ordered to go back to Utah to
collect another atomic bomb. But when he reached
California, the War in the Pacific was already over.

On 12 August Hirohito told his family he had
decided to surrender. The terms offered by the Allies
seemed to leave intact the principle of imperial rule,
so he was ready to capitulate. He seems to have been
moved more by the frightening prospect of a Soviet
invasion than by the nuclear bombs. He authorised
prime minister Togo to inform the Allies that Japan
would accept their terms on one condition only –
that 'the prerogatives of His Majesty as a Sovereign
ruler' would not be compromised. Never mind the
tens of thousands of civilians, the loyal subjects,
who had died in the nuclear bombings, or the tens
of thousands more who might yet die in bombings
that might come tomorrow or the next day...

If mass murder was done here, if a war crime
was committed, who was the more to blame, the
Americans or the Japanese? President Truman or
Emperor Hirohito?

'WHAT THE HELL IS GOING ON?'

MY LAI (1968)

My Lai was an obscure cluster of hamlets in South Vietnam. Its name became associated with one of the most infamous episodes in the Vietnam War – the My Lai massacre, which took place on 16 March 1968.

Perhaps 700 people were living there, before the massacre. Shortly after dawn on 16 March, three platoons of American troops from C Company, 11th Brigade, arrived after being dropped by helicopters. 1 Platoon was commanded by Lieutenant William Calley and was ordered to go to My Lai village. They were part of a search-and-destroy task force with an order to search for members of the NLF, known as Vietcong, or 'VC', to the US soldiers. The village was in an area where the NLF had been very active.

As the troops from 1 Platoon moved through the village, they began firing at the villagers. The villagers were clearly non-combatants, as the young men had gone out to the paddy fields to work; left in the village were the women, the children and the elderly. One of the soldiers who was at My Lai said in 1973 that he saw nobody who could have been considered to be of military age. He also said that the villagers offered no resistance. An army photographer accompanying the expedition, Ronald Haeberle, saw an American soldier shoot two young boys who could have been no older than five. Photos taken at the scene show the bodies; they can only have been young children and no-one in their right mind could have mistaken them for combatants.

Those returning to the village after the massacre claimed it took them three days to bury all the bodies. They reported that some of the children had their throats cut and that other bodies had been mutilated. Many of the victims had been tortured and sexually abused.

The massacre only came to light when in November 1969 Paul Meadlo, a US soldier, was interviewed on television. He admitted killing ten or fifteen men, women and children. This admission led to pressure being put on the US military to investigate the incident. In fact the US military already knew about it and had launched an investigation into My Lai in April, a clear six months before the general public knew anything. What emerged fairly quickly was that hundreds of villagers had been killed. The precise number could not be established, but it was not less than 175. Figures commonly given are 347 and 504. The official US army investigation came up with the figure of 347, while the memorial at My Lai lists the names and ages of 504 individuals.

Twenty-six US soldiers were charged with committing offences at My Lai, but all were acquitted except Lieutenant William Calley. He was sentenced to life imprisonment with hard labour. After serving only three years under house arrest and four months in a military prison he was released. In August 2009, William Calley took a significant step in making a public apology for the massacre:

There is not a day that goes by that I do not feel remorse for what happened that day in My Lai. I feel remorse for the Vietnamese who were killed, for their families, for the American soldiers involved and their families. I am very sorry.

Calley and his supporters for many years maintained that he was simply following orders. The defence that he offered at his trial was that he was in My Lai to search for Communists and to destroy

Communism, and that he was only carrying out his orders to hunt out the NLF. Colonel Henderson ordered his officers to 'go in there aggressively, close with the enemy and wipe them out for good.' Colonel Barker allegedly ordered 1st Battalion commanders to burn the houses, kill the livestock, destroy the food. On the day before the attack took place, at a briefing session, Captain Ernest Medina told C Company that nearly all the civilian residents of the hamlets in the area would have left for market by 7 am, and that anyone remaining would be NLF or NLF sympathisers. Some of the soldiers, including the platoon leaders, understood these orders to mean that they were to kill all guerrilla combatants and 'suspects', which would include women and children. The Captain was quoted as saying, 'They're all VC, now go and get them.' How would they identify the enemy? Anyone who was running away from them. So the men going into My Lai understood their orders to be to kill everyone they found there.

There was substantial popular support in America for Calley, a young and inexperienced junior officer who was seen as a scapegoat. Seymour Hersh, a journalist who was among the first to report the massacre, thought Calley was as much a victim as the people he shot. It is perhaps possible to understand something of what was in Calley's mind from a remark he made about the nature of the war, 'My troops were getting massacred and mauled by an enemy I couldn't see, an enemy I couldn't feel, I couldn't touch.'

Because of the nature of the fighting, the American soldiers knew that anyone they encountered could be an NLF fighter or at least sympathiser: anyone of any age or either sex. The people in the villages all wore the same style of clothing, so Vietcong could not be distinguished by their appearance. The NLF left lethal booby traps all over the place, so the soldiers knew that at any moment they might be blown up and suffer terrible injuries. They might be killed at any moment. C Company was under stress. Within a few weeks of going on patrol, the company had lost five men and seen others wounded in twenty-eight separate incidents involving booby traps.

One of the soldiers at My Lai, Varnado Simpson, said, 'Everyone who went into the village had in mind to kill. We had lost a lot of buddies and it was a VC stronghold. We considered them either VC or helping the VC.' Sergeant Isaiah Cowen said the men who had been dropped by helicopter in Son My, the district where the village of My Lai was, had been told that everybody there was Vietcong. 'He [a captain] stated that everything that was there was VC or VC sympathisers. There was no doubt in my men's minds that they [the My Lai villagers] were VC.' What this amounts to is an admission of conditioning; they were going into an area having persuaded themselves and one another that everyone they would encounter there was going to be an enemy. There was also an admission that reprisal was a motive: 'We had lost a lot of buddies.' It is interesting that 'sympathisers' were lumped together with fighters; that presumably made it permissible to kill not only a Vietcong fighter, but his wife and children too. My Lai, it had been decided before the helicopter landed, was harbouring Vietcong. A mindset had been created within which a heartless and pointless massacre could take place.

A US Marine wrote later that the nature of the Vietnam War made it likely that civilians would be killed. 'In a guerrilla war, the line between legitimate and illegitimate killing is blurred. The policies of free-fire zones, in which a soldier is permitted to shoot at any human target, armed or unarmed, further confuse the fighting man's moral senses.'

The soldiers fired first at what they thought was a Vietcong position. During the initial shooting some villagers were killed or wounded. After that the soldiers started shooting anything that moved and the scale of the massacre spiralled, the level of brutality increasing by the moment as the soldiers went berserk. Women were stripped and gang raped. Families huddled for safety in huts, but they were shown no mercy. Those who came out into the open with their hands held up in surrender were also killed out of hand. Dozens of villagers were herded into an irrigation ditch and mown down with automatic fire. About seventy-five villagers, rounded up into a large group by the 1st Platoon in the middle of the village, were killed by William Calley and by soldiers ordered to fire by Calley. Calley also shot two other large groups of civilians with a weapon taken from a soldier who refused to do any further killing.

It is important to emphasise that there were some US soldiers at My Lai ready to disobey orders and refuse to kill villagers. Michael Bernhardt, who was a sergeant, was one of those who refused to participate in the killing. He put himself in danger by doing so and by additionally telling Captain Medina that he would write to his Congressman about the incident; he believed that his action – or inaction – at My Lai led to his being assigned to more dangerous duties afterwards. Later he would be called as a prosecution witness in Medina's trial.

The 2nd Platoon went to another two hamlets a few hundred metres away and killed more than sixty people there. After these initial sweeps by the 1st and 2nd Platoons, the 3rd platoon went through killing any person or animal still living in the area, including shooting dead any wounded found among the heaps of bodies. Over the next two days, the soldiers continued the work of burning and destroying dwellings.

Most of the soldiers in the area had not taken part in the atrocities, but most of them did not protest or try to prevent them either; probably they did not dare to, given the ambiguous nature of the orders. Three soldiers who did try to stop the massacre and protect the wounded were afterwards denounced by US Congressmen; when they returned home they received hate mail and death threats. They were only honoured for their efforts many years afterwards.

A helicopter pilot, Warrant Officer Hugh Thompson, was flying over the village and saw large numbers of dead and dying civilians. He radioed for help for the wounded. 'It looks like a bloodbath down there! What the hell is going on?' He landed.

Then Thompson and his crew witnessed Captain Medina kicking and shooting an unarmed woman, though Medina later claimed that he thought she had a grenade. Thompson was shocked and confused as he encountered a soldier with some people in a ditch; when he asked the soldier, a sergeant, if he could help the people out of the ditch, the sergeant answered that he would 'help them out of their misery'. Thompson had a conversation with Calley, who said he was following orders. As Thompson took off again, he saw the sergeant firing into the ditch.

Thompson saw another group of villagers in a bunker and being approached by US soldiers. He landed again and told his crew that if the US soldiers fired at the Vietnamese civilians they were to open fire at the soldiers. Thompson had an unsatisfactory conversation with a lieutenant who thought the only way to get the people out of the bunker was with a hand grenade. According to Thompson's testimony, he told the lieutenant to hold his men where they were while he got the children out. He found about fifteen people in there, persuaded them to come out and led them to his helicopter; he stood with them while they were flown out in two groups. Thompson went back to My Lai, landed again and went to the ditch. Among the bodies there he and his crew found an unharmed boy, who was flown to safety. Thompson then reported what he had seen at My Lai to his company commander, Major Watke, describing 'needless and unnecessary killings'. Thompson was awarded the Distinguished Flying Cross and his crew Glenn Andreotta and Lawrence Colburn the Bronze Star. In 1998, they were additionally awarded the Soldier's Medal 'for heroism above and beyond the call of duty while saving the lives of Vietnamese civilians'.

But another version of My Lai was being propagated. General Westmoreland congratulated the unit responsible for carrying out an 'outstanding job'. An army magazine described an action in which 'US infantrymen had killed 128 Communists in a bloody day-long battle'. Colonel Henderson was nevertheless ordered to investigate what had happened. He interviewed several of the soldiers involved and wrote a report saying that about twenty civilians had been inadvertently killed during the operation. This was at a time when the US army was still presenting My Lai as a military victory. As the months passed, though, individual soldiers filed complaints about incidents of brutality they had witnessed. One letter of complaint was from a twenty-one-year-old soldier, who claimed US soldiers were guilty of routine and pervasive brutality against Vietnamese civilians, though without specifically naming My Lai. Colin Powell, then a thirty-one-year-old major, investigated the letter and, at the time, minimised the maltreatment of Vietnamese. By 2004, when he was a powerful political figure, US Secretary of State, he was prepared to admit that 'horrible things happen every now and again, but they are still to be deplored.' But the massacre might still have gone unnoticed if a member of C Company, Ron Ridenhour, had not written about My Lai to President Nixon, and copied the letter to the Pentagon and numerous Congressmen. Many ignored it, but not all.

It was not until September 1969 that Calley was charged with several counts of premeditated murder; twenty-five other soldiers were later similarly charged. William Calley was convicted in March 1971 and sentenced. President Nixon controversially decided to release Calley from prison pending appeal. Captain Medina was tried separately, and he denied giving the order that led to the massacre. He was acquitted. Most of the enlisted men who were involved in the My Lai massacre had already left the army and, within American law, therefore exempt from prosecution.

Some commentators have argued that the outcome of the My Lai courts-martial was the reverse of the principles set out in the Nuremberg War Tribunal after the Second World War. Calley's sentence was reduced because he honestly believed that what he was doing was a part of his orders. This reasoning is a direct contradiction of the code set at Nuremberg and Tokyo – where both German and Japanese soldiers were executed for committing similar acts under similar circumstances. 'I was only carrying out orders' was not an allowable excuse in the aftermath of the Second World War.

PART FOUR

BREAKING POINT KILLERS

'WE GENERALLY KILLS
THEM WHERE WE GO'
ALTON COLEMAN (1984)

Alton Coleman was a spree killer who, unusually, was sentenced to death four times in three states, Illinois, Indiana and Ohio (twice). Because of the complexities of the American legal system, Coleman was executed in 2002 for murders that he committed during a killing spree long before, in 1984. He was executed specifically for the murder of a forty-four-year-old woman, Marlene Walters of Norwood, Ohio, though he actually killed seven people. Altogether about twenty people were brutally attacked.

Alton Coleman had a partner in crime, Debra Denise Brown. She too was sentenced to death in Ohio, but her sentence was commuted in 1991 to life imprisonment. She is serving this sentence without any prospect of parole in the Ohio Reformatory for Women in Marysville, Ohio.

It was in the summer of 1984 that Alton Coleman and Debra Brown, then twenty-eight and twenty-one years old respectively, launched into their killing spree. Most of the victims were black Americans, like Coleman and Brown themselves. It is not clear why. One theory is that the killers believed they would merge into the background more easily, and stand a better chance of escaping, if they murdered within their own racial group. Another theory is that there was a strange, anti-black, racist motive. A retired FBI profiler has argued in favour of a racial element in the killings. During one vicious assault, Coleman was heard to rant incoherently about the way black people were forcing him to murder other blacks.

Alton Coleman had a disturbed and deprived upbringing. His mother was a prostitute who often had sex with her clients in front of him. Not surprisingly, this unsettled the boy's sexual development and between 1973 and 1983 he was charged with sexual offences six times. Two cases were dismissed, in two he was acquitted, in two he pleaded guilty to lesser charges. He had been charged with raping a fourteen-year-old girl and was about to go on trial in Illinois for this offence, when he went on his rampage of killing.

Debra Brown too had a disturbed and unsatisfactory unbringing. She was one of a family of eleven, had suffered a head injury as a child, had low intelligence and was described as having a dependent personality. She met Coleman in 1983 and moved in with him. She went along with and participated in Coleman's assaults and murders, but she had never been involved with any crime before. She does not appear to have been naturally disposed to violence and had never, until then, been in trouble with the police. When her death sentence was commuted to life, Governor Celeste drew attention to her low IQ – she scored around 60–70 in tests – and he pointed to her slave relationship with Coleman as an extenuating circumstance. Governor Celeste was a vigorous and committed opponent of capital punishment and she was perhaps fortunate that she was one of eight prisoners on death row in Ohio to have their sentences commuted, just before Celeste left office. But Debra Brown should not be portrayed as an innocent victim of circumstances. She is, reportedly, not sorry for her actions. At her first trial in Ohio, she sent a note to the judge which included the comment, 'I killed the bitch and I don't give a damn. I had fun out of it.'

In May 1984, Coleman befriended Juanita Wheat. She lived in Kenosha, Wisconsin and had a nine-year-old daughter called Vernita. On 29 May, Coleman kidnapped Vernita and took her to Waukegan in Illinois. The child's body was discovered three weeks later in a derelict building that was just four blocks away from the apartment of Coleman's grandmother. Vernita's body was badly decomposed, but it was evident that she had died by strangulation with a ligature. On 31 May, which was probably the day after he murdered Vernita, Coleman befriended Robert Carpenter and spent the night at his home in Waukegan. The following day, Coleman borrowed Robert Carpenter's car, ostensibly to go shopping, and never returned.

In June 1984, Coleman and Brown turned up in Gary, Indiana. There they met two little girls, Annie and Tamika Turks, aged nine and seven. On 19 June, at about the same time that Vernita's body was discovered, the body of little Tamika was also found and the cause of death was the same. Annie was lucky to survive the attack, though she was sexually assaulted by both Coleman and Brown.

On the same day that Tamika's body was discovered, Coleman made friends with Donna Williams, a young woman living in Gary. A month later, her badly decomposed body was found in Detroit, and her car was nearby. The cause of death was the same as with the other victims: strangulation with a ligature. On 28 June, Coleman and Brown went into the home of Mr and Mrs Palmer Jones at Dearborn Heights, Michigan. Coleman handcuffed Mr Jones and gave him a beating; Mrs Jones was attacked as well. Then Coleman stole their money and their car.

In July 1984, Coleman and Brown arrived in Toledo, Ohio. There Coleman befriended Virginia Temple, who had several children. When relatives stopped hearing from Virginia, they became concerned about the welfare of her children and called at her house. They found the younger children alone, abandoned and frightened. There was no sign of Virginia or the eldest child, nine-year-old Rachelle. Their bodies were found in a crawl space; both had been strangled. On the same morning as the Temple murders, Coleman and Brown entered the home of Mr and Mrs Duvendack (Frank and Dorothy) in Toedlo. Coleman tied the couple up with cords cut from appliances. As in the Jones attack, Coleman and Brown took the cash and the car. One of Mrs Duvendack's watches was taken and later found, apparently deliberately placed, under the body of a later victim, another repeating motif.

That same day, Coleman and Brown had a non-violent encounter, this time when they appeared at the home of the Revd and Mrs Millard Gay in Dayton,

Ohio. They stayed with the Gays and then went with them on 9 July to Lockwood, Ohio, to attend a religious service. The next day, the Gays dropped the pair of mass murderers in downtown Cincinnati, and drove off unscathed. They were lucky.

By this stage, the police had worked out the pattern of criminal activity and who was responsible for it. On 12 July 1984, the FBI added Alton Coleman to its Ten Most Wanted List. The authorities understood that they were dealing with an extremely dangerous man. Meanwhile the killing spree continued, as Coleman and his partner cycled into Norwood, Ohio, on the morning of 13 July. By midday they were driving away in another stranger's car, leaving Marlene Walters dead and her husband Harry unconscious; it was Harry's car they were driving. Harry Walters survived to become a key witness in the case against Coleman and Brown. The two killers had come to him to enquire about a camper van he had offered for sale. While they were discussing the details, Coleman picked up a candlestick and hit him violently over the head with it, breaking his skull. Sheri Walters, the Walters' daughter, arrived home in the middle of the afternoon to find her father unconscious at the foot of the basement steps and her mother dead. Both had ligatures round their throats, both had their wrists tied together behind their backs. For some reason the killers had covered Mrs Walters' battered head with a sheet. The post mortem revealed that she had been beaten over the head twenty-five times, an extraordinarily savage attack. Pieces of a broken bottle were found in the living room, bearing Coleman's fingerprints. In the basement bloody footprints from two different kinds of shoe were found.

Two days later, Coleman and Brown appeared in Williamsburg, Kentucky, driving Mr Walters' car. There they abducted Oline Carmical, a college professor, and drove back to Dayton with Mr Carmical locked in the boot. They abandoned the car and Mr Carmical was rescued by the police. Coleman and Brown went back to the home of the Revd Millard Gay and his wife. By this time Coleman was the focus of a nationwide manhunt, so Mr Gay recognised Coleman, not just as someone who had befriended him but now as a killer as well. Coleman and Brown produced guns. Mr Gay asked why they wanted to treat them like that – a question that probably no-one could answer – and Coleman said, 'I'm not going to kill you, but we generally kills them where we go.'

It is not clear why the Gays were spared, but perhaps it was their association with the church that did it. A residual element of respect. But Coleman and Brown took the Gays' car when they went, and drove it back towards Evanston. On the way they stole another car, killing its elderly owner. They changed cars frequently to avoid detection. In the same way they kept changing tee-shirts, during journeys.

In Evanston on 20 July, someone who knew Coleman by sight stopped at a traffic light. Coleman and Brown crossed the street in front of him. Noting where they were going, the driver drove on to a petrol station where he told the police. A description was broadcast and it was not long before a detective spotted the two killers in an otherwise empty park. When officers approached Coleman, Brown was seen to walk away towards another park exit where she was stopped by police. The two were taken into custody without any violence and driven to the Evanston Police Department. Fingerprints were taken and their identity firmly established.

A week later, over fifty law enforcement officials from the six different states involved met to plan how to prosecute the killers most effectively. Michigan was rejected as a starting-point because it did not impose the death penalty; Ohio was chosen instead, giving the best chance of a quick imposition of the death penalty. Successful convictions for 'sample' murders were achieved in mid-1985. But Coleman's case was taken to the US Supreme Court several times over the next seven years. Coleman's appeals, based on the assertion that his conviction and death sentence were unconstitutional, did not persuade the judges to alter the sentence.

Ohio planned to allow a large number of victims' family members and survivors in to witness the execution. So many were being allowed that closed-circuit television was being installed to allow some to witness Coleman's death from outside the execution house. Coleman's final appeal was based on the idea that this would turn his execution into a 'spectator sport'. It was to no avail. He died by lethal injection in the state prison at Lucasville on 26 April 2002, without expressing any remorse for the killings.

'I WISH I HAD STAYED IN BED'
THE HUNGERFORD MASSACRE (1987)

On 19 August 1987, just two months before the Great Storm struck southern England, a man went berserk in Hungerford in Berkshire, and shot dead sixteen people. The man was Michael Robert Ryan. He was a twenty-seven-year-old unemployed labourer and antiques dealer. He was an only child and his father, Alfred Ryan, had been fifty-five when Michael was born. Alfred Ryan died in Swindon in 1985. At the time of the massacre, Michael Ryan was living with his mother, who had a job as a dinner lady at the local primary school. The press made much of this, suggesting that the mother-son relationship was unhealthy. But it may have been that there was a mutual dependence resulting from their circumstances, she recently widowed and therefore feeling vulnerable, he unemployed and therefore feeling insecure and anxious. One newspaper headline called Ryan a 'mummy's boy', but that is no better than name-calling: it explains nothing.

Far more serious was Michael Ryan's obsession with firearms. The press reported that he had magazines about guns and survival skills. But much that was in the press was unfounded. One claim was that Ryan was obsessed with the Rambo film First Blood, but there is no evidence that he had ever seen the film or owned a video recorder. Ryan acquired a shotgun certificate in 1978 and in 1986 he acquired a licence that allowed him to own two pistols. Then he applied to have this amended to include a third pistol. This was granted in April 1987. In July 1987 he applied for a licence variation to include two semi-automatic rifles, which was also granted. He now owned, legally owned, two semi-automatic pistols, two shotguns and two semi-automatic rifles. At the time of the massacre, one of the pistols was being repaired. No questions appear to have been asked by the authorities about the reason for amassing this substantial arsenal.

Michael Ryan's appalling killing spree began in Savernake Forest, seven miles west of Hungerford, just after midday on 19 August 1987. A thirty-five-year-old woman, Susan Godfrey, had driven her two small children from Reading to the forest for a picnic. Hannah was four years old and James was two. Ryan held the family at gunpoint, made Susan put her children in the car, then forced her to walk into some bushes. There he shot her thirteen times in the back. Hannah got out of the car and went off to get help. She approached a pensioner, Myra Rose, and told her that a 'man in black has shot our mummy'. Myra Rose called the police.

Meanwhile, Michael Ryan was back in his silver Vauxhall Astra and driving along the A4 back towards Hungerford, stopping for petrol at an out-of-town petrol station. There he waited for a motorcyclist to leave the garage before putting petrol into his tank. He fired at the assistant standing at the till, Mrs Dean, and missed. He went into the shop and tried to shoot her from closer range, but the rifle magazine had fallen out. He drove off towards Hungerford. Mrs Dean had a lucky escape, like some others that day, though a very frightening experience. The motorcyclist had seen the attempted shooting; he stopped in the village of Froxfield and called the police to say that he had seen an attempted armed robbery.

At 12.45 pm, Michael Ryan was seen at his home in Hungerford. He piled his weapons into the Astra and found that the car would not start. It says a lot about his state of mind that his reponse to this setback was to get out and go round to fire five shots into the back of the car. Neighbours watched anxiously as he moved in an agitated way between the car and the house. He went back into the house and shot the family dog. Then he doused the house with petrol and set it on fire. The fire eventually spread to and destroyed three adjoining houses.

Neighbours Roland and Sheila Mason were in the back garden of their house. Ryan took the shotguns from his car boot and killed them. He shot Sheila once in the head and Roland six times in the back.

Because the Astra would not start, Ryan went off on foot to the town's common. He shot and wounded Marjorie Jackson as she watched him from her living room window. He shot and wounded a teenager, Lisa Mildenhall, as she stood outside her house; he shot her in both legs. Lisa remembered Ryan smiling at her before he crouched and fired.

A seventy-seven-year-old woman protested to Ryan about the noise he was making, and was lucky not to have been shot – perhaps her response was too surreal to register. Marjorie Jackson went and pulled the protesting woman into her home and then phoned George White, a friend who worked with her husband. She told him she had been shot. Her husband decided to go home and George White offered to drive him.

Ryan met a family walking their dog. When Kenneth Clements saw that Ryan was heavily armed, he understood what was happening. He raised his hands in the surrender gesture while his family scrambled over a wall and ran for cover. Ryan ignored the surrender gesture and shot Mr Clements, who fell down dead, still holding the dog lead.

Going back to the carnage of his burning home, Ryan encountered a police officer, PC Roger Brereton, who was arriving in a car after the reports of shooting. Ryan shot PC Brereton, whose car swerved and crashed into a telegraph pole. He radioed to his colleagues that he had been shot, then died sitting in his patrol car. Then, moments later, a Volvo turned into the road driven by Linda Chapman with her teenage daughter Alison as her passenger. Ryan fired repeatedly at the Volvo. Alison was hit in the right thigh, Linda in the left shoulder. While Ryan was reloading, Linda was able to reverse the car, get away from Ryan and drive to the local doctor's surgery, crashing into a tree outside. Then George White's Toyota arrived, with Ivor Jackson in the passenger seat. Ryan fired, killing George White and seriously injuring Ivor Jackson. The Toyota crashed into the back of the police patrol car. Ivor Jackson wisely decided to pretend to be dead. He remained very still, hoping that Ryan would not come over and look more closely.

Ryan moved off along Fairview Road. Abdul Rahman Khan was mowing his lawn; Ryan shot him dead, then shot and injured his next-door neighbour, Alan Lepetit. Ironically, Mr Lepetit had helped Ryan build the unit in which Ryan displayed his guns. Then he fired at an ambulance, shattering one of its windows and injuring paramedic Hazel Haslett as it arrived. Hazel accelerated away before Ryan was able to fire again.

Not surprisingly, people had started to come out to see what was happening. A crowd gathered; others looked out of windows. Ryan fired randomly at people as they appeared on the street, and at the windows. Then Ryan's mother Dorothy arrived in her car, to see her house in flames, her son armed to the teeth, wrecked cars and the bodies of dead and injured people lying all over the place. A scene of carnage. Instinctively, she went to help. She opened the door of George White's Toyota and Ivor Jackson – with four bullet wounds and still feigning death – heard her say 'Oh, Ivor'. Then she went to try to reason with her crazed son. He took aim. She raised her hands and pleaded with him not to shoot, but he shot her just the same and she fell down dead.

Mrs Betty Tolladay came out of her house with the intention of complaining about the noise Ryan was making. She assumed he was doing target practice. He shot and wounded her, and she ran off towards the common.

By this stage the police understood the situation and decided to evacuate the area, but the plan to do this was ineffective. The police helicopter assigned to track Ryan's movements did not take off until an hour after the massacre started, if we see it as marked by Ryan setting his mother's house on fire. The police helicopter was then hampered by the activity of media helicopters. One police officer observing Ryan's behaviour and the extent of his arsenal advised that armed police should be used; he was too heavily armed for Hungerford police station to deal with.

Ryan shot and killed Francis Butler as he walked his dog on the common. He fired at teenager Andrew Cadle, but missed; Andrew was able to cycle away at speed. A taxi driver, Marcus Barnard, slowed down as Ryan crossed the road in front of him; Ryan shot him in the head and killed him. Mr Barnard had responded to a a police diversion towards the common. This reflected the poor level communication between the police helicopter and the police on the ground. An ambulance repairman, John Storms, was sitting in his parked van when Ryan shot him in the face. Mr Storms crouched low inside the vehicle, hoping that was the end of the shooting. He felt two more bullets punch into the van, but he was not wounded again. Bob Barclay, a local builder, courageously ran out to drag Mr Storms from his car and into the safety of his house.

Ryan walked next towards the centre of town, which police were trying to evacuate. On his way, Ryan shot and killed Douglas Wainwright and injured his wife as they sat in their Datsun. Kathleen Wainwright saw that her husband was dead. She also saw that Ryan was reloading and approaching the car. She unbuckled her seatbelt and ran from the car. The couple were visiting their son, who was a Hungerford policeman. It had been PC Wainwright who had signed the extension to Ryan's firearm licence a few weeks before. The next driver to be attacked, Kevin Lance, was wounded in the arm. Eric Vardy, a fifty-one-year-old handyman, was driving along Priory Avenue, when he encountered Ryan. Mr Vardy's passenger, Steven Ball, saw a wounded young man – it was Kevin Lance – running into a side street while clutching his injured arm. He was distracted by this sight when Ryan started firing on

Mr Vardy's van. The windscreen shattered and Mr Vardy was hit twice in the neck and upper body and crashed the van into a wall; he later died of his injuries. Steven Ball had no serious injuries.

At about 1.30 pm, Michael Ryan fired a single shot at a passing Renault, fatally wounding the driver, twenty-two-year-old Sandra Hill. A passing soldier, Carl Harries, tried to help her, but she died. Then Ryan shot his way into a house in Priory Road, shooting the couple inside, Jack and Myrtle Gibbs, and killing them both. From inside the Gibbs's house, Ryan fired into neighbouring houses, injuring Michael Jennings in one house and Myra Geater in another. Ryan moved on down Priory Road and saw Ian Playle. The thirty-four-year-old was in his Ford Sierra, driving his wife and two small children home from a shopping trip. Ryan shot Mr Playle, and the Ford crashed into a parked car. Carl Harries was again there to try to give Mr Playle first aid. It was to no avail, though Mrs Playle and the children were unhurt.

Shortly afterwards, Michael Ryan broke into the Community Technical College, which was empty and closed for the summer holiday. Ryan had been a pupil there, which may have some significance. He went into one of the classrooms and barricaded himself in. Police surrounded the building. A number of ground-staff were present and they gave advice on entering the building and its possible hiding places. Ryan fired at circling helicopters as negotiators got themselves into position. Attempts to persuade Ryan to come out failed and towards 7 pm he committed suicide. During the negotiations, Michael Ryan said, 'Hungerford must be a bit of a mess. I wish I had stayed in bed.'

There was a great deal of heart-searching afterwards, especially about the police response. The police were hampered in several ways. The telephone exchange could not deal with the large volume of emergency calls coming through. The Thames Valley firearms squad were training forty miles away. The police helicopter was being repaired. Only two phone lines were in use at the police station.

The Hungerford Massacre ranks with Dunblane (1996) and Cumbria (2010) as the worst firearm atrocity in British history. The inquiry that followed revealed that Michael Ryan had owned his weapons entirely legally and that led on directly to the Firearms (Amendment) Act of 1988, which banned the private ownership of semi-automatic centre-fire rifles and placed greater restriction on the use of shotguns with a capacity greater than two rounds.

'NO-ONE GETS AWAY FROM ME'

PORT ARTHUR MASSACRE (1996)

The Port Arthur Massacre claimed the lives of thirty-five people. Twenty-one other people were wounded, mostly at the historic Port Arthur prison colony, a major tourist focus in the south-east of Tasmania. Because of the scale of the mayhem, this ranks as the worst killing spree in Australia's history, and one of the worst of its kind in modern times globally.

The killer was Martin Bryant, a twenty-eight-year-old man from New Town, a Hobart suburb. At first sight he seems an unlikely candidate for a mass murderer. Often spree killers are hard-luck cases of one sort or another. Often they are people without financial resources or people who have been marginalised socially. But Bryant was not quite one of these, as he inherited a great deal of money from a friend, Helen Harvey. He used some of this to do a lot of travelling from 1993 onwards. But he also used some to buy an AR-10 semi-automatic rifle through a newspaper ad in Tasmania. In March

1996 he had this repaired at a gun shop and was making enquiries at other gun shops about buying an AR-15 rifle. Meanwhile, he was buying cleaning kits for a shotgun and a sports bag that would be stout enough to carry a large amount of ammunition.

A factor that cannot be overlooked is that he was a man of low intelligence; he had an estimated IQ of sixty-six, which puts him in the lowest two percent of the population. At the time of the massacre, he was receiving a Disability Support Pension on the basis that he was mentally handicapped. He had, on the other hand, never been diagnosed with schizophrenia or any other mental illness. Even so, it is worrying that someone functioning at his mental level was able to hold a driving licence, let alone buy guns. These were issues – the Australian gun laws in particular – that would become the subjects of heated debate in the aftermath of the shootings.

Bryant's father tried to purchase a seaside holiday accommodation property called Seascape. Before he could organise his finance, David and Noelene Martin bought it. This was a great disappointment to Bryant's father, who grumbled about what he saw as the Martins' 'double-dealing' in acquiring Seascape. Martin Bryant tried to help by offering to buy the Martins another property nearby, but they declined his offer. It is not known how much this episode contributed to the father's depression and later suicide. Bryant believed that the Martins had bought the property out of spite, to thwart Bryant's father. He believed that the Martins were reponsible for driving his father into depression and suicide, describing them as 'very mean people ... the worse people in my life'. He had turned himself into a victim, a victim with a grudge.

The day of the killing spree began unusually, with Martin Bryant's alarm clock going off at 6 am. His girlfriend Petra and others who knew him intimately said he had never been known to use the alarm; he had no job to go to and no other commitments. At 8 am Petra left the house to visit her parents. Bryant too left the house, which had been left to him by his employer, setting the house security alarm at 9.47 am.

At 10.30 am, he bought a cigarette lighter from a newspaper shop, paying with a large-denomination note and not waiting for the change. He bought a bottle of tomato sauce from a supermarket, which he paid for with coins. Then he drove to Forcett Village, stopping at a service station for a cup of coffee. He told an attendant he was going surfing at Roaring Beach, but the attendant thought it unlikely as it was a very calm day: there would be no surf.

He stopped at another service station to buy petrol and the attendant there noticed Bryant staring at the calm waters of the bay. He had a surf board on his roof rack, and the attendant again noted that the conditions were no good for surfing.

He drove on to Port Arthur, arriving at Seascape, the seaside accommodation that his father had wanted to buy, at 11.45 am. Bryant entered, killing the new owners, David and Noelene Martin. A visiting couple arrived outside and Bryant went out to them. They wanted to view the accommodation, but Bryant made an excuse not to let them in. The visitors found him rude and unco-operative, so they left. Bryant locked the doors of Seascape and drove into Port Arthur. He stopped to speak to Roger Larner, a farmer who did not at first recognise him as they had not met for over fifteen years. Bryant told Larner he had bought a property called Fogg Lodge and was hoping to buy some cattle from Larner; he also spoke about buying the Martins' place next door, which in one sense at least he was now able to do. He asked if Marian Larner was at home and asked he could drive up to the farm to see her. Larner agreed, but said he would come too. Bryant changed his mind and left, saying he would come back in the afternoon.

Bryant parked at the historic waterfront site and carried a large bag and a video camera to the café. He ordered a large meal, which he ate on the deck outside; people holding the door open for him commented on the large amount of food. He said he was hungry from surfing. He started conversations with several people, but mostly mumbled nervously to himself, looking both towards the car park and into the café, perhaps assessing the numbers of people. The café was unusually busy. When he had finished his meal he went back into the café to return his tray, then pulled a rifle out of his bag. He shot and killed twelve customers and wounded ten more in only fifteen seconds. Because the café was so crowded, most of the customers did not know what was happening. Some people who heard the gunshots assumed they were blanks, fired as part of a re-enactment, the sort of thing that often happens at heritage sites.

Bryant moved on to the gift shop, which gave many people time to hide under tables and behind shop displays. He shot and killed two young women who worked in the shop. Others were shot as they tried to escape through a locked door. Bryant fired back into the café and one of those hiding in the gift shop, Jason Winter, thought it was safe to emerge into the open, seeing Bryant just too late; Bryant shot him dead. Then Bryant went into a corner of the shop where he found several people hiding and shot three more.

By the time Bryant left the café and the gift shop, twenty people lay dead – and the spree had only lasted two minutes. Some of the café staff had been able to get out through the kitchen and warn people outside what was happening. There were several coaches outside with lines of tourists. Many of them hid inside the coaches or in nearby buildings. Some did not react, not fully understanding the situation. Bryant walked towards the coaches and shot one of the drivers in the back; Royce Thompson managed to roll under the coach, but died later of his wounds. Brigid Cook urged people to move down between the coaches and along the jetty area to safety; she worried that she was making a fuss about nothing, but certainly saved many people's lives by her action.

Bryant fired randomly among the tourists, following some of them as they tried to escape along the waterfont. But he changed direction, went back to his vehicle and changed weapons. He sat in his car for a moment, then went back to the coaches, firing several more shots. He found one of his earlier victims lying wounded, unable to move; he shot her again and she died later. He boarded one of the coaches and found a woman hiding there; he shot her dead. Then he shot and wounded a man he saw standing in the next coach. He chased Neville Quin, firing at him twice before Mr Quin boarded a coach. But Bryant followed him, pointed his gun at his face and said, 'No-one gets away from me.' Mr Quin knew Bryant was about to shoot and ducked. The bullet hit his neck. He was sufficiently wounded for Bryant to leave him. Mr Quin was then able to go and find his wife, who was also injured. She died, but Neville Quin survived. A difficulty in evading Bryant was that the shots were very loud and it was impossible to tell where they were coming from. Bryant was also moving about very erratically.

Bryant got into his car and drove out of the car park, towards the toll booth. As he overtook a young woman with two small children who were trying to escape, he slowed down and opened his car door. Nanette Mikac moved towards the car, instinctively believing she was being given an opportunity to escape. She did not know he was the gunman. Others nearby shouted, 'It's him!', but it was too late. Bryant got out of his car, held her by the shoulder and told her to kneel. She did, saying, 'Please don't hurt my babies.' He shot her in the temple, killing her instantly, and then with unbelievable brutality shot dead the two little girls, Madeline and Alannah.

On seeing this appalling incident, people further up the road started running for their lives. Things had happened very quickly and, at this stage, the staff at the toll booth had no idea what was happening. Bryant drove up and blocked the path of a BMW that was stopped at the toll booth. One of the occupants protested at Bryant's behaviour, and Bryant shot him dead at point blank range. Another occupant got out of the BMW and went towards Bryant. He too was shot dead. Bryant went to the BMW, pulled two women out, and shot them dead too. It was evidently the BMW that Bryant wanted. He transferred most of his ammunition and other gear, including handcuffs, rifle and a container of fuel, into the BMW.

Bryant shot at the driver of another car as it drove up, Graham Sutherland. Mr Sutherland was able to reverse up the road and reach the nearby service station, where he tried to warn people what was happening. But Bryant arrived almost at once, blocking a white Toyota as its driver, Glenn Pears, tried to get out onto the road. Bryant pointed his gun at Mr Pears, pushed him towards the BMW and made him get into the boot; Bryant locked him inside. Glenn Pears' girlfriend was meanwhile trying to reach the driving seat of the Toyota. Bryant shot and killed her. The incident was seen by everyone at the service station. Some ran to hide in the scrubland. Those inside were told to lie down by the attendant, who locked the doors and grabbed his rifle, but before he could load it Bryant had driven off. Several minutes afterwards, a policeman arrived and set off in pursuit of the killer.

Bryant drove down to Seascape and got out of the BMW, firing randomly at five passing cars, and wounding two of the drivers. Then he drove down the Seascape drive to the house, pulled Glenn Pears from the boot and handcuffed him to the stair rail inside the house. At some point, perhaps just after this, Bryant set fire to the BMW.

By now it was 2 pm. The only two policemen in the area had been radioed with a message to go to Port Arthur and look out for Martin Bryant's Volvo. As they approached in different cars by different routes, they were told to look out for the BMW. One of the policemen drove past Seascape, passing one of the gunfire-disabled cars. He radioed the second officer and they converged on Seascape, where they could see the burning BMW. Bryant fired at them and they took cover in a ditch. Whenever they tried to move from their position, Bryant fired, so they were trapped there for several hours.

Bryant answered the phone. It was a woman journalist who was making random phone calls to try to get information about what was happening. By chance, Bryant himself answered the phone when she called Seascape. Bryant said his name was Jamie. What was happening? 'Lots of fun!' But then he said that if she called again he would shoot his hostage.

In the evening, at about 9 pm, a team from the Tasmanian Police Force's Special Operations Group arrived. Using bullet-proof jackets, riot shields and the cover of darkness, they were able to rescue the two officers trapped in the ditch. Then followed a stand-off lasting eighteen hours. During this time, the police negotiated with Bryant by phone. He asked for a helicopter to take him to a plane; he wanted to be flown to Adelaide in South Australia. If the police would supply the helicopter, he would release one of his hostages, Mr Pears. He would only keep the other hostage, Mrs Martin. He could see SOG officers moving about and approaching the house, and demanded that they be moved back. The police were uncertain how he knew what they were doing, and assumed there some sort of night-vision surveillance system at the property, though none was later found.

Late in the night, Bryant's cordless phone began to run out of power. The police tried to persuade him to put the phone on its charger, but he would not. Then the phone went dead and there were no further communications.

The next morning Bryant started a fire in the guest house and shouted to the police to come and get him. The police believed that Mr Pears was already dead, but still did not risk going into the house. They assumed the fire would eventually force him out. The ammunition was igniting and exploding randomly as the fire spread. Eventually Bryant ran out with his clothes on fire, preoccupied with removing them. He was arrested and taken to hospital. The police then confirmed that Mr Pears was dead. He had been shot during or even before the stand-off. The bodies of the Martins were also found.

Martin Bryant's account of events to the police was very garbled. He denied shooting anyone. He did not take the BMW from the area of the toll booth. The man he took hostage was from the BMW, and he must have died in the boot when the car exploded. In his mind there was no distinction between the car fire and the house fire. The guns the police found were not his, though he admitted that the gun found in his own car, abandoned near the tollbooth, belonged to him. He had not been to Port Arthur that day. He was either telling lots of lies or he genuinely did not really know what had happened. At one level or another, Martin Bryant was in denial on a grand scale.

Bryant pleaded not guilty to committing the thirty-five murders and laughed when the judge read out the charges. Later he changed his plea. He was found guilty, without trial, on every charge and is currently serving thirty-five life sentences for the murders plus 1,035 years of cumulative penalties for the other associated offences. The order is that he is never to be released. The removal of the possibility of parole, which is very rare in Australia, is a recognition that this was one of the worst cases, globally, of a mass killing spree.

Spree killers usually commit suicide at the climax of their sprees, but Bryant did not. Nor was he shot by police marksmen, as he might have been. Instead, he survived to stand trial and receive thirty-five life sentences for his crimes. It may seem pointless to speculate about factors that might have made a difference. But might Michael Bryant's state of mind have been altered if there had been a good stiff breeze – if it had been a good day for surfing? Or was there some inner time-bomb ticking away, that would have made it happen then, whatever the weather?

'I Can't Wait To Join You'
THE FORD HOOD SHOOTINGS (2009)

On 5 November 2009, a gunman killed thirteen people and wounded thirty others. This mass killing took place at Fort Hood, a huge US army base just outside Killeen in Texas.

The killer was Nidal Malik Hasan, who was a psychiatrist in the US army, holding the rank of major. Hasan was of Palestinian origin, an American-born Muslim extremist. Other army officers had become aware of Hasan's growing interest in radical Islam from 2005 onwards. He was in e-mail contact with the Yemen-based cleric Anwar al-Awlaki, who declared Hasan an Islamic hero: 'Fighting against the US army is an Islamic duty'. The e-mail correspondence was known about by the FBI terrorism task force in 2008, but the FBI made the judgement, wrongly as it turned out, that Nadal Hasan was not a threat. The FBI believed that the questions Hasan addressed to Anwar al-Awlaki were consistent with the pursuit of medical research.

But that was before the shootings. Subsequent to the shootings, the US authorities have classified al-Awlaki as a Specially Designated Global Terrorist; the UN identified al-Awlaki as an associate of al-Qaeda. Yet even after the attack and after months of investigation it is still unclear whether Hasan was a terrorist or the victim of a severe mental health issue. He has still not been conclusively linked with any radical group.

Just after 1.30 pm on 5 November 2009, Major Hasan arrived at his post, the Soldier Readiness Centre. This is a health centre where soldiers receive routine medical treatment immediately before deployment, and on their return. Hasan sat at an empty table with his head bowed for a few seconds before standing up and opening fire. He is said to have shouted 'Allahu Akbar!' and begun firing at soldiers who were processing through cubicles in the centre. He also fired on a crowd gathering for a college graduation ceremony that was due to begin in a nearby theatre at 2 pm. He aimed particularly at people in army uniforms. He had two handguns and a revolver.

Captain John Gaffaney tried to stop Hasan, apparently by rushing at him with a chair, but he was otherwise unarmed and Hasan shot and killed him.

A civilian assistant physician, Michael Cahill, also tried to charge Hasan with a chair, and he too was shot and killed. An army reserve specialist, Logan Burnette, tried to stop Hasan by throwing a table at him. He was shot in the hip and fell, crawling into a nearby cubicle.

Called out by reports of an emergency at the centre, a Civilian Police officer stationed at the base, Sergeant Kimberley Munley, met Hasan coming out of the building as he pursued a wounded soldier. Hasan shot Sergeant Munley twice, in the thigh and knee, which took her to the ground. She still had her pistol in her hand, and may have fired a shot at Hasan, but he kicked the pistol out of her reach. As the shooting continued outside, medics went into the building and secured the doors with a belt so that they could tend the wounded in relative safety. Then another Civilian Police officer arrived, Sergeant Mark Todd. Segeant Todd saw Hasan firing at people as they were trying to run and hide. Then Hasasn turned and fired at Todd. Todd fired back and Hasan fell. Todd kicked the pistol out of Hasan's hand and put handcuffs on him; then Hasan lapsed into unconsciousness.

The incident had lasted only ten minutes, but in that time, Hasan had fired 146 times and killed thirteen people. In the confusion, it was at first thought that there was some sort of terrorist conspiracy and that three soldiers were involved in the shootings, but the other two who were under suspicion were subsequently released. The Fort Hood military base and the surrounding area were closed off by military police and the US Army CID for the rest of the afternoon. Troopers and deputies from the surrounding area were drafted in, and FBI agents were sent in. The extent of the subversive attack was not known. Was just one terrorist involved – or ten?

Hasan, the gunman, was taken to a hospital in Temple, Texas, and later moved to Brooke Army Medical Centre at Fort Sam Houston, where he was heavily guarded. He had been hit by at least four bullets. Hasan survived the shooting, but is now paralyzed from the chest down. The injured victims were taken for treatment to Temple and Killeen hospitals. Eight more soldiers were treated in hospital for shock.

Hasan was thirty-nine years old at the time of the shootings. He was a practising Muslim whose religious views intensified after the deaths of his parents in 1998 and 2001. He was also affected by some of the stories he heard from people returning to America from Afghanistan and Iraq. These developments could have contributed to increasing antipathy towards official US strategy in the Middle East. They could have made him more hostile to the wars and to the US Army itself, though he was never heard to make any anti-American remarks. Hasan is not known to have associated with any Muslim extremists, though it is said that in 2001 he attended the Dar al-Hijrah mosque at Falls Church, Virginia, at the same time as two of the 9-11 hi-jackers, Nawaf al-Hazmi and Hani Hanjour. According to law enforcement officers, on his computer Hasan visited websites propagating radical Islamist ideas. But that could have been nothing more than curiosity. None of these points is in itself incriminating, but there was an earlier occasion on which he behaved aberrantly. He was supposed to be giving a medical lecture to a group of psychiatrists, when he launched into a diatribe about Islam. Non-believers would be sent to hell, set on fire, have their heads cut off, have burning oil poured down their throats.

According to media reports, officials at the Walter Reed Medical Centre had expressed anxiety about Hasan's behaviour during the six years he worked there, ending in July 2009. By the spring of 2008, officials were meeting to discuss how to handle the problem. It seemed that Hasan's behaviour showed indications of a psychiatric disorder. Words like 'paranoid' and 'schizoid' were used. Yet the staff at Fort Hood seemed not to be aware of Hasan's instability, if that is what it was. One military activist commented that it was odd that his psychiatrist colleagues failed to notice how deeply disturbed he was, even though he was right in their midst.

Then there was the evidence of the eighteen emails exchanged between Hasan and al-Awlaki. In one e-mail Hasan said, 'I can't wait to join you', apparently meaning in the afterlife. A military analyst, Lieut-Colonel Tony Shaffer, interpreted the e-mails as meaning that Hasan was 'either offering himself up or had already crossed that line in his own mind'. Hasan asked al-Awlaki when jihad was justified and whether it was permissible for innocent people to be killed in a suicide attack. Although all this was known before the killing spree, Hasan was still considered to be no threat. Nor was there enough evidence to justify further investigation.

In the wake of the shootings, the US authorities seem to prefer to see Hasan as a lone madman rather than a terrorist. This may be, as al-Awlaki has said, because they wish to cushion the reaction of ordinary Americans. He, al-Awlaki, evidently prefers to see the shootings as an al-Qaeda attack. It is still not clear where the truth lies.

What was the trigger, the breaking-point, for Nidal Hasan? It seems that it was the news that he was to be deployed to Afghanistan just three weeks later, on 28 November. This was revealed by a spokesperson for a US Senator, though Hasan's family apparently knew nothing about it. Perhaps Hasan knew and was brooding about it. Given his growing fundamentalism, he would no doubt have found it deeply compromising to his beliefs to be directly involved in the US military initiative in Afghanistan.

Nidal Hasan was a man in deep internal conflict. Evidence may emerge to show that he was a regular terrorist, but the events of the day bear most of the hallmarks of the workplace mass murder, a lashing-out under stress at those nearest. One analyst has commented that the attack was less like a terror attack, more like the Virginia Tech Massacre. It may be that this was an in-between attack. Some spree killers self-radicalise as a result of a volatile mix of personal distress, psychological issues, and an ideology that can be sculpted to justify and explain their anti-social leanings.

'Everything Seemed Normal'

THE APPOMATTOX SHOOTINGS (2010)

Christopher Speight described himself in court papers as someone who was not quick to anger; he was dependable, hardworking and proud of his ability to find ways out of problems without using force or violence. When in 1995 he applied for a concealed weapons licence, at the age of twenty-four, he explained that firearms had been a hobby for many years and that he took seriously the responsibility of handling them. As someone else once said in a very different context, 'Well, he would say that, wouldn't he?' As is always the case in these spree shootings, there was a good deal of heart-searching afterwards about the adequacy or otherwise of the gun laws.

To get his gun licence, Christopher Speight needed references. One of his referees wrote in support that Speight had taken part in a National Rifle Association high-powered rifle competition, in which he excelled. 'I can tell the character of a man after coaching him for two days on the rifle range,' wrote the referee. 'Chris did very well with high scores to prove his ability with the rifle.' This is a back-handed recommendation. What it implies is that if the young man were so minded, and he chose to shoot to kill, he would be lethally dangerous – a skilled assassin. But his friends were ready to describe him as 'very mature and responsible' and as 'an upstanding, Christian young man'.

But in the years after that his friends noticed a change in him. That change seemed to start with the death of his mother in 2006. One of his co-workers, David Anderson, said that Speight spoke of a 'zinging' in his ears. He had been to a therapist but Speight knew it had not helped him much. His condition had deteriorated. David Anderson and other people who worked with him believed that this worsening was to do with tensions in the house where Speight lived in Snapps Mill Road, the house his mother had left to him and his sister. Speight had become quieter.

There was circumstantial evidence that something was happening within Christopher Speight, something that was turning him into a different sort of person. As Mr Anderson put it, something must have been building.

In a sudden eruption of violence one morning, on 20 January 2010, several people were shot dead: Christopher Speight's sister, Lauralee Sipe, and his brother-in-law, Dwayne Sipe, along with his niece and nephew, fifteen-year-old Morgan Dobyns and four-year-old Joshua Sipe. Also shot were four family friends: fifteen-year-old Emily Quarles, who was a friend of Morgan's, Emily's mother and father Karen and Jonathan Quarles, and sixteen-year-old Ronald Scruggs, Morgan's friend. That fateful Tuesday, eight people died in and round Speight's house. Four of the victims were found inside the house, three immediately outside it and another in the middle of a road nearby.

Speight was known for his love of shooting, so the sound of gunfire from his property on the day of the massacre attracted no attention at all. The neighbours said he regularly did target practice in the woods or, they assumed, hunted deer and rabbits. But on the morning of the shootings, Tammy Lee Randolph, a neighbour, was driving past the Speights' house when she saw a body in the middle of the road. Her first thought was that this was someone who was drunk; she associated the Speights' house with partying, so it seemed a likely explanation. She got out and looked. It was a man lying face down, wearing a grey hoodie covered in blood. She made an emergency call and waited until a sheriff's deputy arrived. Then they looked along the Speights' driveway, where there were several parked cars. Tammy Lee Randolph cried, 'Oh my God, there's another body!' More emergency vehicles were summoned. Then someone poked a gun barrel out of a window and fired seven shots. The deputy shouted into his radio that shots were being fired, and they both ran.

Later, the seventeen-year-old Dakota Henderson said that he had shot with Speight in his back yard the previous summer while he was going out with Speight's niece, Morgan. Dakota Henderson reflected that he had lost three friends in the massacre, all of them students at Appomattox High, including his girlfriend, Morgan. He had been at the house as recently as the previous Saturday, three days before the shootings. Although the school was in session on the Tuesday, it was a day when staff were required to attend, but not students; this is why there were students at home on a weekday.

Dakota said the house was always clean and orderly. There were lots of family photographs on the walls. He had got on well with Morgan, who he described as 'a very classy person and easy to get along with'. He had got on well with Speight too. He was always polite, friendly, ready to play video games with him: he was fun. Dakota Henderson commented, 'Everything seemed fine. Everything seemed normal.'

But not everyone thought everything was fine or normal. The people who worked at the store with Speight saw a change in him that last weekend. Although he may have put on a mask of bonhomie at home for the benefit of Dakota and others around him, at work he appeared preoccupied, more so than usual. One of the store employees said that he seemed more distant the last time she saw him. Mr Anderson also noticed that he seemed withdrawn. He had been pacing up and down. Mr Anderson commented that he was going to wear a trench in the floor. Speight said, 'I know, I know.'

Christopher Speight was unmarried and his sister was his closest family member. But he may have felt marginalised in a household dominated by his sister and her family – and their circle of friends.

The motive for the killing is still obscure. Tension within the family seems the likeliest explanation. Speight's friends said that he spoke of a dispute with his family about the ownership of the house and the land it was built on. The house sits among woods and farmland. The documentary evidence shows that Speight's mother left the property, which amounts to thirty-four acres, jointly to Christopher and his sister Lauralee. Speight thought his sister and brother-in-law were trying to get him out of the house, in effect to dispossess him. They had come from Georgia, moving into the house a few months before. Now he was sleeping in a basement bedroom and feeling that he was expected to move out.

Clearly there was enough land to accommodate a second house, which he could have, and the sister and brother-in-law promised they would help him build it. They cleared the site, though Speight felt that he had done most of the work in felling the trees. Then the house itself was not built. Speight was left feeling that he had chopped a great deal of wood just to fill the stove. This was the version of events that he described to Mr Anderson.

After the shootings, Speight fled into the woods, where he used a high-powered rifle to hold the police back. He even fired some well-aimed shots at a police helicopter. Six shots hit it. The fuel tank was pierced and the helicopter had to make a forced landing. The next day, wearing a bullet-proof vest and camouflage trousers, he emerged from the woods and gave himself up to the police.

He was charged with one count of first-degree murder. Police officers searched Speight's home with bomb-sniffing dogs; seven explosive devices were discovered.

The people who had worked with Christopher Speight as a security guard at Anderson's store were astonished by the allegations that were made against him. They saw him as a calm, committed Jehovah's Witness. He liked to shoot, though evidently not to hunt; guns were one of his main interests. Speight worked for Mr Anderson and the two men had become friendly over several years. Speight did some work on Mr Anderson's cabin and they did target practice together both at Mr Anderson's place and on the 200-yard range Speight built on his own (and his sister's) property.

Speight had an impressive, some would think alarming, collection of firearms – at least twenty-five of them. Perhaps his favourites were the AR-15 semi-automatic rifles. As well as gun safes full of weapons, Speight had a good deal of other military and paramilitary gear. He had night-vision goggles, Kevlar vests and ghillie (camouflage) suits. He also started to dig a twelve-foot bunker on his land. Speight's comment to Anderson was that it was a stupid idea to build it. In the end, when

Speight's huge dog died, he decided to bury it in the unfinished bunker. But the crucial point is that Speight's interest in guns went far beyond mere target practice. He evidently had a well-developed fantasy life in which guerrilla warfare of some kind took place. Who was he fighting in his head? Who did he want to shoot?

Following the massacre, Christopher Speight was ordered by Judge Richard Blanton not to stand trial but to be sent to a psychiatric hospital for treatment and evaluation. It was important to establish his mental state because the charges against him carry the death penalty. In May 2010 Speight's lawyer said that he was still unable to communicate rationally with his client. One of the lawyer's investigators had visited his client, who had talked of 'being tortured by other entities that were battling over him and he demanded that the torture stop.' Christopher Speight is in a strange and precarious state. He is in a state-run mental health institution where efforts are made to restore him to sanity. Judge Blanton has ordered that if at any point the staff believe he is competent to stand trial they must report to the court. Then, presumably, he will be made to stand trial.

'ONE DAY I'M GOING TO GET A GUN'
DERRICK BIRD (2010)

Some breaking-point murders seem to be the culmination of the pressures of working in a strongly competitive urban society, but not all. The shootings in Cumbria in 2010 happened in what outwardly appeared to be a peaceful, stress-free rural setting. What drove Derrick Bird, a self-employed taxi-driver from Rowrah, to take his gun one morning and shoot twelve people dead? The question was still being asked long after the shootings, and there is still no clear answer.

The incident started early one morning, when Derrick Bird drove from Rowrah to Lamplugh and called at the house of his twin brother, David. He shot David, then drove to Frizington, where he shot dead Kevin Commons, the family solicitor, on the driveway of his house.

The police were alerted at 10.20 am to the fact that a major incident was under way. Derrick Bird then drove to Whitehaven. At 10.33 there was a shooting incident near the taxi rank there and it later became clear that the taxi driver who had been shot was known to Derrick Bird – and Bird answered to the witness descriptions of the man who had shot him.

The police urged people living in the towns of Whitehaven, Egremont and Seascale to stay indoors. The gates of the Sellafield nuclear reprocessing plant were shut as a precautionary measure; staff on the afternoon shift were told not to attempt to come to work. It was evident that Derrick Bird was on the rampage with his gun and could kill anybody he encountered – which is exactly what happened next. He drove through several towns and villages shooting randomly. In Egremont he shot dead two people in the street. In the village of Wilton a couple were shot dead; a mole-catcher was killed in a field at Carleton. At Boonhead near Gosforth a former semi-professional rugy player, Garry Purdham, was shot dead outside the Red Admiral Hotel. In Seascale, Bird killed three more people: two people on foot and a man driving a car.

At 12.30pm the police confirmed that there had been several fatalities in the area and that they were searching for a suspect, the driver of a dark grey Citroen Xsara Picasso. This was Derrick Bird's car. He abandoned it in the village of Boot and evaded the police on foot. Not long after this, at 2 pm, the police confirmed that they had found a body, which they believed to be Bird's, together with a shotgun. It was now safe for people to go about their normal activities again. One man had been single-handedly responsible for all the shootings.

The first victim was Derrick Bird's twin brother David and the second their solicitor Kevin Commons. Then Darren Rewcastle, a taxi-driver, was shot dead in the street in Whitehaven; his fellow driver Don Reed was only injured and managed to crawl away from the scene. Kenneth Fishburn, a retired Sellafield security worker, was shot dead on the old bridge in Egremont. Susan Hughes, a pensioner, was killed while walking home with her shopping in Egremont. Jennifer Jackson was shot in Wilton, then her husband James while he was looking for her. Garry Purdham was shot dead while working in a field in Gosforth. Jane Robinson was shot while delivering shopping catalogues. Jamie Clark, a twenty-three-year-old estate agent, was shot while driving through Seascale and killed in the resulting crash. Isaac Dixon, a part-time mole-catcher, was shot dead while working in a field. The final victim was Michael Pike, a retired shipbuilder, who was shot while riding his bicycle in Seascale.

The Prime Minister, David Cameron, happened to be taking his first Prime Minister's Questions in the House of Commons that afternoon. At 3 pm, just one hour after Bird's body had been discovered, Mr Cameron announced that at least five people had died, including the gunman. Because the situation in Cumbria was still chaotic and the shootings had happened in so many different locations it was at that time still unclear how many people had died. But by the evening it was clear that twelve people had been killed, another eleven had been injured and the suspect had killed himself. The police announced that two different weapons had been used in the attacks and that thirty crime scenes were being investigated.

Then, out of the chaos, a semblance of a pattern, or at least a part of a pattern, began to emerge. The killings took place along a 24-kilometre stretch of the Cumbrian coast, and they were all committed by one person, Derrick Bird. Certainly the first two killings looked as they would (eventually) be explicable; the murders of his twin brother and his solicitor were clearly not random killings. But were any of the other killings going to turn out to be meaningful, in terms of the selection of the victims? Was the attack on two fellow taxi-drivers in Whitehaven a deliberate revenge attack on commercial rivals – a taxi-rank quarrel?

Derrick Bird was fifty-two years old and had a son by a woman from whom he separated in the 1990s. He became a grandfather in May 2010. No-one seems to have thought him in any way odd, or potentially dangerous. He was described as quiet and popular. But there were unconfirmed reports that he had sought help at a local hospital for his fragile mental state. What might have been the cause of this fragile state? Perhaps he felt inadequate and unsuccessful by comparison with his twin brother. Siblings, and twins especially, are prone to compare their performance, first at school and then in their careers. As a self-employed taxi-driver, Derrick Bird may have felt that he was a failure compared with his brother David. Another factor may have been anxiety over his financial affairs. He was being investigated by HM Revenue & Customs for possible tax evasion, which does not of course mean that he had been dishonest but he might well have been feeling under considerable pressure. One of Bird's fellow taxi-drivers, who had known him for fifteen years, said that Bird told him he had £60,000 stashed away in a secret bank account and was worried that he might be sent to prison for hiding this money from HM Revenue and Customs.

There were also things in Bird's past that may contain clues. He had worked at the Sellafield nuclear power plant as a joiner. There had been an allegation that he had stolen wood from the plant, which led to his resignation. He was subsequently given a twelve-month suspended sentence.

There was some speculation that the killing spree might have been prompted by a desire to get even with employees who helped him to lose his job, and three of the victims were former Sellafield employees, but there seems to be no connection.

Another possibility is that Bird felt that he had been made a fool of by a Thai woman. This story came from one of the other taxi drivers, who described himself as a friend of Derrick Bird's, though Bird shot him in the hand on the day of the killings. Bird had met the Thai woman while on holiday in Pattaya. Another friend confirmed this and added that Bird had sent £1,000 to the woman, who eventually sent a text message ending the relationship. This may have been a serious blow to his self-esteem.

But the fact that the first two victims were his brother and their solicitor gives credence to the theory that the Derrick Bird was in dispute with his brother and the family solicitor, Kevin Commons, over a will or possibly over a threat (real or imagined) that they were going to 'stitch him up' over his tax affairs. He was making plans to leave the country. Just the evening before the killings, he apparently told a friend, Gary Kennett, that he was likely to be imprisoned for tax evasion and that he feared the outcome of a meeting the next afternoon with his brother David and Kevin Commons. Gary Kennett thought Bird was in a paranoid and depressed state, convinced that when he turned up for this meeting they would have him put away and take all his money. Apparently there was wild talk of withdrawing his money out of the bank account and running away to Thailand. Stress on this scale could easily have triggered the massacre.

A grudge of some kind was evidently developing. Some nine months before the shootings, Bird had offered a warning. He held long-standing grudges against members of his family, friends and acquaintances. He confided his intentions to two close friends during a diving holiday in Croatia. One of the friends was Bob Cullen, who was told, 'One day I'm going to get a gun and shoot them all.' Bob Cullen did not believe him. It was just casual remark, he thought.

Bird had a criminal record, but he was also

a victim of crime. In 1998 he was the victim of a theft from his taxi, and also there was an incident in which a passenger ran off without paying the fare. In 2002 he made a complaint of assault, but later withdrew it. Five years later, the year when when he obtained a firearms licence for his .22 rifle, he was again assaulted. The year after that he reported criminal damage to his taxi. These repeated crimes against him may have contributed to making him more vulnerable, more paranoid.

A conspicuous feature of the case was the fact that Bird held a gun licence. There was renewed debate, as there invariably is following an incident of this kind, about British gun laws. There were similar discussions in the wake of the Hungerford and Dunblane shootings. But Bird held a shotgun licence from 1995 onwards and a firearms certificate for a rifle from 2005. Although it seems he was technically, legally, entitled to hold firearms licences, there were questions as to whether the local police carried out enough checks to make sure that Bird was still psychologically fit to hold such licences, particularly after he was forced to leave Sellafield charged with theft and after he had repeatedly been the victim of crime.

A thirteenth victim, Jason Carey, was spared when

his dog barked at Bird, frightening him off. Jason Carey was an instructor at a local diving club. The local story was that Bird had a grudge against Carey after Bird was accused of taking an inexperienced diver too deep. When Bird knocked at the Careys' door in Wilton, Carey was still in bed. His wife was up, but unable to answer the door straight away because their dog was barking. By the time she had opened the door, Bird was walking away. Instead of shooting Jason Carey, Bird shot Jennifer Jackson, apparently at random, just yards away, and then killed her husband Jimmy too.

Derrick Bird was a man suffering from stress from a range of different and unrelated sources, and he seems to have wanted to settle several scores. The attacks on his brother and solicitor were partly to do with financial difficulties that he feared might be exposed. The attacks on the fellow taxi drivers were to do with commercial competition that he considered unfair. The attack on Jason Carey, if it had happened, would have been revenge for criticism. The other attacks were, it seems, completely random.

There were questions about the effectiveness of the police operation. One of the questions concerned the length of time it took the forty-two armed police officers to catch up with Bird. After the armed officers responded to the first 999 call, ten of the victims were shot over the course of one hour. Part of the explanation was that it was difficult to have the police in the right place at the right time because they had no idea where Bird was going. The police were able to confirm that Bird was indeed the subject of a tax investigation by HM Revenue & Customs.

'DID THE MEDIA HELP TO PULL THE TRIGGER?'

RAOUL MOAT (2010)

Raoul Moat, a Newcastle man, was thirty-seven years old when he was released from Durham Prison on 1 July 2010. From February to July that year, he had been serving an eighteen-week sentence for assaulting a relative, a nine-year-old child. He was armed with a sawn-off shotgun when, just two days after his release, he shot his former girlfriend Samantha Stobbart and her new partner, Chris Brown, a twenty-nine-year-old karate instructor.

Moat had been in touch with Samantha and she knew that Chris was in great danger from Raoul. She warned Chris to stay away, especially after Raoul made threatening phone calls. Chris's answer to the threat was to try to protect Samantha by taking her to stay at a friend's house close to where her parents lived in Birtley.

But Moat found them. He arrived in the early hours of 3 July outside the house in Birtley which Samantha Stobbart was visiting with her new partner.

According to Moat himself, he crouched, hidden beneath the open living room window for an hour-and-a-half listening to the conversation between Stobbart and Brown. They were talking about him, mocking him, he said. Presumably he attracted their attention in some way, because at 2.40 am, Chris Brown went outside to confront him. That was when Chris Brown was shot at close range with Moat's shotgun. Moat then shot Samantha in the arm and abdomen. Samantha's mother meanwhile was desperately phoning for the police.

Moat also shot a police officer, David Rathband, who survived but was permanently blinded. Samantha Stobbart was seriously injured and spent a long time in hospital. Chris Brown was killed outright in the attack.

After the shootings, Raoul Moat fled. He was on the run for six days, while a major manhunt was organised by Northumbria Police across the entire Northumbria area: the two counties of Northumberland and Tyne and Wear. Around 160 armed officers were involved. Eventually he was spotted by the police and contained in an open space near the River Coquet. A stand-off followed, during which the police tried to negotiate with him. At the end of this, Moat shot and fatally injured himself. He was pronounced dead at Newcastle General Hospital.

Moat shot Samantha Stobbart and Chris Brown in Birtley in the early hours of 3 July 2010. It was almost twenty-four hours later, at 12.45 am on 4 July, that he shot PC David Rathband. The policeman was on traffic duty, sitting in his parked patrol car on the roundabout of the A1 and A69 at East Denton. David Rathband was taken to Newcastle General Hospital in a critical condition with upper body and head injuries. It emerged that Moat had phoned the police twelve minutes before shooting David Rathband, to tell them what he was going to do. He phoned them again about an hour later. He showed little remorse, and complained that the police did not take him seriously enough.

The reason for this attack is not known. It may be that, while Moat was in prison and out of fear for what Moat might do to her new partner, Samantha Stobbart told Moat, untruthfully, that she was in a relationship with a policeman. This could easily have caused Moat to develop a grudge against police officers. He also blamed the police for the failure of his business. Straight after his release from prison, Moat posted threats to the police on Facebook. He also made threats in letters and phone calls. He said he had no grudge against the general public but he would go on shooting policemen until he was dead. David Rathband just happened to be in the wrong place at the wrong moment: an available target.

The police held a press conference held the following day, in which they directly addressed Raoul Moat, assuring him that they did take him seriously. They insisted that Chris Brown was not a police officer. They urged him to give himself up, for the sake of his three children. The implication was that if he remained on the run the episode would end with Moat's children losing their father, which is what happened.

There were other factors in the situation, such as the build, personality and temperament of the perpetrator. Raoul Moat was a big powerful man, six foot three tall, stocky and weighing seventeen stone. He had been a panel-beater, a tree surgeon, a bouncer and a body-builder. It was said by his relatives that he was prone to outbursts of anger produced by his use of steroids – so-called 'roid rage'. He had apparently tried to get psychiatric help. He had one previous conviction for common assault, and had been arrested twelve times relating to charges on seven separate offences.

During the manhunt, some of Moat's relatives

made appeals for him to give himself up. The police did the same. They thought Moat must be evading capture and even managing to stay completely out of sight by living rough, and in due course they found his abandoned camp-sites. Several people were arrested during the man-hunt, suspected of helping Moat to evade capture. There was an armed robbery on the night on 5 July at a fish and chip shop at Seaton Delaval, and it was believed that Moat was involved; a man answering Moat's description carried out the raid.

The next day, the police announced that they believed he was in Rothbury. There had been several misdirected raids, false leads and false alarms, but from that point on the police focus was Rothbury. A two-mile-wide ground exclusion zone was established round Rothbury. Two men were then discovered. It was at first thought they might be the (imaginary) hostages, released by Moat. When later it was realised that they were not, they were arrested. Moat was seen as a threat to the public in general in his present state of mind, and armed guards were posted outside schools in the area. Several sightings followed, and these led to the final confrontation at Riverside in Rothbury.

On 5 July the police admitted that they had been

warned by Durham Prison three days earlier that Raoul Moat intended to harm Samantha Stobbart: the day before the shootings. Northumbria Police referred what may have been a case of negligence on their part to the Independent Police Complaints Commission. Meanwhile, Northumbria received a rambling communication forty-nine pages long from Moat. He warned that they were 'gonna pay for what they've done. . . The public need not fear me but the police should as I won't stop shooting them until I'm dead.' He said his children, his house, his freedom, his ex-partner and their daughter had all been taken away from him. He admitted he was running out of options, but said he was never violent towards his children.

In an effort to stop Moat killing more police officers, the police relayed a message from Samantha Stobbart to make sure that he knew that she had been lying about having a relationship with a policeman. Chris Brown had never been a policeman or had any connection with the police. In a recent interview, Samantha has said that Raoul phoned her on the night of the shootings to say that he had learned everything about Chris Brown. According to her, he said, 'I know he isn't a cop. I know he does karate. He's an instructor.' Samantha's half-sister Kelly saw that Moat had updated his Facebook profile, adding a hit list; it included her and other members of her family. He would take out any police officers who got in his way.

For some reason, the police were under the impression that when Moat fled he abducted two men as hostages, but asked for a media blackout on this particular information. On 6 July they announced that they were dealing with 'a complex, fast-moving hostage situation'. The cordon round Rothbury was lifted at around 9 pm, though armed patrols checked vehicles entering and leaving the village.

On the morning of 7 July, the police held another press conference. The police said Moat was still at large and they thought he was hiding in open countryside near Rothbury. At a secluded spot at Cartington, they had found one of Moat's camps. In it they found an eight-page letter to Samantha. They also confirmed that the man who raided the chip shop was indeed Moat and they offered a £10,000 reward for information leading to his arrest. Another event was a video appeal from Paul Stobbart, Samantha's father, urging Moat to give himself up.

Then on 8 July the police cryptically announced that they had arrested two more men in Rothbury.

The implication was that Moat had friends who were helping and supporting him. Det Chief Superintendent Neil Adamson, speaking for Northumbria Police, said they now saw Moat as a bigger threat to the general public than they had originally thought, but gave no reason for saying so. After Moat's death, it emerged that the police had had to ask the media to reduce their reporting regarding Moat's personal life; he had threatened to kill a member of the public every time there was an inaccurate press piece.

That same day, the police arrested a couple in Blyth.

Then, on 9 July, the police threw a cordon round the National Trust's Cragside Estate, apparently in the belief that Raoul Moat was living rough within this area. In the early evening of 9 July, Rothbury residents were warned to stay indoors, as a major security operation was under way. There were news reports that a man who looked like Raoul Moat had been surrounded by police; he was holding a gun to his head. The police were negotiating with him and had taken him food and water. With the police was Moat's closest friend, Tony Laidler; the idea was that he might take notice of the voice of a friend. Mr Laidler joined the police in attempting to persuade

Moat to surrender. At one point, the footballer Paul Gascoigne arrived at the scene, claiming that he knew Moat, but he was not allowed to approach him.

In the middle of the night, at 1.15 am on 10 July, a shot was fired in the area of the stand-off beside the River Coquet. About twenty minutes later, the police confirmed that 'a shot or shots' had been fired and the suspect had received a gunshot wound. A statement from Northumbria Police said no shots had been fired by police officers; the suspect had shot himself. Raoul Moat was pronounced dead at 2.20 am, just after arriving at the hospital.

An unusual feature of this case was the number of arrests made during the manhunt – and following Raoul Moat's death. The man from Sunderland who was arrested in North Kenton on 5 July was later released without charge. The man arrested in Wrekenton the next day was similarly released.

The two men arrested on the same day in the street in Rothbury and initially thought to be Moat's hostages, were arrested on suspicion of conspiracy to commit murder and possession of a firearm with intent. The two men were named on 8 July as Karl Ness, a body-builder from Dudley, and Qhuram Awan from Blyth. It was alleged that they had supplied the gun to Moat, that they were with him when he shot PC Rathband, and that Ness had gone with Moat to the shooting of Samatha Stobbart and Chris Brown. The prosecution additionally alleged that the two men had actively helped Moat search for policemen to shoot.

Two extra suspects were arrested in the Rothbury area on 7 July, suspected of 'assisting an offender'. Later they were released on bail. The couple arrested in Blyth on 8 July were similarly suspected of assisting Moat. Afer Moat's death, three more people were arrested on the same suspicion on 13 July. This went on until there were in all twenty arrests.

Some aspects of the police operation are being investigated by the Independent Police Complaints Commission. One point at issue is whether the police should have warned Samantha Stobbart that she was in danger from Moat. Another equally serious matter is the firing of two Tasers at Moat by the police in the moments before Moat's death. The police motive in firing the Tasers was evidently to prevent Moat from killing himself, but it is unclear whether the Tasers were fired before or after Moat turned the gun on himself. If before, Moat could have decided to kill himself because he was being fired on.

The type of Taser used was a long-range XREP Taser, which operates without wires. The Home Office explained that the XREP Tasers were 'currently subject to testing by the Home Office Scientific Development Branch'. In September, it emerged that Pro-Tect Systems, the company supplying the Tasers, had been in breach of its licence when it supplied the weapons directly to the police while they were still in their experimental stage. The Home Secretary, Teresa May, revoked Pro-Tect's licence after confirming that the Tasers had not been officially approved for use.

One of Pro-Tect's directors, Peter Boatman, had been a policeman himself and had only wanted, as conscientiously as he could, to help the police to resolve the Raoul Moat crisis. He was distraught and ashamed at the outcome and on 1 October he was found dead at his home – an unintended extra victim of Raoul Moat.

A major concern about the Raoul Moat shootings is that they came exactly one month after the Derrick Bird shootings in Cumbria. They may be connected. The Derrick Bird shootings were given saturation-level news coverage by the press, radio and television. One journalist in The Independent was brave enough to suggest that the news coverage of Derrick Bird's killing spree might have played a significant part in sending Raoul Moat off on his own spree. The piece was headed 'Did the media help to pull the trigger?' In America the phenomenon of copycat killings has been seen repeatedly in cases of mass murder. An American forensic psychiatrist has concluded that in America the news coverage of a mass murder usually leads to the commission of one more mass murder in the following two weeks. Research carried out in Britain has a similar thrust.

The mass media coverage does not merely give unstable and volatile people the idea of committing mass murder – it encourages them to think that this is a fast route to celebrity and therefore supplies them with another reason for doing it. If you are in despair because you think you are a nobody, here is a way to become somebody, fast. The parallel growth of the celebrity culture in the Western world generally makes this association all the more dangerous. What is needed is the development of a clear distinction in people's minds between fame and infamy. Well-known media people who are well-known for behaving very badly are infamous, notorious, and not in any sense to be celebrated. Yet there they are, still in the limelight. There were even elements of this in the press coverage of

Raoul Moat. As one Twitterer crisply put it, 'I see Raoul Moat has got his own TV show. *The News.*' To substantial numbers of misguided people, Moat became, through his self-created victimhood, a kind of folk-hero. He did not deserve that accolade – nor does any killer.

PART FIVE

SCHOOL MASSACRES

'NO CAUSE TO SUSPECT'
THE BATH SCHOOL DISASTER (1927)

The Bath School Disaster of 1927 was the first of a series of school massacres. The school massacre seems to be a distinctively twentieth century development; as far as is known, there were no mass murders of this kind in earlier centuries. Yet the Bath School massacre was by no means typical; the murderer was not a pupil, nor even a teacher, but a member of the school board.

The disaster happened on 18 May 1927 in Bath Township, Michigan, and on that day three bombs exploded, killing thirty-eight children and seven adults, and injuring at least fifty-eight others. The children were mainly between seven and twelve years old, and they were attending the Bath Consolidated School. The perpetrator of the bombings was a member of the school board, a man named Andrew Kehoe. The cause of his anger was the property tax that had been imposed to fund the building of the school. He blamed this tax for the financial difficulties in which he found himself and for the foreclosure proceedings against his farm.

On the morning of 18 May, having first murdered his wife, Andrew Kehoe set his own farm buildings on fire. As the fire-fighters arrived at his farm, there was an explosion at the school. It wrecked the north wing of the school, killing many of the children inside. Kehoe had set this up over a period of several months, secretly planting dynamite and hundreds of pounds of pyrotol inside the school building; he used a detonator to set the explosives off. Rescuers arrived at the school, and then Kehoe himself drove up in a vehicle loaded with shrapnel, stopped and detonated a bomb inside the vehicle. This killed him, the school superintendent and several other people as well. As the rescue operation continued, more dynamite and pyrotol were found, planted in the basement of the school's south wing; fortunately these explosives did not detonate.

Bath Township was a small, mainly agricultural community. In 1922, the community voted to fund and build a consolidated school. When it opened, there were 236 students on the roll. At that time there were still many small one-room schools, where children of different age groups were taught together in the same room. The decision was made that children would learn more effectively if they attended larger schools where students of different age groups or grades could be taught separately, in separate rooms. This new structure would allow schools to be better equipped and more appropriately staffed. This is what was meant by a consolidated school. The new school building was funded by raising a levy on local landowners like Andrew Kehoe.

Kehoe was born in Michigan in 1872. His mother died when he was young. When his father remarried, Kehoe is said to have quarrelled frequently with his stepmother. When he was fourteen, his stepmother was somehow set on fire – an accident with an oil stove was blamed – and Kehoe threw a bucket of water over her, which caused the flames to spread more rapidly. She died later of her injuries.

In 1912, Andrew Kehoe married Ellen Price and in 1919 they bought a farm outside the Bath Township. Neighbours saw Kehoe as intelligent but quick to anger if crossed. They also thought him cruel to his animals: he had beaten a horse to death. But he was careful with money and his reputation for thrift got him elected treasurer of the Bath Consolidated School board. While on the board, Kehoe argued continually for lower taxes. He blamed the property tax levy for his own poor financial situation and repeatedly accused the school superintendent, Emory Huyck, of mismanaging the school finances.

Another element in Andrew Kehoe's psychological stress was his wife's medical condition. Ellen Kehoe had tuberculosis and her frequent hospital stays may have put an additional strain on the family's finances. Kehoe had stopped making mortgage repayments, stopped paying home insurance premiums, and now the mortgage lender had started proceedings to foreclose.

The bombings were by no means a spur of the moment decision. The way the explosives were acquired and planted shows that the disaster was planned for across several months, perhaps as much as a year. Early in 1926, the board asked Kehoe to carry out maintenance work inside the school building. He had a reputation as a handyman. As a board member assigned to undertake repairs, he was able to go anywhere in the building without being questioned. From the middle of 1926, Kehoe was buying pyrotol, an explosive used in the First World War and then commonly used by farmers for excavation. In November Kehoe drove to Lansing, the nearest larger settlement, to buy two boxes of dynamite. This too was also in common use on farms. Because Kehoe bought small amounts of explosives in different places on different dates, he roused no suspicion. He was behaving just like the classic Victorian poisoner, buying small quantities of arsenic for allegedly harmless purposes, and storing it away until it became a massively lethal dose for his – or her – victim. When neighbours heard explosions on Kehoe's farm, he explained that he was removing tree stumps.

As Kehoe's preparations approached completion, he started giving warning hints. He said to one of the teachers, Bernice Sterling, that if she wanted use his grove for a picnic she had 'better have it at once'. In the days leading up to 18 May, Kehoe loaded the back seat of his car with metal: tools, nails, rusty farm machinery – anything that would produce deadly shrapnel in an explosion. Then he placed a lot of dynamite behind the front seat. Ellen Kehoe was released from hospital in Lansing on 16 May. Some time during the next forty-eight hours, Kehoe killed her with a massive blow over the head and put her body in a wheelbarrow at the back of the chicken coop.

Kehoe put home-made pyrotol fire-bombs in all the farm buildings. The livestock were tied up in their pens to make sure that they too died. Kehoe set of the firebombs at his farm at 8.45 am.

An hour later came the explosion in the school building. Bernice Sterling described the explosion as being like an earthquake; the floor seemed to go up several feet and the air seemed to be filled with children and flying books and desks. The children were tossed high in the air, and some were thrown right out of the building. Firefighters and rescuers turned from the Kehoe farm to the school; parents too converged on the school.

The school's north wing had collapsed. As the walls had given way, the edge of the roof went down onto the ground. A pile of five- or six-year-old children was pinned under the roof edge, unrecognisable as individuals because they were covered in plaster, dust and blood. The distraught parents were unable to lift the roof to free the children's bodies. One witness volunteered to go back to his farm to get a heavy rope to help move the roof. As he drove to his farm, the witness saw Kehoe in his car heading in the opposite direction. Kehoe waved to him and gave him a big grin, showing all his teeth.

In no time, as many as a hundred men were at work clearing away the debris. The mothers ran round trying to find their children, breaking down when they saw the bodies lying on the grass, while others tore at the wreckage trying to find traces of their young. Half an hour after the school explosion, Kehoe drove up to the school and spotted Superintendent Huyck. Kehoe called him over. As Huyck approached, Kehoe pulled out a rifle and fired it into the back seat. This ignited the dynamite. The explosion killed Kehoe and the superintendent; it also killed postmaster Glenn Smith and Smith's father-in-law, a retired farmer called Nelson McFarren. An eight-year-old girl, Cleo Claton, who had survived the first school explosion and managed to scramble out of the collapsed building, was killed by shrapnel from Kehoe's car explosion.

The dead were taken to the town hall, which was turned into a mortuary. Within hours, thirteen ambulances arrived at the town hall to take the bodies to undertakers.

The search for bodies was halted for a time while a search was made for possible further explosives. A cache was found in the south wing, and there was a further delay while this bomb was disarmed. With the second device was found an alarm clock timed to set the bomb off at 9.45 am. It was not clear why this bomb had failed to go off.

When investigators went over Kehoe's farm, they first found the barely recognisable body of fifty-two-year-old Ellen Kehoe. Then they found sufficient quantities of unused equipment and materials to pay off the Kehoes' mortgage. They were in debt unnecessarily. Kehoe had wired his last message to the farm fence. It said, 'Criminals are made, not born.'

News of the Bath School Disaster and the ensuing funerals (eighteen on one day) filled the front pages of the national press in America until it was displaced on 23 May 1927 by Lindbergh's solo flight across the Atlantic.

The coroner's inquest concluded that no-one had been to blame for the disaster and the forty-five deaths except Kehoe himself, because Kehoe had 'conducted himself sanely and so concealed his operations that there was no cause to suspect any of his actions.' Meanwhile, pyrotol was quietly taken off the market.

'INTENTIONS TOWARDS THE BOYS'

DUNBLANE MASSACRE (1996)

The Dunblane Massacre of 13 March 1996 is, so far, the best-known of only a very small number of school massacres to have taken place in the United Kingdom. The perpetrator was forty-four-year-old Thomas Hamilton, and he murdered sixteen children and one adult before committing suicide.

In the wake of the killings the police investigated Hamilton's background to try to find out why he had committed the murders, and could find nothing definite to explain them. He had at one time been a shopkeeper. He was licensed to carry guns. There had been some complaints to the police about his behaviour towards the boys who went to the youth clubs he ran. There were suspicions that Hamilton was sexually interested in young boys. More than one complaint had been made about his taking photographs of half-naked boys.

He had at an earlier stage been a Scout leader. Again there were several complaints about his behaviour. On two occasions boys were forced to sleep with Hamilton in his van during walking expeditions in hill country. In the end, in 1974, when the County Commissioner said that he was 'suspicious of his moral intentions towards the boys', Hamilton's Scout Warrant was withdrawn. But Hamilton's activities in the local boys club continued. George Robertson MP, who was a resident in Dunblane, complained to Michael Forsyth, who was the local constituency MP, about Hamilton's behaviour. Mr Robertson's son had attended the boys club and, following the shootings, he recalled that he had had an argument with Hamilton about his behaviour.

Following Thomas Hamilton's summer camp at Loch Lomond in 1993 Central Scotland Police received several complaints, which were investigated by the Child Protection Unit. As a result of the unit's report, Hamilton was reported to the Procurator Fiscal for consideration of ten charges of offences against children and obstructing the police. But there was no prosecution. It is not known how many complaints were made against Hamilton in all, nor is it known how the police responded in every case, but it is known that on at least one occasion he was give a police caution.

Thomas Hamilton wrote letters in which he complained that rumours circulating about him led to the failure of his shop in 1993, just three years before the shootings. In the final months, when he was trying to organise a boys club he complained that he was being persecuted by the scout movement and the police. He wrote letters of complaint to his MP, Michael Forsyth, and to the Queen.

Thomas Hamilton may have been a paedophile, and he may have had business difficulties, but it is still not clear why his anger was directed against the children. The massacre is inexplicable. What we are left with as an explanation is that Hamilton was a 'madman on the rampage', which is hardly an explanation at all.

In April 1996 he walked into Dunblane Primary School armed with two Browning pistols, two Smith & Wesson revolvers and plenty of ammunition: 743 cartridges. Once inside the school building, Hamilton walked to the gymnasium, where he opened fire on a class of young children. He killed or wounded all the people in the gym except one. Fifteen children were killed, all but one of them only five years old. Their teacher, Gwen Mayor, was killed too as she tried to protect them.

Hamilton went out through the emergency exit

into the playground. From there he started shooting into a mobile classroom. The teacher in the mobile classroom had heard the sound of gunfire moments earlier and realised that something was seriously wrong. She told her class to hide under the tables. The bullets that flew across the room hit books and other equipment, but none of the children were hit. He fired towards a group of children in a corridor and injured a teacher.

Hamilton then went back into the gymnasium, stuck one of his revolvers into the roof of his mouth and fired, killing himself instantly.

Six days later, Hamilton's body was privately cremated. A month afterwards, the gymnasium where the shootings took place was demolished and replaced by a memorial garden; subsequently the school has beeen refurbished.

The implications of the Dunblane Massacre were far-reaching in British culture. A Home Affairs Select Committee later that year came to the conclusion that the rules on gun ownership should be changed so that people like Hamilton (whatever that meant) would be unable to own weapons in future, though it also believed that a complete ban on handguns would be excessive. But the Hungerford Massacre also involved a legal gun owner going on the rampage, so the public mood was turning against the private ownership of guns. This allowed a more restrictive policy on handgun ownership to come into play. Another change was a tightening of security in schools, especially primary schools, in the United Kingdom generally, to make it much harder for deranged people like Hamilton to gain entry. This was a response to Dunblane, but also to two other incidents at about the same time: the murder of head teacher Philip Lawrence at a school in London and the wounding of six children and a teacher at a nursery school in Wolverhampton.

A prisoner undergoes torture at the hands of the Spanish Inquisition, *c.*1500. He is tied to a revolving wheel, under which a fire is being fanned by bellows. The monks in the background are waiting patiently with quill and paper to obtain the prisoner's confession. (Credit: Getty Images)

English executioner Jack Ketch, who was notorious for his incompetent and often sadistic execution technique, is himself taken to be hanged for the murder of Elizabeth White on 31 May 1718. (Credit: Getty Images)

After a seven-day hunt for fugitive gunman Raoul Moat (right), the police finally corner him in the countryside. Despite their best efforts to negotiate with Moat, he committed suicide. (Credit: Getty Images)

Columbine High School shooters Eric Harris (left) and Dylan Klebold appear in this video capture of a surveillance tape released by the Jefferson County Sheriff's Department in the cafeteria of the school. The killing spree, which took place on 20 April 1999, took the lives of thirteen people. (Credit: 1999 Jefferson County Sheriff's Office/Getty Images)

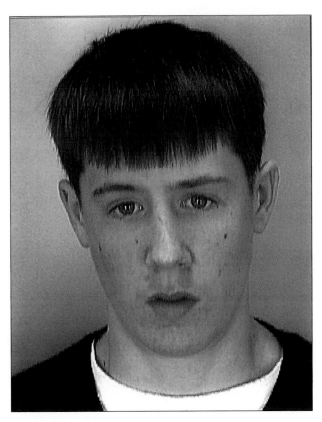

In September 1998, Kip Kinkel confessed to killing his parents in their home on 20 May 1998 and the next day, walking into the Thurston High School cafeteria and spraying students with 50 rounds from a semiautomatic rifle, killing two students and wounding twenty-five others. (Credit: Getty Images)

During the final stages of World War II in 1945, the United States dropped two atomic bombs on the Japanese cities of Hiroshima (above) on 6 August and Nagasaki on 9 August. The after-effects of the two bombs killed 90,000–166,000 in Hiroshima and 60,000–80,000 in Nagasaki. (Credit: Time Life Pictures/Getty Images)

Two women walk past an advertisement board for a local newspaper, giving details of a killing spree that took place on 3 June 2010 in Whitehaven, Cumbria. A fifty-two-year-old man, Derrick Bird, went on a rampage with a shotgun killing twelve people and injuring a further twenty-five before taking his own life, allegedly blaming the rest of society for his shortcomings. (Credit: Getty Images)

Three near simultaneous explosions hit Atocha station in the centre of the Spanish capital of Madrid on the morning of 11 March 2004, just three days before the country's general elections. The blasts killed 191 people and wounded 1,800. (Credit: AFP/Getty Images)

'NO-ONE SHOULD SURVIVE'
COLUMBINE HIGH SCHOOL MASSACRE (1999)

The Columbine High School Massacre is perhaps the best-known of the school massacres. It had an enormous impact on the local community, the little suburban town of Littleton, Colorado, because of its violence and because it came without any warning. In the middle of a school day on 20 April 1999, two boys set out to kill hundreds of their fellow-students. They had prepared themselves and were armed with knives, guns and bombs in order to carry out as many killings as they could.

The two boys were Dylan Klebold and Eric Harris. They were intelligent, had secure family backgrounds, with older brothers who might have been role models. They were seen as well-rounded characters, playing sport and working with computers. There was nothing unusual about them, except that they had been made to feel by their peers that they did not belong. They had met at the Ken Caryl Middle School in 1993, and the problems began when they went on to high school, where various student cliques existed and the two boys did not fit into any of them. Because of this they found themselves treated as outsiders by other students; they became the victims of a certain amount of low-level bullying. This perhaps threw them into each other's company rather more. They worked together in a pizza parlour. After school they liked to play computer games together. Much of their behaviour looked liked normal adolescent behaviour, and not fitting in with their peers very well did not appear to be a huge difficulty.

They systematically deceived everybody round them, the other students and even their own families, about their inner thoughts and intentions. Just a month before the massacre, the Klebold family went on a four-day road trip to the University of Arizona, where Dylan had been accepted for the following year. During the trip, the Klebolds did not notice anything strange or unusual about him. But they had also not noticed the cache of incriminating videotapes, journals, guns and bombs in his room; clearly they had respected the boy's privacy. The Harris family treated Eric in the same way, and he too had a cache of arms in his room and a record of his plans. This raises painful questions about responsibility. 'Am I my brother's keeper?' Parents have a responsibility for their children's social (and anti-social) behaviour, but children in their turn have a right to privacy. The boys were behaving normally enough for there to be no real justification for their parents searching their rooms, but if they had investigated they would have found plenty of disturbing evidence that a massacre was being prepared.

Dylan Klebald was thinking of committing suicide by 1997, and they had both begun discussing a large-scale massacre by April 1998, a year before the event. These things are known because the boys left notes, journals and videos. They purposely left them so that they would be found after they had died, as a record of their insane enterprise of destruction. They had, by that stage, started to behave antisocially, and to get into trouble. In January 1998 they were arrested for breaking into a van. They were given what was termed a 'juvenile diversion programme', which was designed as a rehabilitation scheme. They were first-time offenders, and by agreeing to co-operate with this programme, and completing it, they would have nothing on their criminal record. By participating in this remedial project, Klebold and Harris persuaded the authorities that they regretted what they had done and were on track to become good citizens. But at the same time they were planning the massacre.

What motivated them seems to have been anger. They were angry about being taunted by the school athletes. They hated black students. They hated racists. They hated Christians too. They hated martial arts fanatics. They hated people who boasted about their cars. There were very few people they didn't hate. Harris wrote in his journal:

You know what I hate? Star Wars fans: get a friggin life, you boring geeks. You know what I hate? People who mispronounce words, like 'acrost', and 'pacific' for 'specific'. And 'expresso' instead of 'espresso'. You know what I hate? People who drive slow in the fast lane, God these people do not know how to drive. You know what I hate? The WB network!!!! Oh Jesus, Mary Mother of God Almighty, I hate that channel with all my heart and soul.

The boys spent a lot of time whipping up their own rage.

Using the Internet, the boys found recipes for explosives and pipe bombs. They also collected weapons. They wanted to kill as many people as possible and when they studied the movements of students into the cafeteria they noted that after 11.15 am, when the first lunch break began, there would be more than 500 students in there. Their plan was to plant propane bombs in the cafeteria, and set them to go off at 11.17 am. They would shoot any survivors as they ran out.

There seems to have been some uncertainty about which was the best date for the attack. April 19 was the anniversary of the Oklahoma City bombing, which would be appropriate. April 20 was Adolf Hitler's birthday – he would have been 110 that day. The reasoning is opaque, but they decided on Hitler's birthday.

On that day, the two boys drove to school separately and parked one on each side of the cafeteria. One minute before the lunch break began, they carried two twenty-pound propane bombs in bags and put them next to tables in the cafeteria. They were timed to explode at 11.17 am and there was nothing to distinguish them from any of the scores of other bags students had brought in to the room; nobody noticed the boys placing the bags. Klebold and Harris went back to their cars to wait for the explosion.

There was no explosion. If the bombs had gone off, it is likely that everyone in the cafeteria – all 448 students – would have been killed. After waiting a few minutes, the boys realised that the timers must have gone wrong. They decided to go ahead, using just the weapons. Klebold armed himself with a semi-automatic handgun and a double-barrelled shotgun. Harris had a carbine rifle and a sawn-off shotgun. Both carried knives and bags full of bombs. They wore black trench coats to hide the weapons.

At 11.19, two pipe bombs they had set up in a field some distance away exploded. It was a diversion to distract the police. Then the boys started shooting students sitting outside the cafeteria. A boy was injured and a seventeen-year-old girl was killed. Many of the students did not believe anything serious was happening. It was close to graduation and it was a tradition at Columbine, as at other schools, for seniors to set up a leaving prank. Many students thought the shootings were mock-shootings, just a prank, so they did not immediately run for cover. Three students came out of the cafeteria, saw the guns and assumed they were just paintball guns; they kept on walking towards Klebold and Harris. They were all wounded. Klebold walked over to the injured boys and shot again, killing one of them outright.

One of the staff inside the cafeteria, Dave Sanders, understood that this was not a prank and persuaded the students to move away from the windows and lie down on the floor for safety. Many students went up the stairs to an upper floor. When Klebold looked into the cafeteria, it appeared to be empty.

He rejoined Harris and together they went into the school, shooting as they went. A policeman arrived; he and Harris fired at each other, and both missed. Klebold and Harris walked through the north hallway, laughing and shooting. Stephanie Munson was one of the students walking down the hallway. When she saw the two boys, she tried to run from the building. She was shot in the ankle as she ran, but managed to get away. The two boys turned back towards the entrance. Dave Sanders came down the stairs and rounded a corner to come face to face with Klebold and Harris with their guns raised. He turned back, but they fired and hit him before he could escape. He managed to crawl to safety, and another teacher dragged him into a classroom.

Klebold and Harris went on firing randomly and throwing bombs. They threw two bombs down the stairs into the cafeteria, where fifty-two students and four staff were still hiding. Then they went into the library and told anyone wearing a white cap (an athlete) to stand up. No-one stood up, but Klebold and Harris started firing anyway. Klebold shot and killed a boy sitting at a computer, then fired under a table where three students were hiding: he injured all three. Harris walked to a table under which two girls were hiding, banged on the table, shouted 'Peek-a-boo!', then shot one of the girls. He taunted another girl sitting on the floor, making her plead for her life. Then he was distracted by Klebold calling him over to another table. One of the students hiding there was black; Klebold dragged him out and Harris shot him. Then Klebold shot under the table and killed another boy. The shooting rampage in the library went on, with three more students killed. As Harris stopped to reload he recognised a boy under the table. The boy was on friendly terms with Klebold and he asked Klebold what he was doing. Klebold said, 'Oh, just killing people.' The friend then had the presence of mind to ask Klebold if he was going to be killed too. Klebold told him to leave the library: the friend did not hesitate. Harris shot again underneath a table, killing two more students. After firing a few more rounds and hurling a chair, Klebold and Harris left the library. They had only been in the library seven minutes or so, yet in that time they had killed ten young people and injured twelve more. The thirty-four students who lived and were not injured were lucky to have survived the carnage.

Then there was a kind of intermission when Klebold and Harris walked along corridors, looking into classrooms, but not trying very hard to get into them. The students were taking refuge in the classrooms, with the doors locked, which seemed enough to deter the two boys. It was now just half an hour after the killing spree had started, and Klebold and Harris went back to the cafeteria to try to set off the two large bombs. They shot at one of them, fiddled with the other, but still the bombs would not explode. Klebold threw a small bomb at one of the propane bombs, but it only started a fire, which triggered the sprinklers. They went out to throw more bombs, then came back to find that the sprinklers had put out the fire.

They returned to the library, to find that most of the uninjured students had escaped. By now there were police and paramedics outside the school building and at midday Harris and Klebold fired out of the windows at them. At about 12.05, they shot themselves in the head.

It was difficult for those outside, the police, the families, the injured students who had escaped, to understand what was happening. No-one saw all of the events except the two boys, who were now dead, and no-one outside saw them commit suicide, so it was by no means certain when the massacre was over. It was only as the police gradually cleared the building that this was discovered. The students who had escaped were taken by bus to another school where they gave statements to the police. Then they were put onto a stage to be claimed by their parents. As the hours passed, it became clear to those parents left waiting that their son or daughter must have been injured or killed. In fact the list of those who had died was not confirmed until the following day.

The slowness of the police operation was due to the bombs and explosives used. It was not possible to go straight in and evacuate the students and staff who were hiding inside. Some were stranded for hours waiting to be rescued. One victim who had been shot twice in the head decided to escape from the library window halfway through the afternoon. He fell from the window, two floors up, and luckily was caught by rescuers – and he survived.

The teacher who had helped hundreds of students to escape, Dave Sanders, died in one of the science classrooms. The students with him tried to give him first aid, put signs in the windows to encourage emergency services to come quickly, but no-one came until it was too late.

Klebold and Harris killed thirteen people, twelve students and one teacher. The massacre was terrible, but the massacre that Klebold and Harris had planned was even worse. Of all the bombs they threw, thirty exploded and forty-six did not. They planted thirteen bombs in their cars, which also did not go off. And the two big bombs in the cafeteria never exploded. The death toll, terrible though it was, could have been much higher.

In the aftermath of such an event, people always ask, 'Why?' It is hard to be sure, but the exclusiveness of adolescent peer groups clearly played a part in alienating the two boys, in promoting feelings of rejection and anger. It is also possible that the violent video games the two boys spent a lot of their time playing were part of the problem. It is almost as if Eric Harris and Dylan Klebold acted out in the real world the sort of violent destruction that should have been confined to the computer screen. They graduated from zapping pixels to zapping people. This would help to explain why they showed no awareness of the terrible suffering they were causing to their victims and to their victims' families.

'WE MUST NOT THINK EVIL OF THIS MAN'

AMISH SCHOOL SHOOTING (2006)

The Amish School Shooting took place at a one-room schoolhouse in the Old Order Amish community of Nickel Mines in Pennsylvania. On 2 October 2006, Charles Carl Roberts IV seized hostages at the West Nickel Mines School on White Oak Road. Just over half an hour later, he shot ten girls aged between six and thirteen, killing five of them. Then he committed suicide.

At 10.25 in the morning of 2 October, Charles Roberts backed a pick-up truck to the front of the schoolhouse. He went into the school to ask the teacher and the children if they had seen something in the road that he had lost. Roberts was mumbling and avoiding making direct eye contact. The children had seen nothing and nor had the teacher, Emma Mae Zook. Roberts went out to his truck and returned with handgun, telling the boys to help him carry things into the classroom from his truck. Emma Zook knew something was seriously wrong, and ran off with her mother to a neighbouring farm to get help. Roberts saw them go and told a boy to stop them; he threatened to shoot everyone if the women got away.

Emma Zook and her mother reached the farm, and asked Amos Smoker to call the police. Meanwhile, Roberts and the boys carried a shotgun, a stun-gun, wire, chains, nails, tools, timber and a small bag from the truck into the classroom. Amongst all this equipment was a wooden board with lots of metal hooks attached to it. In the bag was a change of clothes, toilet paper, candles and plastic ties. Roberts used the timber to barricade the front door. He told the girls to stand in a line against the blackboard, telling them, 'Stay here. Do not move. You will be shot.' He allowed everyone else to leave, including four adults and all the remaining boys. One girl escaped. Emma Fisher, who was nine years old, spoke only Pennsylvania German and did not understand Roberts' order to stand in line; she just left the room with her brother Peterli. This left Roberts with ten hostages.

The emergency call to the police was sent at 10.35 am. During the wait for the arrival of the police, one of the men from Amos Smoker's farm took two large dogs across to the schoolhouse, stealthily approaching the back of the building, which had no windows. Hoping he could find an opportunity to help the girls, he slid round the side of the building and observed what was happening through a side window. When he saw the first police patrol car passing the schoolhouse, he ran down to the road to wave it down. The car did a rapid u-turn and stopped. This was at about 10.42 am.

While waiting for reinforcements, police officers tried to communicate with Roberts, using their public address sytems. They asked him to throw out his weapons and come out. Roberts refused, telling the officers to leave. By eleven o'clock a crowd had gathered outside the schoolhouse: police, paramedics and local inhabitants. Roberts continually threatened violence towards the girls.

By now all of the girls understood that they were going to be shot. It was an appalling ordeal for them, but some of them managed to carry on talking to one another throughout, to try to cope with what they had to face. He had told them at the beginning that they would be shot. As they realised the moment was approaching when Roberts was going to open fire, two of the girls, two sisters, Marian and Barbie Fisher, one thirteen years old, the other eleven, asked Roberts to shoot them first so that the others might be spared. It was an extraordinarily selfless, brave, indeed heroic offer for the two girls to make.

Outside, a child's scream was heard. A group of officers hiding behind a shed at the back of the schoolhouse asked for permission to go to the schoolhouse windows, but they were ordered to stay back. Perhaps if the building had been rushed at this point, more lives might have been saved.

Shortly after eleven o'clock, Roberts started shooting his hostages, one by one, in the back of the head. Then the troopers immediately went forward, but they were already too late. As the first trooper reached a window and smashed it, the shooting abruptly stopped. With the eighteenth shot, Roberts had killed himself. Eighteen shots is the number estimated by the police commissioner, though the deputy coroner, who examined the bodies, said she counted at least two dozen bullet wounds in one child before she had to ask an assistant to continue counting for her. She said, 'There was not one desk, not one chair, in the whole schoolroom that was not splattered with either blood or glass. There were bullet holes everywhere, everywhere.' There is therefore a difference of opinion about the total number of bullets fired in the schoolhouse, and therefore also of the nature of the killings. The smaller number of bullets would be associated with an execution-style killing; the much larger number suggests an indiscriminate hail of bullets.

Barbie Fisher lay wounded, and Marian was dead. The police officers broke through the barricade and reached the children. All of them had been shot, four of them killed outright, and a fifth would die of her injury within the day. Troopers and police officers helped the paramedics to administer first aid on the survivors as they lay on the school playground, before they were taken to hospital by helicopter or ambulance.

Charles Roberts was not Amish. He drove a milk lorry, serving several of the Amish farms in the area, including the farms where some of the girls lived. Roberts was married with three children. He left them four letters, one each, which showed that he went into the schoolhouse intending to end his own life there. Jeffery Miller, the State Police Commissioner, interviewed Roberts' co-workers and they said they had noticed a change over the previous two months. But in the week before the shooting he had seemed back to normal. Miller believes this was when Roberts decided to do the shooting and kill himself. It is a common feature of suicides that they tend to be much more upbeat once they have definitely decided on death; they have decided on the 'solution' to their problems and have committed to it.

The five girls who were wounded were taken to Lancaster General Hospital, stabilised and then transferred to hospitals specialising in pediatric trauma care.

The response of the Amish community was remarkable. Amid the grief there was a determination to accept and forgive. The grandfather of one of the murdered girls asked his younger relatives not to hate the killer: 'We must not think evil of this man.' Another parent commented that Charles Roberts 'had a mother and a wife and a soul, and now he's standing before a just God'. Another member of the community said, 'I don't think there's anybody here that wants to do anything but forgive and not only reach out to those who have suffered a loss in that way but to reach out to the family of the man who committed these acts.' Amish neighbours went out of their way to comfort the killer's widow and parents. One Amish man held Roberts' sobbing father in his arms for an hour. The Amish even set up a charitable fund to support Roberts' family and thirty of them attended Roberts' funeral. Marie Roberts wrote to her Amish neighbours to express her gratitude for their grace and mercy. 'Your love for our family has helped to provide the healing we so desperately need. Gifts you've given have touched our hearts in a way no words can describe. Your compassion has reached beyond our family, beyond our community, and is changing our world, and for this we sincerely thank you.'

The schoolhouse was demolished the week after the shootings and returned to pasture. A new school, the New Hope School, was built nearby, in a different architectural style.

Why did Roberts do this terrible thing? He was living at Georgetown, and was last seen by his wife at 8.45 am when they walked their children to the bus stop. Mrs Roberts returned home from a prayer meeting to find the four suicide notes just before 11 am, when Roberts already had the girls captive in the schoolroom and just a few minutes before he shot them. She dialled 911 at once to alert the police, but by then they already knew: it was too late. Using his mobile, Roberts phoned his wife from the schoolhouse and told her, in a very disturbing message, that he had sexually molested two female relatives under the age of five, twenty years before, when he had been twelve years old. Now he was fantasising about molesting young girls again.

So, one element in Roberts' psychological breakdown was a sense of overwhelming guilt and shame about what he had done twenty years earlier; another was fear that he was about to re-offend. Another element emerged in one of the suicide notes. His daughter, born nine years earlier, had died only twenty minutes after being born. This had left him despondent. But then there was a new twist in the mystery. The two female relatives Roberts said he had molested told the police a different story. They said there had been no such abuse. Presumably Roberts was not lying about it – there would be no possible reason to lie about it. It rather suggests that Roberts was seriously mentally ill, that he somehow persuaded himself that he had committed abuse when he had not. This is unusual. It is far more common for people to delude themselves in the opposite direction, to persuade themselves (and others) that they have not committed crimes when really they have.

'WELL-PREPARED TO CONTINUE'
VIRGINIA TECH MASSACRE (2007)

The Virginia Tech Massacre was the worst mass murder in American history as measured by death toll, on or off a school campus. On 16 April 2007, in two separate attacks two hours apart, Seung-Hui Cho killed thirty-two people before committing suicide. The massacre took place at the Virginia Polytechnic Institute and State University at Blacksburg, Virginia.

The perpetrator was a student following an English course at Virginia Tech. Some mass murderers appear to be quite normal, though they lead abnormal interior lives. But Cho was very evidently abnormal, and it had been known for several years that he had serious mental health problems. He had been diagnosed with a severe anxiety disorder, and for much of his school life (middle and high school) he had been having therapy and special education support. Although the staff at his school knew perfectly well about Cho's personality disorder –

they were organising his treatment – they were not allowed to pass this information on to the Virginia Tech staff. The reason was the constraints of federal privacy laws. Cho went to Virginia Tech with a clean slate.

But in 2005, Cho was accused of stalking two female students. There was an investigation, Cho was declared to be mentally ill by a Virginia special justice. He was ordered to attend treatment. One of the professors, a former chair of the English Department, had also told Cho that he should get counselling. Cho's mother looked to the church for help, and a minister advised that 'spiritual power' was needed to help him.

Cho was seen close to West Ambler Johnston Hall early in the morning, at 6.45 am. This building was a co-educational hall of residence housing 894 students. Cho had a mailbox in the building's lobby, so he had a pass card access that operated from 7.30 am onwards. It is not clear how he was able to gain access to the building nearly an hour before that. At 7.15 am, Cho entered the room nineteen-year-old Emily Hilscher was sharing with another student. Cho shot and fatally injured her. Ryan Clark, a twenty-two-year-old male resident assistant, heard the shots and went to try to aid Emily Hilscher. He was shot and killed. Emily died three hours after being shot, yet for some reason during that time no-one from the tech campus, police or hospital thought to notify her family of her condition.

While the police and emergency medical services responded to the double shootings in the dorm, Cho returned to his own room and changed out of his bloodstained clothes. He switched on his computer, deleted his e-mails, then removed the hard drive, apparently to dispose of it. About an hour later Cho is thought to have been seen near the duck pond. The implication is that Cho threw both his hard drive and his mobile phone into the pond, but a search produced nothing.

Two hours after the double shooting, Cho was in a post office nearby, posting a parcel of video recordings and writings to NBC News. This was timed by the postmark at 9.01 am. Then he walked to Norris Hall, for the second and more horrific part of his killing spree. He wore a backpack containing chains, locks, a knife, a hammer, two guns and lots of ammunition. Norris Hall housed the Engineering Science and Mechanics departments. Cho went in and chained shut the three main entrance doors. He left a note on one of the chained doors to say that if anyone tried to open the door a bomb would go off.

Just before the shootings started, a member of staff found the note and took it up to the second floor to show to the college administrators.

At that moment, Cho started shooting students on the first floor. The first emergency 911 call to the police was made almost at once. Before the shooting started, Cho peered into several classrooms. He looked into one of them twice. One of the students thought it odd that at this point in the term anyone could be lost, looking for a class. Presumably Cho was deciding who to kill. His first Norris Hall attack was on an advanced hydrology engineering class that was being taught by Professor G. V. Loganathan. First Cho shot and killed the professor. Then he went on shooting, killing nine out of the thirteen students in the room.

Cho cross the hallway to a room where a German class was being taught by Christopher Bishop. Cho shot and killed Mr Bishop, then four students. Six other students were wounded. By now teachers and students in other classrooms understood what was happening. When Cho tried to get into the next two rooms, he found he was impeded by hastily assembled barricades. In one of the rooms the teacher was a Holocaust survivor; Professor Liviu Librescu held the door shut to give his students time to escape out of the windows. Eventually he died when Cho shot him several times through the door. One student in his room was killed. In the next room, teacher Jocelyne Couture-Nowak and her student Henry Lee were shot dead while they tried to barricade the door.

Cho reloaded and went back to some of the classrooms where he had left dead and wounded. In one of them, students had barricaded the door and were doing what they could to tend the wounded. When Cho came back, Katelyn Carney and Derek O'Dell both received injuries as they tried to hold the door shut. In another room, Cho saw one of the students he had wounded moving and shot him again, killing him. In yet another room, so far unvisited by Cho, the teacher, Haiyan Cheng, saw Cho walking towards them. He and the students pushed a heavy table against the door. Cho fired several shots through the door but was unable to force his way in. Nobody in that room was killed or wounded.

When, up on the second floor, Professor Kevin Granata heard the sound of gunshots on the first floor, he led twenty students out of a classroom, where they were vulnerable, into an office with a lockable door. Leaving them safely locked in,

Professor Granata went downstairs to see what could be done. Cho shot and killed him. None of the students he led to the office were injured.

About ten minutes after the Norris Hall attack started, Cho for some reason decided he had done enough and shot himself in the head. He had fired perhaps 174 rounds, but police afterwards found 203 live rounds in Norris Hall, so he could easily have gone on and killed twice as many people. Police Superintendent Flaherty commented to a state panel, 'He was well prepared to continue.' As it was, he killed thirty people and wounded seventeen; another six were injured as they jumped from first-floor windows to escape. The police arrived in the ground floor of the Norris Building too late to do any good; as they entered, they heard the final shot.

The man who carried out the massacre was a South Korean citizen with permanent residency status in the USA. He was an undergraduate, with a room in Harper Hall, to the west of West Ambler Johnston Hall. As we have already seen, Cho was a troubled and anxious youth well before he arrived at Virginia Tech. As early as three he was described as shy, frail and wary of physical contact. Suggestions that he suffered from autism have been rejected. He was diagnosed as having severe depression and a social anxiety disorder known as selective mutism, which inhibited speech. Cho's family knew there was something seriously wrong and tried to get appropriate therapy for him when he was at school. He may also have been bullied because of his speech difficulties.

The problems began to magnify after Cho's admission to Virginia Tech, and this was in part because of federal privacy laws which prohibited his school from disclosing his mental health problems or special education status. With hindsight it can be seen that this prohibition was unhelpful. On the other hand, Cho was displaying unusual and worrying classroom behaviour even in his first year at Virginia Tech and this should have been interpreted as a sign of mental deterioration. Then he was investigated by the university for stalking two female students. He was declared mentally ill and ordered to seek outpatient treatment.

The various symptoms Cho displayed may point to the fact that he was developing schizophrenia. One symptom of schizophrenia is 'poverty of speech', in other words the sufferer engages in markedly little talking. Cho's manifesto (in the parcel posted to NBC News) provides evidence of paranoid and grandiose delusions, which can also be associated with schizophrenia. So the problem may have been that Cho was an undiagnosed schizophrenic.

When the police investigated Cho's room they found a suicide note in which Cho condemned the students around him, in terms such as 'rich kids', 'deceitful charlatans' and 'debauchery'.

Another element in Cho's worsening state of mind may have been the frightening prospect of leaving the protected environment of school and college, of being turned out into the world of work, money and responsibility. Instead he took refuge in a fantasy that he was some kind of saviour, cleansing and rescuing the world. The investigating panel concluded that his thought processes were so distorted that he began arguing to himself that his evil plan was actually doing good. His destructive fantasy became an obsession.

In the aftermath of the shootings, many questions were raised about the gun laws and the state of Virginia closed the legal loopholes that had allowed a person diagnosed as mentally ill to buy handguns. The purchase, or attempted purchase, should have been picked up by the National Instant Criminal Background Check System (NICS). The massacre led to the passage of the first major federal gun control measure for over thirteen years. The law strengthening the NICS was signed by President Bush in January 2008. The Virginia Tech Review Panel, a body created to review the massacre, reported that there were weaknesses in the mental care system and the privacy laws which had led to the killer's deteriorating mental condition going untreated.

Virginia Tech cancelled classes for the rest of the week and closed Norris Hall for the rest of the term. Counsellors were drafted in to help students and staff come to terms with what had happened. Thirty-two separate endowment funds were set up to commemorate each of the victims. Norris Hall is being revamped in such a way that it will no longer house classrooms.

The State Governor, Timothy Kaine, set up an eight-member panel to review all aspects of the massacre, including the university's delay in warning students of the danger they were in after the bodies of the first two victims were discovered, and its delay in 'locking down' the campus at that time. In August 2007, the panel announced its findings. One, among many, was that the campus police department had not responded with sufficient action when first alerted. The major finding was that Cho was responsible for what happened, and that he was accountable. But the review panel supported the general public criticism of the university's response to the initial double murder. It took the view that lives could have been saved if the university authorities had at that point immediately suspended classes and given staff and students clear warning of the presence of a gunman on the campus.

Federal government passed a significant modification to gun control law. State reporting to the National Instant Criminal Background Check System was improved in order to stop convicted criminals and those declared mentally ill from buying guns. There was an existing gun control law, but it was inadequate. The existing 1968 federal law was enacted in response to the assassinations of Robert Kennedy and Martin Luther King, and it prohibited anyone 'adjudicated as a mental defective' from purchasing guns. This particular exclusion applied to Cho when a Virginia court declared that he was a danger to himself in November 2005, and in the same judgement ordered him to accept psychiatric treatment. At that moment, Cho technically acquired mental defective status. But the problem was that a crucial gap existed between federal law and the state law of Virginia, and the state of Virginia did not report the change in Cho's legal status to the NICS. As a result, Cho's insanity did not emerge when he purchased guns, with disastrous consequences. The new measure was passed by the US Senate in December 2007 and signed by President Bush in January 2008. Measures were also considered to create a better balance between the right to individual privacy and the need for public safety, in matters of sharing education records.

In South Korea, there was a sense of horror and shame that a South Korean could have committed this terrible crime. Cho's family members expressed their shock and grief, and their sympathy for the families of the victims; they also described Cho's history of mental and behavioural problems.

In America, the gun laws debate was reactivated yet again. The White House issued a statement saying that, 'The president [George W. Bush] believes that there is a right for people to bear arms, but that all laws must be followed.' Campaigners for the prevention of gun violence claimed that it was too easy for people to get hold of powerful weapons; they wanted increased control over gun ownership. Representatives of the National Rifle Association advocated an end to gun-free zones. Virginia Tech was a gun-free zone, and the NRA view was that in other incidents mass shootings have been ended by law-abiding gun owners. The Governor of Texas,

Rick Perry, proposed that licensed owners of guns should be allowed to carry their guns anywhere in the state of Texas. The issue was, and remains, a very complex one. The Governor of Virginia, Tim Kaine, expressed his condemnation of the gun politics debate being pegged to the massacre:

To those who want to make this into some sort of crusade, I say 'Take this elsewhere'.

'FOR FUN — BECAUSE IT'S FUN!'

WINNENDEN SCHOOL SHOOTING (2009)

The Winnenden school shooting took place on 11 March 2009 at a secondary school at Winnenden in south-west Germany. The killing spree resulted in the deaths of sixteen people, including the suicide of the perpetrator, Tim Kretschmer, a seventeen-year-old ex-pupil of the school. Several others were injured in the shootings.

Tim Kretschmer started shooting in the Albertsville Secondary School at 9.30 am, using a Beretta pistol he had taken from his parents' bedroom. He headed for two classrooms and a chemistry laboratory on the top floor of the building. In the classrooms, Kretschmer shot and killed eight girls and one boy, as well as a woman teacher. The fact that most of the victims were female caused some observers to speculate that the boy may have been deliberately targeting females.

The school's headmaster broadcast an announcement in code – 'Mrs Koma is coming' – to alert his staff to the situation. 'Koma' is 'amok' spelt backwards. This coded message was agreed throughout German schools in the aftermath of the Erfurt school massacre of April 2002. On hearing it, the teachers locked their classroom doors.

One of the students made an emergency phone call at once, timed at 9.33 am, and three police officers arrived on the scene just two minutes later – by any standards an excellent response time. They were able to interrupt Kretschmer's killing spree. He fired at the police, then fled from the building. In the entrance hall he happened to see two women teachers and he shot them dead before leaving the building.

In a nearby park, Kretschmer shot and killed the caretaker of a nearby psychiatric hospital. Meanwhile, large numbers of policemen converged on the school and then began searching Winnenden for Kretschmer. They searched for hours without finding him. At 10 am, Kretschmer hi-jacked a Volkswagen minivan in a car park. He sat in the back seat, and ordered the driver, Igor Wolf, to head towards Wendlingen, which was twenty-five miles away. This drive took them west into the suburbs of Stuttgart, through Waiblingen, Fellbach, Bad Cannstatt, the Heslach Tunnel, then on by autobahn towards Tubingen. Igor Wolf naturally asked the boy why he was doing this, and the young gunman answered, 'For fun, because it is fun!' The boy was loading his pistols during the journey and asked, revealingly, 'Do you think we will still find another school?' Fearing for his own safety, just before reaching the autobahn junction for Wendlingen, Herr Wolf took the car onto the grass verge, stopped, jumped out of the car and ran towards a police patrol car.

Kretschmer also got out of the car and ran towards a nearby industrial area. He went into the main entrance of a Volkswagen showroom, where he threatened a salesman and demanded keys for one of the cars. The salesman managed to escape while Kretschmer was distracted. Kretschmer shot and killed one of the other salesmen and a customer, firing thirteen shots into them. He paused to reload and as he did so another sales assistant and another customer managed to escape through the rear of the building.

At about 12.30 pm Kretschmer emerged from the car showroom and shot randomly at a passing car; the driver was not hurt. Then the police arrived from nearby Nürtingen and the gunman engaged them in a shoot-out. A police officer fired eight shots at him and succeeded in wounding him once in each leg. Kretschmer went back into the showroom, firing twelve shots at the police who were beginning to surround the building. He escaped out of the back of the showroom, running across a yard into a business complex. There he shot and wounded two policemen in an unmarked police vehicle. Now Kretschmer was firing at random, at anyone he saw, at adjacent buildings. He reloaded his pistol, then shot himself in the head. Altogether, during the whole shooting spree Kretschmer had fired a total of 112 rounds. Kretschmer's spree cost the lives of fifteen people, including nine students, three trainee teachers, one caretaker and one car salesman.

Tim Kretschmer was born in 1991. He had recently left the Albertsville Realschule, in 2008, with relatively low grades, and these go a long way towards explaining his resentment towards the school. Because of the low grades, he had not qualified for the apprenticeship that he wanted. Instead he was attending a commercial high school in Waiblingen. The course there would prepare him for an apprenticeship and then he could have a commercial career.

One of Kretschmer's friends described him as 'a lonely and frustrated person who felt rejected by society'. Another noticed that he was not only quiet but had begun to withdraw from his peers. Kretschmer was a keen table tennis player and had nursed hopes of becoming a professional player. One of his coaches remembered him as 'a bit spoilt'; he demanded a lot of support from his parents. The same coach said Kretschmer had great difficulty in accepting defeat. If he lost a game he might throw a tantrum. He would also openly denigrate his opponents. When the coach tried to discuss the boy's attitude with his mother, he was surprised to hear her taking her son's side.

Kretschmer was another loner who was dependent on video games. More significant perhaps is his interest in air guns. He fired these both in the woods behind his home and in the basement of the house.

Tim Kretschmer had no criminal record. But he did have a medical record. He had received treatment as an in-patient at a psychiatric clinic. After he was discharged, he was supposed to continue his treatment as an out-patient but he decided to terminate the treatment. According to the police and the staff at the clinic, Kretschmer was treated for clinical depression, repeatedly, in 2008. His family rejected this version of events, maintaining that he never received psychiatric treatment. But the psychiatric report prepared for the prosecutor's office says that Kretschmer met a therapist five times, on which occasions he talked about his mounting anger and urges towards violence; and the concerned therapist had then contacted Kretschmer's parents about the matter.

Then there was the matter of the gun. How was it that Tim Kretschmer, a boy with a history of clinical depression, had access to guns? The police visited the Kretschmer family home at 11 am on the day of the shooting. It emerged that Tim's father owned fifteen guns. He was a member of a local shooting club. The police found that one Beretta handgun was missing, together with several hundred rounds of ammunition. Fourteen of the guns were kept in a gun safe – but the Beretta had been kept in the bedroom. It had not been kept secure. A few days after the shootings, prosecutors initiated preliminary proceedings against Tim Kretschmer's father for negligence, since the gun had not been properly locked away as required by law. The other fourteen guns were confiscated. The father said he would voluntarily relinquish his gun licence. In November 2009, the Public Prosecutor's Department in Stuttgart announced that the father had been indicted on charges of negligent homicide and violation of the weapons law. In May 2010, the state court upheld the charge relating to weapons law violation, but dropped the homicide charge.

There were demands from politicians for a prohibition on video games that involve shooting and for better monitoring of gun club members, for the storing of ammunition with the police and the storing of guns at club houses. Some of the victims' families wrote to the German Chancellor making smilar demands. They also called for a change in the style of reporting of such events, so that the role of the perpetrator would not and could not be glamorised. Traditional styles of reporting could easily trigger copycat mass killings. There was a serious proposal to ban fighting games such as paintballing, though the draft legislation was never passed. Neither was there, in the end, any legislation to limit the number of weapons owned by individuals – nor any obligation to store guns at shooting clubs.

'LET KIP HAVE THE GUNS'
THE KIP KINKEL SHOOTINGS (1998)

Kip Kinkel was a teenage mass murderer who, at the age of fifteen, first murdered his parents and then, at Thurston High School in Springfield, Orgeon, killed two students and injured twenty-two more.

Kipland Philip Kinkel, nicknamed 'Kip', was born in 1982, the son of William Kinkel and Faith Zuranski. His parents were both language teachers. Bill Kinkel taught Spanish at Lane Community College. Faith taught French at Springfield High School. The Kinkels spent a sabbatical year in Spain when Kip was six years old. At that time, the boy attended a non-English-speaking school in Spain and found it a difficult experience. On returning to Oregon, he went to the Walterville Elementary School Springfield. His teachers there thought him physically and emotionally immature, young for his age. The parents decided it would be best for him to repeat his first year. By the fourth year, he was being diagnosed with dyslexia and put into special education classes.

More worrying than any of this was Kip's developing interest in guns and explosives, which started at a very early age. At first his father denied this interest, but later enrolled him in gun safety courses and bought him guns, a Long rifle and a Glock handgun. William Kinkel claimed that his psychologist had advised him to 'let Kip have the guns: it will be a good outlet.'

Things started to go seriously wrong when in 1998 Kip got hold of a stolen handgun. A friend of Kip's stole the pistol from Scott Keeney, the father of a school friend, and arranged to sell it to Kip. Kip paid 110 dollars for it. It was a Beretta pistol loaded with a nine-round magazine. Kip put it in a paper bag and left it in his locker. When Mr Keeney realised his handgun was missing he reported the theft to the police, giving them the names of boys he thought might have taken it. Kinkel's was not one of them, but staff at the school suspected him and asked him about it. He said, 'Look, I'm gonna be square with you guys; the gun's in my locker.' At that point, on 20 May 1998, Kip Kinkel was suspended from Thurston High School pending an expulsion hearing. He and the friend were arrested, then Kinkel was released and taken home by his father.

Bill Kinkel was angry. That afternoon, on the day of the suspension, he told Kip that if he did not start to co-operate he would be sent to boarding school.

At 3.30 pm the boy went to get his rifle, which was stored in his parents' bedroom, and loaded it. Then he went to the kitchen, where he shot his father in the back of the head. He waited over two hours then for his mother to return. At 6 pm she walked up the stairs from the garage. Kinkel told her he loved her, then shot her twice in the back of the head. He shot her three times in the face and once in the heart. He claimed that he killed his parents to spare them the shame and embarrassment that his expulsion from school was going to cause them.

Kinkel dragged his mother's body from the foot of the stairs into the garage and covered it with a sheet. Then he dragged his father's body into the bathroom, where again he covered it with a sheet. He put on some music, which was still playing when the police arrived to find the bodies.

On 21 May, the next day, Kinkel drove his mother's car to the high school. He was wearing a trench coat to conceal the fact that he was carrying a hunting knife, a semi-automatic rifle and two pistols. He was also carrying an alarming amount of ammunition: 1,127 rounds.

He parked two blocks away from the school and walked into the forecourt area. He fired his rifle, wounding one boy and fatally wounding another. Then he went into the cafeteria and fired the remaining forty-eight rounds in his rifle. This onslaught wounded twenty-four students and killing one. When Kinkel's rifle ran out of ammunition and he paused to reload, Jacob Ryker, one of the wounded students, threw himself at Kinkel. Several other students did the same. Kinkel managed to pull out the Glock pistol and fire one shot with that before he was disarmed. The single pistol shot injured Jacob Ryker again, and another student. The students successfully restrained Kinkel until the police arrived to arrest him. It was an admirable effort on the part of the seven students who were brave enough to tackle the young gunman. They took a major risk, but they succeeded in putting an end to a rampage that could have ended in scores of deaths; Kinkel had enough ammunition to do a great deal of damage. Jacob Ryker was taken to hospital with a perforated lung, but made a full recovery.

The killing spree had ended prematurely as far as Kip Kinkel was concerned. He had envisaged killing more people, and then committing suicide. He had felt like committing suicide after killing his parents but found that when it came to it he was unable to do it. At the police station, he rushed at one of the police officers with his knife hoping that this would force the officer, Al Warthen, to shoot him dead. He shouted at him, 'Shoot me! Kill me!' Officer Warthen subdued him with pepper spray.

Kinkel's lawyers brought in psychiatrists to demonstrate that Kinkel was mentally ill. But Jeffrey Hicks, the one psychologist who had actually treated Kinkel prior to the rampage, declared that he was of the opinion that Kinkel was of sound mind. He had seen Kinkel for nine sessions.

On 29 September 1999, three days before the process of selecting jurors for Kinkel's trial was to begin, Kinkel pleaded guilty to murder and attempted murder. Because of the expert witness evidence, he was not able to try for acquittal on grounds of insanity. The guilty plea meant that he did not stand trial. In November 1999, Kipland Philip Kinkel was found guilty and sentenced – to 111 years in prison, with no possibility of parole. Kinkel apologised for the murder of his parents and for the shooting spree at the school.

But in June 2007, by then aged twenty-four and approaching the maximum age to be held as a juvenile, Kinkel tried to get a new trial. His argument was that his case had been mishandled. His original lawyers should have taken the case to trial, and they should have pleaded insanity on his behalf.

Two psychiatrists were found to testify that Kinkel was showing symptoms of paranoid schizophrenia at the time of the shootings. In August the judge denied him a fresh trial. His lawyer planned to appeal against this decision.

Meanwhile, Kinkel has been moved to the Oregon State Correctional Institution in Salem, Oregon.

PART SIX
WORKPLACE KILLINGS

AN ARMED CITIZENRY?
THE 101 CALIFORNIA STREET KILLINGS (1993)

In the middle of the afternoon of 1 July 1993, a nondescript-looking businessman walked in through the entrance of a granite-faced high-rise office building, 101 California Street in San Francisco, and made his way up to the thirty-fourth floor. There he found the smart offices of the law firm, Pettit and Martin. Gian Luigi Ferri was fifty-five years old, a property developer, and he was dressed in a dark business suit and carrying a black attaché case. He looked like a lawyer himself, perhaps returning to the office after a late lunch. He had been a client of Pettit and Martin for over ten years, and he was unhappy about the way the firm had treated him.

He came out of the lift, set down his case and pulled three semi-automatic pistols from under his jacket. He put on a pair of ear protectors, walked sixty feet towards a glass-walled conference room where lawyers were taking a deposition from a witness in a labour dispute, and started shooting. The glass wall was shattered. Two people died instantly, the plaintiff in the case and her lawyer. Two other people in the conference room were wounded, one of them shot in the arm as she dived for cover behind a chair. Ferri moved round and fired through another glass wall, killing one of the Pettit partners in his office. People fled for cover, hiding behind doors and running to try to escape through exit doors.

Someone set off the fire alarm, which caused confusion as some people thought it was just an emergency drill. SWAT teams arrived in the building. The public address system warned everyone to stay inside their rooms and lock their doors. Ferri roamed about on this level for a time as the survivors vanished before going down a staircase to the floor below, where he carried on shooting. The rampage continued across several floors of the building before the police arrived. About fifteen minutes after he started shooting, Ferri was descending to the twenty-ninth floor when came face to face with the police as they came up the stairs; then he shot himself under the chin, through the roof of the mouth. In just fifteen minutes, he had killed eight people and injured six more. A police official described the incident as the worst mass homicide incident in San Francisco's history.

It was never fully clear why Ferri had committed this crime, though he left behind a garbled letter in which he outlined a long list of complaints. He was evidently deeply dissatisfied with the legal services the company had offered. Gian Luigi Ferri was a loner, an isolate, a would-be property tycoon. He had had some limited dealings with Pettit and Martin in relation to a botched property deal several years before. He irrationally blamed the law firm for his own subsequent failures. He nursed his rage for over ten years. In the rambling letter he left there was a 'List of Criminals, Rapists, Racketeers, Lobbyists', which including Pettit lawyers.

If the targets were intended to be the staff of Pettit and Martin, Ferri miscalculated. He was in the right building and on the right floor, but he was not pointing his gun at the right people. He killed Allen J. Berk, who was a partner in Pettit and Martin, and John Scully, who was a twenty-eight-year-old lawyer with the firm. David Sutcliffe was only a law student who was working temporarily at Pettit & Martin for the summer. So really only two of the victims were employed by the target firm. The other victims were not Pettit and Martin staff at all. Jack Berman was a partner in the firm Bronson, Bronson & McKinnon and a president of the American Jewish Congress; he just happened to be visiting the offices of Pettit & Martin on the day Ferri called to settle his score.

Donald Merrill worked for the Trust Company of the West; Shirley Mooser was a secretary at the same firm. Deborah Fogel was a secretary for Davis Wright Tremaine, another law firm with offices in the same building. Jody Jones Sposato was a young mother.

The shootings, which appeared to be totally random, led to calls for tighter gun control, and there was in fact a tightening up of gun law in response to the Ferri shootings. The state of California brought in some of the toughest gun control laws in America. The state also repealed a law giving gun manufacturers immunity against litigation, following the unsuccessful attempts by victims' families to get compensation from the companies who made Ferri's weapons.

Several organisations were set up, including the Legal Community Against Violence, which acts as a conduit for information about local, state and federal policies on firearms issues. The Jack Berman Advocacy Centre was set up to lobby for gun control and violence reduction. One of the survivors of the shootings was John Heisse. At the time of the shootings, he was a Pettit lawyer, but when Pettit dissolved in the mid-1990s Heisse and a dozen other Pettit lawyers were picked up by a large national law firm, Thelen, Reid & Priest. Interviewed twelve years after the shootings, John Heisse remembered with emotion having to step over the body of the young law student who had been working for him. He remembered the several friends who had died that day. Heisse found a worthy cause in anti-gun activism. He became one of the co-founders of the Legal Community Against Violence.

Although Pettit no longer exists as a firm, the transfer of lawyers to Thelen has meant that now Thelen sees the shooting tragedy as part of its own institutional history. That sense of historic mission, of a flame carried on from Pettit, prompted Thelen in 2004 to join Mayor Michael Bloomberg of New York to wage a landmark lawsuit against over thirty gun manufacturers and distributors, who together constituted virtually the entire US firearms industry. New York, with Thelen's and ultimately Pettit's help, took on the might of the American gun industry.

In May 1997, a San Francisco judge dismissed a lawsuit against one of the gun-makers. He said the manufacturer was not responsible for the Gian Luigi Ferri rampage. This was disappointing, because two years earlier Superior Court Judge James Warren had ruled that victims and survivors could try to prove that firm in question had designed the semi-automatic pistol precisely for mass killing – and had marketed the pistol in such a way that it would appeal to criminals. Dennis Henigan, the director of the Legal Action Project, argued that the manufacturer had marketed a weapon that was 'designed to be spray-fired from the hip' and marketed it 'as an assault-type pistol'. It urged the court to find that the manufacturer owed a duty of care that was violated by its decision 'to sell a military-style weapon to the general public'. One of the three judges on the panel agreed that the evidence showed that 'no responsible user would have any use for this weapon'.

Gun lobbyists argue that it is people who kill, not guns. They argue that manufacturers of knives, for example, are not hounded in the way that some would like to see gun manufacturers hounded. Knives are often sold even without warning labels – yet we know that they can kill.

The autopsy report on Gian Luigi Ferri concluded that he was not on any drugs at the time of his death and he was not under the influence of alcohol. Little is know about Ferri's motives or state of mind, beyond the incoherent and uninformative suicide note that he left. One thing that can deduced from it is that Gian Luigi Ferri did not have a great capacity for reasoned analysis. This is part of his strange and troubled message:

*There is this condescending attitude in business that
when you get emotionally and mentally raped, well 'you
get screwed' and the accepted result is the victim is now
supposed to go to work at 7–11 or become homeless and
the rapist is admired and envied as 'a winner'. I have
always admired and tried to copy winners, but rape of
any kind is deplorable and against the law. Remember
the time when the same sneakering, laughing attitude
was bestowed upon drunk drivers, and the victim got
no sympathy? Remember the time when the person
raped physically did not dare to report it because of the
humiliation and ridicule that the legal system put the
victim thru. It is understandable that business people
compete with each other. When you hire a consultant
or an attorney you don't hire for the purpose of getting
raped and then having all your efforts toward legal
recourse totally thwarted by a corrupt legal system
of 'esquires.' Esquires in the dark ages roamed the
country-side to steel from the working people and give
to the prince. Do attorney want us to call them esquires
because their allegiance to the monarchy?*

*One possibility of the deceit of P & M is old racial
[illegible] and ethnic prejudice: two of our investors are
African, one Spanish, one Muslim.'*

The Ferri shootings revived the simmering debate

about gun control laws. The clash is always the basic conflict between the essential need for public safety and the customary rights of Americans to possess and carry guns. Alarmingly, one of the arguments offered today by the gun lobby in favour of gun ownership is the eighteenth century one – that an armed citizenry is a defence against tyranny. Thomas Jefferson said it, so it must be true.

The Gian Luigi Ferri killings resulted in the loss of eight human lives. The death toll due to gun ownership in America is alarmingly high. In the year 1995 alone, 35,957 people were killed by guns in America, in homicides, suicides and accidental shootings. This is a huge toll taken on American society, a huge and unnecessary loss in human life and suffering. The cost of direct medical care in the treatment of gunshot victims in 1993 in America was 703 million dollars.

'I HOPE THIS WON'T RUIN YOUR TRADING DAY'

THE ATLANTA DAY-TRADER KILLINGS (1999)

On 29 July 1999, Mark Orrin Barton killed nine people and injured thirteen others during a shooting spree at two locations in Atlanta, Georgia. Barton was a day-trader who had lost 105,000 dollars during the previous two months' trading. The shootings took place at two day trading firms in Atlanta, Momentum Securities and the All-Tech Investment Group. Barton was seen by the police at a petrol station in Acworth, Georgia, and ordered to stop. He committed suicide before the police could reach him.

Afterwards, police officers visited Barton's home, where they discovered that he had murdered his family before going on the shooting spree, so the rampage was in effect spread across three different locations. Barton had bludgeoned his second wife Leigh Ann to death with a hammer, and then murdered his son and daughter in the same way, twelve-year-old David and nine-year-old Mychelle. He had then put the children to bed, arranging them as if they were asleep. Barton left a note explaining that he had killed his wife on 27 July and his children on 28 July. After killing his wife, he had hidden her body in a cupboard, so that the children would not see it. Even before the mass murder, Barton had been regarded as a suspect in the murders of his first wife, Debra Spivey, and her mother Eloise. Those murders had taken place in 1993 in Cherokee County, Alabama. He was not charged with either of those murders. In the light of the 1999 spree killings, it now looks very likely that Barton was responsible for the earlier murders, which were also beatings to death. The note he left with the bodies of his children and second wife denied the earlier murders; 'There may be similarities between these deaths and the death of my first wife Debra Spivey. However, I deny killing her and her mother. There is no reason for me to lie now.' In spite of this flat denial, he must still be regarded as the prime suspect for the earlier killings. If he committed the earlier murders, Barton can be regarded as a serial killer as well as a mass murderer.

Mark Barton was the only child of Air Force parents. After working as a manual labourer and making a false start in a college course, he went to the University of South Carolina, where he took a chemistry degree in 1979. He married his first wife, Debra Spivey, in 1979. He had met her, a fellow student, while he was working as a night porter at a local hotel. They moved to Atlanta, Georgia, and then to Texarkana, Texas. In 1988 he founded a company, TLC Manufacturing, with some friends. Just two years later, he and TLC parted company. Barton explained in his deposition that although officially he had been sacked it had been a way for the company to save face and avoid frightening off suppliers. But it was not even that straightforward. After Barton's last day at TLC, there was a break-in. Somebody got into the TLC offices, stole secret formulae and wiped computer files. Barton was the chief suspect, and the police went round to arrest him for burglary. One of the detectives investigating the case believed the burglary was 'not intended for the theft of the product formula but to hide kickbacks, discrepancy in inventory or the possible sale of chemicals for drug activity'. The same day, a member of the TLC board called the police to say, without any further explanation, that the company had come to an agreement with Barton. The charges against Barton were dropped.

Then he took a job as a salesman for a chemical company. At work he got to know a young receptionist, Leigh Ann Lang. She was married, though not happily. Barton commented that 'she liked older guys; she made that known to everybody.' Mark Barton and Leigh Ann Lang started having an affair. By May 1993 he was making it obvious to his wife that something was going on. He was buying new clothes and keeping up his tan. Debra became suspicious, jealous, accusing. Barton took out a life insurance policy on her. He hoped to make it one million dollars but could not afford the premium, so he settled for 600,000 dollars. He assured the insurance company that this was Debra's idea, and that it was reflection of her 'extreme sense of self-worth', as Barton described it.

Barton speaks to us in part through the note he left with his murdered second wife in 1999, but also through a deposition made in 1995. The earlier deposition is a description of his life in sober but self-serving terms, written in the wake of his first wife's murder. At that time he was trying to collect the 600,000 dollars of insurance on his first wife. The police had understandably identified Barton as a suspect, and the insurance company had, equally understandably, refused to pay out until they were convinced that Barton had had no hand in Debra's death. This was why the deposition was necessary.

In June 1993, Barton and Leigh Ann went on a trip to Charlotte, North Carolina, where they had dinner with friends of Leigh Ann's. During the meal, Barton declared that he had never loved anyone more than Leigh Ann. He would be free to marry her by 1 October, he said. In August, Leigh Ann was taking steps to end her own marriage, moving in with her sister. A few days afterwards, Debra went to Alabama to spend the weekend with her mother in a lakeside trailer. Barton stayed at home with their children, Mychelle and Matthew, or at any rate that was the alibi that he later gave the authorities. By the end of that weekend, the bodies of Debra and Eloise were found in the trailer, bludgeoned to death with an axe-like tool that was never found.

The police suspected Barton at once, arriving at his home looking for evidence immediately after Debra's funeral. He teased the police investigators. They sprayed the house with Luminol, a chemical that causes blood traces to glow in the dark. Barton was a chemistry graduate and knew about the substance, but he claimed he had never heard about it. Then he added that he had seen it in an episode of the TV detective series *Columbo*. The investigators got some interesting results with Luminol, picking up blood traces inside Barton's car, on the seat belt and ignition switch. He could not explain why there was blood in his car, but he directly challenged them: 'If there is a ton of blood in my car, why aren't you arresting me? Well, now, why am I not in handcuffs?' The police officers admitted there was not enough blood to warrant an arrest.

Later, in spite of his bravado, Barton drove to Alabama to offer the police an explanation for the presence of the blood in the car. It had occurred to him that he had cut his finger during the summer before his wife's murder. If there was blood in the car, it would be his own. Playing along with this suggestion, the police asked for blood or saliva samples from him for DNA testing; Barton refused. They proposed a lie-detector test; he refused. The police developed a strong feeling that Barton was guilty, but there was too little evidence to justify a charge. There were no witnesses to his visit to the lakeside trailer. There were no fingerprints and only the most tenuous forensic evidence. Before the blood traces in the car could be tested, Barton successfully removed them, claiming that he accidentally spilt a soft drink in the car and had to clean it up. The small amount of evidence had been brazenly destroyed by the murderer. If the blood traces had been analyzed, doubtless the DNA test would have revealed that the blood belonged to Debra or Eloise; Barton would have been convicted of their murder and sent to prison, and the 1999 shooting spree would have been averted.

With Debra out of the way, Leigh Ann was able to spend nights at Barton's house with him and his children. Just a month after Debra's murder, Leigh Ann's divorce was final. After six months, the two were living together. Barton had moved to Morrow, where the neighbours knew nothing about his first wife or her violent death. But the new marriage was far from idyllic. Leigh Ann often walked out, and the neighbours were very aware that there were major domestic difficulties. In early 1994 the little Mychelle, not yet three years old, told a care worker that her father had sexually molested her. Some psychological evaluations followed, and one of the reports indicated that Barton was capable of committing murder. A key problem in bringing the case to court was Mychelle's age; it was difficult to treat a child under three as a key witness – to anything. The local district attorney commented in 1999 that it been disturbing enough to read the reports on the Barton child abuse case back in 1994; re-reading them after the massacre, in which little Mychelle was one of the murder victims, was even more so. 'It's absolutely chilling to think about it now.'

The insurance company seems to have been in a quandary regarding the pay-out on Debra's death. The insurers were clearly still ready to believe that Barton had murdered Debra, and were reluctant to pay. On the other hand, the law enforcement authorities were not going to bring any murder charge against Barton because they had too little evidence. The insurance company was in limbo. They decided on a compromise. They would not pay out the full 600,000 dollars. They would pay 450,000 dollars. They calculated that if the case went to court a jury might vote in sympathy with the children, who had lost their mother. In an attempt to protect the children's interests, the insurance company stipulated that 150,000 dollars of the pay-out must be put in trust for Mychelle and Matthew.

Barton found himself 300,000 dollars richer and took to gambling on the stock markets. He tried his hand at increasing his wealth hunched over a computer termminal, betting on the daily fluctuations of share prices. He became a full-time day-trader. But he lost money. In the run-up to the killing rampage Barton lost 105,000 dollars, mostly on Internet stocks, according to Momentum Securities, through which he was trading. According to some reports, his account at Momentum Securities was closed after he was unable to put up cash to cover a debt caused by falling share prices. In order to get his account reopened, Barton wrote a cheque for 50,000 dollars. The cheque bounced and he was denied access to trading facilities for another two days (the Wednesday and Thursday of the fateful week of the shootings). Momentum Securities was Mark Barton's first stop when he started his shooting spree on the Friday. Barton had not traded with the All-Tech Investment Group, the other company he attacked, for some months, but he had lost considerable sums over the previous year and evidently some of those losses had been with All-Tech. It is estimated that Barton lost, overall, in the region of 300,000 dollars in the course of one disastrous year – and he blamed Momentum and All-Tech.

When Mark Barton walked into their office on the Thursday afternoon, the manager and secretary of the All-Tech office in Atlanta recognised him. They greeted him by name and he commiserated with them over a major slide on the Dow Jones index. He seemed to be behaving perfectly normally. There was nothing to indicate that he had murdered his wife on Tuesday and his son and daughter on Wednesday; nothing to show that he had just come from a building across the street where he had opened a conversation with similar small talk, then opened fire with two handguns, killing four people. The small talk was about to end at All-Tech too.

Barton fired five shots in the meeting room, seriously wounding the manager and his assistant. Barton walked onto the main trading floor with a gun in each hand. Fifty-three-year-old Nell Jones glanced up from her computer screen. Barton was ten feet away from her. He raised a gun, pointed it at her and fired at her head. The shot narrowly missed her, hitting her computer. He was calm and determined and went on firing. As he left he said, 'I hope this won't ruin your trading day.'

Five people died at All-Tech. By nightfall, Barton himself was dead at a petrol station in the suburbs, and his complex and horrific story began to unfold, a story of not just one set of murders, but two.

The notes he left offer explanations and justifications, but it is hard to know how much value to put on them. His remarks about the killing of his second wife make little sense. 'I killed Leigh Ann because she was one of the main reasons for my demise. She couldn't really help it, and I love her so much anyway.' Did he have any reason to kill his children? He referred to Mychelle as 'my sweetheart' and Matthew as 'my buddy'. But he hit them over the head with a hammer as they slept, then held them underwater in the bath to make sure they were dead. They died 'with little pain', he said. He sentimentally placed a teddy bear on the girl's body, a video game on the boy's.

'I have been dying since October. I wake up at night so afraid, so terrified that I couldn't be that afraid while awake it has taken its toll. I have come to hate this life and this system of things. I have come to have no hope. The fears of the father are transferred to the son. It was from my father to me and from me to my son. I'm sure the details don't matter. There is no excuse, no good reason, I am sure no-one will understand. If they could I wouldn't want them to. You should kill me if you can.'

'GOING POSTAL'
THE POSTAL SERVICE MURDERS (1983-2006)

There was a series of violent incidents starting in 1983 in which postal service workers in America committed mass murder. They shot and killed supervisors, managers, co-workers, members of the general public and even policemen. Between 1986 and 1997 there were at least twenty incidents of workplace rage, in which over forty people were shot down by spress killers.

The peculiar association between mass murder and the postal service has led to the coining of a new phrase for going berserk under conditions of excessive stress – 'going postal'.

On 20 August 1986 a postman, Patrick Sherrill, who worked from the Edmond, Oklahoma post office, shot and killed fourteen co-workers. Sherrill then put his gun to his own forehead and shot himself.

Patrick Sherrill's nickname was Crazy Pat, because of his very unusual behaviour. It was said that Sherrill was often seen at night, prowling about in combat fatigues, tying up dogs and peering into neighbours' windows. He would mow his lawn at midnight. He had done many different jobs and exhibited the same bizarre behaviour throughout. He is said to have behaved oddly even when a boy, but the descriptions of his behaviour sound like normal adolescence. He was reclusive yet showed no interest in study. His main interest was in sport. In 1960, when he was nineteen years old, Pat Sherrill won a wrestling scholarship at Oklahoma University, but he dropped out during his first year. He joined the Marine Corps and was stationed in North Carolina. He failed to show the necessary skill levels in everything except firearms, and he was discharged after two years. Back in the civilian world again, Pat Sherrill tried enrolling at Edmond Central State University. As before, his grades were low and he left university.

He went from one odd job to another. He succeeded in none of them, mainly because he was unco-operative and rude. Employers did not like him; he did not take kindly to being told what to do. He preferred to be left alone, without supervision. He was a difficult employee. In 1985, Pat Sherrill managed to get a job with the postal service as a postman. He had worked for the postal service once before, but it had been a failure: he did not have the right skills. But he needed the money, so he went back. His mother had died, and although she had left him the house he now had to maintain it.

To begin with, he work hard, but his rude behaviour was a problem, to both co-workers and customers. Most of his co-workers ignored him, which made the problem worse. He started to make mistakes and he was reprimanded. But Sherrill had been employed as a relief carrier. In other words, he was covering for regular postmen who had more or less fixed routes; he was made to work different routes on successive days. This pattern of work made it far likelier that he would make delivery errors. He was also, for the same reason, delivering mail later than customers were used to receiving it. On the afternoon of 19 August, Sherrill was formally reprimanded by two supervisors. That same afternoon, he spoke to a female clerk in the post office, a woman who had been kind to him. He asked her if she was coming in to work tomorrow. She said, 'Of course.' Sherrill told her she should stay at home. It was his way of repaying her kindness; he did not want her to be injured.

Sherrill believed the supervisors had conspired to sack him. He was angry and he decided to teach them a lesson. On the morning of 20 August 1986, he put two Colt semi-automatic guns and a .22 pistol, together with ammunition, into his mail satchel. He walked in through the rear entrance of the Edmond Post Office and approached the two supervisors who had reprimanded him the previous day, Richard Esser and Patty Jean Husband, holding a gun in each hand. He shot the two supervisors at close range. Then he walked round the building firing randomly. People fell, shot, wounded and screaming, as other employees scrambled to escape from the spray of bullets. As he progressed through the building, he shut and locked doors behind him, to make sure no-one would escape. He paused to reload, then went on shooting.

The rampage lasted for fifteen minutes, during which time he fired fifty rounds. Then he turned the gun on himself. When the police arrived on the scene, they found the bodies of fourteen postal workers, both men and women, and another six people with bullet wounds. Some of those who survived did so by playing dead. It was one of the worst mass murders committed by a single gunman in America's history.

On 10 October 1991 a former postal worker, Joseph Harris, shot and killed two employees at the post office at Ridgewood, New Jersey. Harris left a note in which he referred to the Sherrill shootings at Edmond, which he clearly knew about and understood, and explained what he saw as his own unfair treatment by the Postal Service. He had had a personality conflict with Carol Ott, a supervisor at the Ringwood post office where Harris worked at night as a clerk. He had served in his job for twelve years, during which time he had shown no mental aberrations. Nevertheless, the supervisor had insisted that he should take a psychological examination with a doctor nominated and paid for by the Postal Service – in order to demonstrate his fitness for duty. Joseph Harris regarded this as insulting treatment and little more than a ruse to get him sacked. He refused to comply with what he was sure was just a pseudo-psychological ruse. His refusal to co-operate played just as well into the supervisor's scheme; she began proceedings that resulted in Harris's dismissal in April 1990.

In Harris's view, his union did not make adequate efforts to have him reinstated.

It was then that Joseph Harris took the situation into his own hands. He assembled an arsenal, consisting of a 9mm Uzi handgun, a .22 machine gun fitted with a silencer, three hand grenades, some home-made bombs and a Samurai sword.

Then he booby-trapped the front door of his flat before driving to the suburban home of Carol Ott. He forced his way in and found Miss Ott wearing only a T-shirt. He took his sword and swung it round in a great arc, cutting deeply into her left shoulder. As she staggered backwards, he continued thrusting with the sword. He stepped over her lifeless, half-naked body and crept down the stairs. Her boy-friend, Cornelius Kasten, was in the basement, watching television. Harris stole up behind him and shot him behind the right ear.

At 2 o'clock in the morning of 10 October, Harris went in through the back entrance of the Ridgewood Post Office. He shot and killed two mail handlers, then barricaded himself in the basement. Marcello Collado arrived at the back door and became suspicious when nobody appeared to help him unload his van. Harris shot at him and missed. Mr Collado escaped unhurt and took his van to the nearest police station to report that an incident was under way. At 2.20 am, two police officers arrived and tried to get into the post office. When Harris threw one of his bombs at them they were forced to retreat and wait for additional support to arrive.

Before long the Bergen County SWAT team surrounded the building. Officers attempted to phone Harris, but he refused to answer. He managed to keep the SWAT team at bay for four hours before surrendering to a police negotiator. At 7 am, the police visited Harris's flat and removed the bomb attached to the door. Inside the flat, they found the note giving an account of his grievances.

The Postal Service declined to give details of Joseph Harris's personnel file to journalists. This is hard to intepret. It could be argued that the employer was protecting its employee's right to privacy, and therefore behaving very ethically. Or it could arouse the suspicion that there were things on Harris's file that might prove embarrassing to the employer. The Postal Service brought in social workers and psychologists to advise employees in ways of protecting themselves from the press. The Postal Service presented a business as usual front and was largely successful in keeping the story out of the press. Only one national newspaper picked up on the story.

Joseph Harris was subsequently convicted of first degree murder and sentenced to death. He died on death row in 1996.

On the day when Harris went on his killing spree to get some sort of redress or revenge for his grievances at Ridgewood, a senator was meeting with the Postmaster General to discuss complaints from employees and customers about another post office. Senator Carl Levin of Michigan met Anthony Frank, the Postmaster General, to explore the reasons why so many customers and employees were unhappy with the management of the Royal Oak Post Office in suburban Detroit. Senator Levin later commented that 'The Postal Service acknowledged management problems in the Royal Oak operation'. The Postmaster General promised an inquiry.

On 14 November 1991, only a few weeks after this, a postal worker went berserk at the Royal Oak Post Office. A recently sacked postal worker shot and killed four people. He was Thomas McIlvane. He had previously been suspended for getting into altercations with postal customers on his delivery round. Then he was sacked for insubordination. After his revenge attack on four co-workers, McIlvane shot himself.

A Congressional committee reviewing the case said that McIlvane was a powder keg just waiting to explode. He had been goaded into his killing rampage by the behaviour of managers at the Royal Oak Post Office, according to the review. He had been subjected to pettiness and intimidation. He had, for example, been reprimanded for taking his lunch at inappropriate locations, ordered to have his vehicle inspected for a brake light problem that clearly did not exist. He was provoked into swearing at a supervisor, and then dismissed for that offence.

McIlvane's co-workers saw McIlvane himself as ultimately responsible for firing the hundred rounds that killed four and injured four, but many of them expressed sympathy for him. One of the people injured in the shooting reflected, ten years after the event, 'I don't absolve him, but I know he didn't get to that point by himself. Tom was the one with the gun. He aimed it at me and put a bullet in my chest. But I know he was driven to that point. He was persecuted.'

A union official, Charlie Withers, spent twelve years trying to get the investigation reopened. He wanted the management's responsibility for what happened to be uncovered. Mr Withers took the grievance process as far as he could, arguing that postal managers created the hostile workplace that provoked the shootings, and afterwards prospered from the promotions, medical retirements and workers' compensation. Mr Withers' campaign failed.

An investigator has questioned wether McIlvane's answer-phone was tampered with. One message on his phone is obscured by a series of electronic bleeps, implying that someone has deliberately erased the message. The investigator believes that a supervisor may have phoned to harass McIlvane immediately prior to the rampage. On the other hand, the Postal Service has denied that there was any sort of cover-up.

Two entirely unconnected postal mass killings took place on the same day, on 6 May 1993. One took place at a post office in Dearborn, Michigan, where Lawrence Jasion wounded three people and killed two (including himself).

Lawrence Jasion was a forty-five-year-old Postal Service mechanic who had worked for the US Postal Service for twenty-four years. At 8.45 am, Jasion started his killing spree in the garage area of the Dearborn Post Office in Michigan. He was carrying a shotgun and a .38 revolver. Using the .38, he shot dead Gary Montes, another Postal Service mechanic, and wounded Harvey Kruger, a supervisor and June Collins, an administrative clerk. Another employee escaped being shot, fleeing for safety, but fell and was injured while running from the building. Jasion carefully picked his victims, then turned the gun on himself. After the incident, employees at the post office told journalists that they hoped this tragedy would lead to a change in the post office's authoritarian structure.

The other Postal Services shooting that happened on the same day took place at Dana Point, California, where Mark Hilburn first killed his mother and then shot two postal workers dead.

Another shooting happened on 9 July 1995, at the mail processing centre at City of Industry, California. Fifty-seven-year-old Bruce Clark, who had worked as a Postal Service clerk for twenty-two years, punched a supervisor in the back of the head. The supervisor, fifty-year-old James Whooper, left the work area to report the incident immediately to the management. Clark also left the work area. Minutes later, Bruce Clark came back with a paper bag. Whooper asked Clark what was in the bag. Clark took a .38 revolver out of the bag and shot Whooper with it twice at close range, in the face and upper body. James Whooper fell down dead. Seventy-five postal workers saw what happened. Two of them went forward and took the gun away from Clark and held him until the police arrived. Clark pleaded guilty to a charge of second degree murder and was given a twenty-two year prison sentence.

In response to these two incidents, from 1993 the Postal Service employed 85 Workplace Environment

Analysts to work in its 85 postal districts. The idea was to help with the prevention of violence and the improvement of the workplace. In early 2009, the Postal Service decided to scrap these positions as an economy measure.

Two months after the Bruce Clark shooting in California there was another Postal Service shooting in Illinois. On 29 August 1995 Thomas Dorsey, a fifty-three-year-old clerk, walked into the sorting office at Palatine, Illinois. Without a word Dorsey fired a semi-automatic pistol five times at a fellow postal clerk, forty-one-year-old Mike Mielke, seriously wounding him. Remaining very calm, Dorsey walked down to the lobby and fired the two bullets left at Steve Collura, another forty-one-year-old worker. He too was wounded. Having run out of ammunition, Dorsey went outside to his car and drove twenty miles. Police arrested him near his home at Northlake, Illinois.

A clerk who had known and worked with Dorsey (and his victims) for twenty years, Maude Kelly, said, 'I can't figure out why he did it. He was just a beautiful guy. We would joke and laugh together.' Another postal worker, Willie Little, said to reporters, 'Don't make it seem like he was some type of vicious person, some fiend, because he was just a nice guy.'

On 30 January 2006, at a large sorting office in Goleta, California, a former postal worker, Jennifer San Marco, shot six postal workers with a handgun before she committed suicide. She was forty-four years old and had worked for six years at the large mail sorting office at Storke Road in Goleta.

Afterwards, police found a seventh victim lying dead in the condominium where Jennifer San Marco had once lived. This incident was the worst of all of the postal service killings. It is also believed to have been the worst workplace killing in American history, in terms of death toll, to have been committed by a woman. According to press reports, the Postal Service had either sacked her or forced her to retire in 2003, on the grounds of her worsening mental state. Judged unfit for work, she tried at first to make the best of it, returning to New Mexico where she had been born and trying to start up a small business. When that foundered, she tried to start up another, but she evidently did not have the appropriate business skills.

Jennifer San Marco had a history of racial prejudice, which may have influenced her choice of targets during her killing spree. She tried to obtain a business licence in New Mexico for a newspaper that would act as a platform for her ideas. It was to be called, very explicitly, *The Racist Press.*

The businesses she tried to launch were unsuccessful. It was obvious to her that where she really belonged was back in her old job in the Postal Service. What she needed was the job that had been taken from her. The more she thought about her situation, the angrier she became about being dismissed. She had to go back to put the situation right. On 30 January 2006 she visited the condominium complex in Santa Barbara where she had once lived. There, with a 9mm handgun, she shot dead Beverly Graham, a fifty-four-year-old former neighbour. Beverly Graham had once complained about her behaviour. Now Jennifer was getting her own back.

Some hours later, at about nine in the evening, Jennifer San Marco drove to her former workplace. She managed to break through the gate security by quickly following through behind another car. She then managed to gain entry to the building by holding an employee at gunpoint and taking their employee's identification badge. In all, Jennifer San Marco reloaded at least once and shot dead six postal workers before committing suicide.

Someone in the building made an emergency call to the police. When the Goleta Valley Patrol arrived, they found two victims in the car park, one just outside the property, one just inside. The deputies evacuated to the fire station opposite any employees who had not so far been able to get out. SWAT teams were sent in to search for victims and find the perpetrator. They found three more bodies, including that of San Marco, who had died from a self-inflicted gunshot wound.

Questions were asked about the security at the sorting office. Should there have been an armed guard on duty? Should the gate have been designed in such a way that only one vehicle could get through at a time? Was the USPS doing enough to protect its workforce from this kind of attack?

On 4 April 2006, Grant Gallaher, a forty-one-year-old postman in Baker City, Oregon, murdered his supervisor. He appears to have taken a revolver to the post office with the intention of killing the postmaster. Baker City post office was a workplace with a history of employee stress. In 1998, a postal worker who was also a union steward had committed suicide.

Gallaher apparently snapped as a result of a stepping-up of work pressure. He had been working as a letter carrier on a new mail route for three weeks and his supervisors, irritated by his outspoken nature, subjected him to a week-long scrutiny of his work, a work-time study. He felt pressured by this, which is probably what was intended. He had also had an extra twenty minutes added to his route. On the day when he went berserk, he was apparently ahead of schedule, and the supervisor 'rewarded' him by bringing him more mail to deliver. According to a union official, Gallaher then 'got a little snippy with her'. He decided to take the matter up with the postmaster, Michael McGuire, on his mobile phone.

Gallaher was by then in such a rage that he went home. Without telling his wife, Kelly, what he was going to do, he picked up his Magnum revolver. Then, just after 4 pm, he drove the three blocks back to the post office, where he spotted his supervisor on foot in the car park. He ran her over, several times. Then he went into the building to find the postmaster. Unable to find him, Gallaher went back outside and shot his supervisor several times at close range to make sure he was dead. Then he fired at the supervisor's car. There was a huge reservoir of anger, frustration and hatred to release. Three bullets went through the bodywork of the car, three through the windscreen.

The gunshots were audible above the general noise level of the industrial neighbourhood. They could be heard above the clatter of hydraulic wrenches at the tyre depot. Even employees changing tyres heard the gunshots. They went outside to look and saw Gallaher standing in the car park at the Wheeler Building. They watched him as he threw his gun towards the river.

A witness working at Ragsdale Mobile Glass across the street from the Post Office heard the gunfire. 'There were two sets of shooting: the first four, then two more.' She also saw Gallaher giving himself up to a police officer. 'He gave himself up, came walking right up to him. They frisked him on the police car, handcuffed him and put him in the car.'

Gallaher was charged with intentional murder of the supervisor and attempted aggravated murder in the alleged attempt to kill Postmaster McGuire. Both charges carry mandatory minimum sentences, of twenty-five and ten years.

The list of single murders and mass murders in the postal service sounds significantly long. Researchers nevertheless have found that the homicide rate per 100,000 workers at US postal facilities are lower than in other occupations. Of the major occupational groups, the highest homicide rate is in retailing: 2.1 homicides per year per 100,000 workers. The second highest rate is in public administration, which includes the police force: 1.7 homicides per year per 100,000 workers. The homicide rate in the postal service is only 0.26.

The nature of the workplace murders varies considerably from one occupation to another. Taxi drivers are far likelier to be murdered by their passengers than by other taxi drivers. Shop owners and their assistants are likelier to be murdered by robbers than by other retailers. In the postal service, on the other hand, employees are most likely to kill each other. A study of homicides in the US in the 1980s showed that 13 percent of the employee-directed murders were carried out at postal facilities by co-workers or former employees, and this in an occupation employing only 0.7 percent of the workforce. So the statistics show that, for whatever reason, in the postal service workers are more likely to kill one another.

'I Can't Give You Excuses'
THE HUNTSVILLE SHOOTINGS (2010)

The shootings at Huntsville, Alabama in February 2010 were unusual in several ways. First, the killer was a woman, and second, the setting was a university department meeting. There is no mystery about the identity of the killer – Amy Bishop – but there is a mystery about her 'career profile' as a killer. Her mass murder was not nearly as spontaneous as it at first appeared.

On 12 February, at the University of Alabama in Huntsville, Amy Bishop gave a lecture to an anatomy and neurosciences class. A student in the class said later that the lecturer had seemed perfectly normal. Amy Bishop then attended a routine meeting of the Biology Department on the third floor of the Shelby Centre for Science and Technology. There were about twelve people in the room, sitting round a large oval table, and the meeting ran as normally for around thirty or forty minutes. Again Bishop's behaviour was described as normal, right up to the moment when she suddenly stood up and started shooting the people nearest to her with a handgun.

Joseph Ng was one of the academics in the room who saw what happened. 'She started with the one closest to her, and went down the row shooting her targets in the head.' Another of the survivors, Debra Moriarity, said, 'This wasn't random shooting around the room; this was execution style.' Those who were shot were on one side of the oval table used during the meeting; the five people on the opposite side of the table, including Jospeh Ng, were able to drop to the floor.

After Amy Bishop had fired a number of times, she pointed the gun at Debra Moriarity, pulled the trigger and there was only a click. The gun had either jammed or run out of ammunition. Bishop was first angry and then confused, uncertain what to do. Seizing the initiative, Debra Moriarity rushed towards Bishop and told her to stop, and she and the other professors succeeded in forcing Bishop out of the room and shutting the door.

Bishop fled, leaving the gun in a cloakroom on the second floor on her way out, and she was arrested a few minutes later after she had left the building. She denied the incident. When questioned about the deaths of her colleagues, she said, 'There's no way. They're still alive.' The police interviewed her husband, James Anderson, when it emerged that she had called him to collect her after the shooting, but they had no reason to charge him with complicity on that score. Anderson mentioned that his wife had borrowed the gun she had used in the shooting, and that he had gone with her to a shooting range in the weeks before the shootings.

Amy Bishop's grievance was that her job at the university was about to come to an end. She had been denied tenure, and was just beginning her final term at the university.

Three members of Amy Bishop's department were dead: Gopi Podila, the chairman of the biology department, Maria Ragland Davis, a biology professor, and Adriel Johnson, also a biology professor. Two other members of staff were shot and injured: Stephanie Monticciolo, a staff assistant, Luis Rogelio Cruz-Vera, a biology professor, and Joseph G. Leahy, also a biology professor.

Amy Bishop was forty-five at the time of the shootings and the mother of four children. After doing a research degree and publishing various scientific articles, she was an instructor in Medicine at Harvard Medical School and then joined the Department of Biological Sciences at Huntsville as Assistant Professor in 2003. It was said by a fellow member of a writing group in Massachusetts that

Amy Bishop had written three novels, all unpublished. One of these was about a female scientist who was trying to defeat a potential pandemic virus while struggling with thoughts of committing suicide at the prospect of not achieving tenure. She is the novelist John Irving's second cousin and may have seen novel-writing as a way out of the academic rat-race. She took herself seriously enough as a writer to get an agent. Members of her writers group said she frequently mentioned her degree from Harvard and her kinship with John Irving as a way of inflating her credentials as a writer. She was inclined to be abrasive when interacting with other members of the writers group, and seemed to feel entitled to praise.

Many co-workers were concerned about her behaviour, interrupting meetings with bizarre and strange asides. Some commented that she was out of touch with reality. When one of the co-workers used the word 'crazy' about her she filed a complaint with the Equal Employment Opportunity Commission, alleging gender discrimination. The professor concerned did not retract his comment, but repeated it. Then in 2009 several of her students made complaints about ineffective teaching and unsettling manner; this led to a petition that was sent to the department head. No action was taken – until the day of the attack. After the shootings, she was suspended and at the end of that month dismissed. By that stage no explanation was necessary and none was given.

Amy Bishop had been denied tenure, in other words the security of a permanent post at the university, in March 2009. She therefore knew that her teaching contract would not be renewed after March 2010. She appealed against the decision, but the university administrators decided that the decision-making process had been properly followed and denied her appeal. An eccentricity of the episode is that the meeting at which she shot three of her colleagues was nothing to do with the issue of her tenure.

James Anderson explained that the refusal of the university to give her tenure had been a major issue for his wife. She was fighting to get tenure. In his view his wife was more than qualified to be awarded tenure and she was distressed at the prospect of losing her job. She had hired a lawyer to help her lodge an appeal, but he had found one problem after another. There was for example a technical point regarding the date of publication of two of her research papers. Had they been published in time to count towards qualifying for tenure, or not?

The incident led to a review of previous episodes in Amy Bishop's life. In 1986 she shot her brother dead at Braintree, Massachusetts, in an incident which at the time was ruled an accident, based on testimony from her mother, a Braintree town official. The unfortunate brother, Seth Bishop, was eighteen at the time, and Amy twenty-one. On that occasion, Amy fired at least three shots from a pump-action shotgun. First she fired into her bedroom wall, then she fired into her brother's chest while she was in the kitchen with their mother. Then she fired the third shot into the ceiling as she ran from the scene. Later she pointed the gun at two employees in a car dealership in order to acquire a car, pointed it without firing. As a result of her mother's favourable testimony, the District Attorney decided not to charge Amy Bishop with any offence, in spite of the fatality. According to the Braintree police chief, the papers relating to this case have disappeared, taken from the files. Even if the mother's testimony is respected, there would appear to have been a subsequent public firearms offence (holding up the car dealers) for which charges should have been brought. She could have been charged, just for that part of the episode, with assault with a dangerous weapon, carrying a dangerous weapon, and unlawful possession of ammunition.

Then in 1994 she and her husband were interviewed about a letter-bomb incident that was directed at her lab supervisor at that time. In a third incident, in 2002, Amy Bishop was charged with assault after striking a woman in the head during a dispute at a restaurant, the International House of Pancakes at Peabody, Massachusetts. According to the police report, Bishop punched and verbally abused a woman who had taken the last seat in the restaurant. She was charged with misdemeanour assault and disorderly conduct, and she pleaded guilty. Prosecutors recommended that Bishop should be put on probation, and made to attend anger management classes. But it is not clear what the outcome was. James Anderson said Bishop had never attended anger management classes.

The earlier incidents, as cold cases, are hard to evaluate, but law enforcement officers are concerned enough to want to re-investigate them. These unsettling episodes had not been known to the university when appointing her.

Committed police investigators have uncovered procedural irregularities at the time of Seth Bishop's death. Those investigating Seth's death were kept in the dark about the later incident at the car dealership. District Attorney William Keating announced that a fresh inquest would be held on Seth Bishop in the spring of 2010. Judge Mark Coven held the inquest in April. As a result of that, on 16 June 2010, Amy Bishop was finally charged with first degree murder, twenty-four years after her brother's death. William Keating said, 'I can't give you any explanations, I can't give you excuses, because there are none.'

The letter-bomb case was equally unsettling. Paul Rosenberg, who was Harvard Medical School professor and a physician at the Children's Hospital in Boston, received a packet containing two pipe bombs. Luckily they failed to explode. Rosenberg was Bishop's supervisor at a lab at the Children's Hospital. Amy Bishop was concerned that she might get a negative appraisal from him; she had been in some sort of dispute with Rosenberg. She resigned from the position because she felt she could not live up to his expectations of her, and as a result was upset. This time James Anderson was involved, and in a way that he seemed not to be with the other incidents. During the period immediately before the letter bomb was sent he is said to have told a witness that he wanted to do harm to Rosenberg. The police investigators had Bishop and Anderson in their sights as the prime suspects for the letter bomb attack on Rosenberg, but in the end had to close the case for lack of positive evidence. The couple's attitude was unco-operative – they refused to let investigators in, refused a search of their home, refused polygraph tests – but none of these amounts to a proof of guilt. Nobody wants the police rooting about in their home. The chief federal prosecutor in Boston reviewed the case after the Huntsville shootings, but in the end decided Bishop and Anderson would not be charged with the attempted letter bombing in 1993. The case remains formally unsolved.

Meanwhile the case against Amy Bishop on three counts of murder and three of attempted murder could hardly be stronger. The main question seems to be not whether Amy Bishop committed these crimes but what her mental and psychological status is – and what her mental and psychological status was at the time of the shootings.

'NOT BECAUSE OF NAME-CALLING'
HARTFORD DISTRIBUTORS KILLINGS (2010)

The Hartford Distributors shooting was a mass murder committed by a discontented former employee. The gunman entered his former workplace, a Budweiser beer distribution company called Hartford Distributors, on 3 August 2010, shooting and killing eight people before shooting himself.

The gunman was thirty-four-year-old Omar Thornton. He was summoned on a disciplinary matter. Thornton had been caught before on a surveillance video stealing beer in the warehouse. It was a repeat offence, and Thornton was given the choice of resigning or being dismissed. He duly signed a letter of resignation and was to be escorted out of the building. But instead of leaving he took two guns out of his lunchbox and started shooting.

There were perhaps forty people working in the building at the time, so there were plenty of people to shoot at. Within the space of a few minutes, he had killed eight of his co-workers and seriously wounded two others. There was a flurry of emergency calls as employees dialed 911 on their mobiles; some of them actually named Thornton as the gunman. The first police arrived on the scene within three minutes of the first 911 call, and went into the building a few minutes after that.

Thornton hid in an office and locked himself in. As the police came into the building, Thornton phoned his mother to tell her what he had done. He also told her he was going to shoot himself. The police closed in on him. He called 911 and explained to the operator that he was carrying out the massacre because of the racial discrimination he had experienced at work. He also said he wished he had killed more people. Shortly after ending this call, Thornton put the gun to his head and pulled the trigger.

The employees at the warehouse were mainly white, and Thornton was an African American. Members of Omar Thornton's family confirmed that he had complained to them that he was experiencing racial discrimination at the warehouse. His girlfriend said Thornton had told her about toilet graffiti directed against him: a racist comment and a drawing of a noose. But everyone else denies that there was any racial discrimination directed against Omar Thornton. The company denies it; the union officials deny it; the workers at the warehouse deny it. The union officials commented that Thornton never made a formal complaint to the union or to a government agency: such a complaint would have been logged. The racism claim, in this case, looks very much like an excuse for criminal behaviour. A psychiatrist commented, 'I've evaluated plenty of murderers during my carer, and I can tell you that people don't commit atrocities because of name-calling.' It looks as if Thornton was dismissed fairly and squarely because of thefts at the workplace. Two people, Christy and Sean Quail, were arrested on a charge of receiving stolen property – the property thought to have been stolen by Omar Thornton. Sean Quail was later arrested on a further eight charges when he allegedly attacked journalists who were trying to cover the case.

The Omar Thornton shootings were the worst workplace massacre in Connecticut's history.

PART SEVEN

MISSION MURDERS

'AS GRUESOME AS YOU CAN'
CHARLES MANSON AND HELTER SKELTER (1969)

Charles Manson was the notorious leader of a pseudo-commune in California in the 1960s. The crimes this group committed under Manson's leadership were many, complex and among the most horrific in modern times. They are also difficult to classify. There were incidents that were spree killings – several victims were killed in quick succession – and those crimes justify inclusion in this book. But there were also lengthy cooling-off periods separating the crimes from one another, and from that point of view the perpetrators may be regarded as serial killers.

Some members of the Family acted out of fear. They were afraid that if they did not do want Manson told them to do he would kill them too. There is a case for regarding their participation in the murders as being under duress. To an extent some members of the Family were hostages and therefore victims of a kind too. Within US law each member of a conspiracy is guilty of crimes committed by the fellow conspirators. Such was Manson's power over the Family that the law needed this rule in order to ensure his conviction of the crimes he ordered the Family to commit. It also meant that the weaker, junior members of the conspiracy, who were only present because they dared not escape, also became culpable of some terrible crimes, some of the worst murders in American history.

Charles Milles Manson was born in 1934. 'Helter Skelter' was a phrase Manson borrowed from a Beatles song. It was fashionable in the 1960s to read all kinds of cryptic meanings into Beatles song lyrics, and Manson for some reason decided that the words of *Helter Skelter* were about an apocalyptic race war. The murders he organised were intended to bring on that race war. This association, which existed only in Manson's mind, gave him and the Family a peculiar status in popular culture; he became an icon of insanity and violence – and the dark side of the psychedelic pop world.

As the Family was beginning to develop, and before the mass murders happened, Charles Manson was already a seasoned criminal. He had by then already spent half of his life in prison for a range of offences. He had also had some experience as a singer-songwriter on the margins of the Los Angeles music industry, thanks to a chance association with

Dennis Wilson, the drummer and founder member of the Beach Boys. One macabre aspect of Manson's weird twilight career is that after he was charged with the very serious homicides, recordings of his songs were released commercially. In the decades since then, various singers have produced cover versions of his songs.

Manson was sentenced to death, but in 1972 a decision by California's Supreme Court abolished the death penalty. When that happened, Manson's sentence was automatically commuted to life imprisonment. The abolition was temporary, yet when the death penalty was re-introduced Manson's sentence was not 'un-commuted'. Manson is currently confined in Corcoran State Prison.

Manson's early life was deeply troubled and unstable, and it goes a long way towards explaining why he became such a disturbed and dysfunctional adult. His mother was an unmarried sixteen-year-old girl called Kathleen Maddox. For a time after he was born, his mother was married to a labourer, William Manson, and the boy was given his surname. The natural father seems to have been a man called Scott, against whom Kathleen Maddox filed a paternity suit. There was an agreed judgement in 1937. It seems Charles Manson never knew his natural father. Manson spent a few months in 1951 at the National Training School for Boys in Washington, DC, and notes on his case file from that episode give a little more about his origins: 'Father unknown. He is alleged to have been a coloured cook by the name of Scott, with whom the boy's mother had been promiscuous at the time of pregnancy.' When the prosecuting lawyer, Vincent Bugliosi, asked Manson about these records in 1971, Manson was emphatic in his denial; his biological father had not been black. But within this family mystery may lie the roots of Charles Manson's obsession with race. He had psychological problems about his unknown black father. Manson's own pseudo-autobiography describes his father as 'a young drugstore cowboy, a transient labourer working on a nearby dam project.'

Kathleen Maddox was said to have been a heavy drinker. One of Manson's relatives recalled that she had once sold her son for a pitcher of beer to a childless waitress. The boy's uncle had to get him back a few days later. In 1939 Kathleen Maddox and her brother were convicted of robbing a service station in Charleston, West Virginia, receiving sentences of five years in prison. Then Manson was sent to live with an aunt and uncle in McMechen in West Virginia. Kathleen Maddox was given parole in 1942. She took her son and they lived together in seedy hotel rooms. Charles Manson remembered the hug she gave him on her release from prison as the best moment in his childhood, the one truly happy memory.

But Kathleen Maddox did not want to keep her son. By 1947, she was trying to get him placed in a foster home. None was available. A court placed him in Gibault School for Boys at Terre Haute in Indiana. After spending ten months at the boys' school, he fled, returning to his mother, only to find that she did not want him. Now he was virtually pushed by circumstances into a life of crime. He burgled a grocery store in order to get the cash he need to rent a room. This led on to a series of burglaries and he was eventually caught red-handed. This led to his being sent to a juvenile centre in Indianapolis. He was there for one day before escaping. He was recaptured and sent to an institution called Boys Town. He was there for four days before escaping with another boy. They committed two armed robberies as they made their way to the home of the second boy's uncle.

Manson broke into two more grocery stores and was caught. This time he was sent to the Indiana Boys School. He was now thirteen. He was subjected to sexual abuse. Again he made efforts to escape. After several failed attempts he managed to get out with two other boys in 1951. The three boys were stopped by the police in Utah as they drove towards California in stolen cars. They had robbed several petrol stations on their way. Now Manson had committed a federal crime; he had taken a stolen car acorss a state border. Now he was sent to the National Training School for Boys in Washington. He was found to be illiterate, in spite of spending four years at school and having an IQ measured (then) at 109; his IQ when measured later was found to be 121. A caseworker found him aggressive and antisocial. But with a background like his, the boy could not be expected to behave normally.

In October 1951, following the recommendation of a psychiatrist, Manson was sent to a low-security institution, Bridge Honour Camp. He was due for a hearing that might lead to parole in February 1952, but a few weeks before it he committed an offence against another boy, holding a razor blade against the boy's throat while he sodomised him. Instead of parole, he was transferred to the Federal Reformatory at Petersburg, Virginia, where the staff considered him 'dangerous'. More offences followed and he was transferred again, to an institution with higher security, the Federal Reformatory at Chillicothe in Ohio.

A startling change came over Charles Manson in Ohio. Within a month he had become a model inmate. He developed good work habits and his educational standard jumped from fourth to seventh grade. In May 1954 he was awarded parole. Initially he obeyed the parole's condition that he go and live with his uncle and aunt in West Virginia, but then he moved in with his mother. In January 1955 he married a hospital waitress and was for a time happy, though he was supporting himself by stealing cars.

When he and his pregnant wife arrived in Los Angeles in a car stolen in Ohio he was again charged with a federal crime. A psychiatric report led to his being given five years' probation. But then there was another identical charge filed in Florida; he failed to appear at the hearing. He was arrested in Indianapolis and his probation was revoked; he had to serve three years in prison on Terminal Island at San Pedro, California. While he was in prison, his son, Charles Manson, Jr, was born. His wife Rosalie was now living with his mother in Los Angeles. In March 1957, because the visits from his wife had ceased, his mother had to tell him that Rosalie was living with another man. Just before a parole hearing was due, Manson tried to escape by stealing a car. He was given five years probation, and the parole was denied.

In September 1958, Manson was given five years parole; Rosalie had now formally divorced him. Within weeks he was acting as a pimp to a sixteen-year-old girl. In 1959 he pleaded guilty to a charge of trying to cash a forged cheque. This carried a ten-year suspended sentence. Manson married a prostitute called Leona, and he took her and another woman to New Mexico with the idea of making a living out of prostitution. He was arrested in relation to the prostitution and then again because he had violated his probation. Now he was ordered to serve his ten-year sentence.

He tried to appeal, and a report on him in 1961 mentions that he had a 'tremendous drive to call attention to himself.' In 1963, Leona was granted a divorce from Manson. He was released from prison in March 1967. He had reached the age of thirty-two and had spent half of his life in prisons. In fact so institutionalised had he become that when the time came for his release he requested that he be allowed to stay: prison had become his home. The request was denied.

On release, he asked to move to San Francisco, which was agreed. He had been taught to play guitar by a fellow-prisoner, and he made a living by busking or begging. He made the acquaintance of Mary Brunner, a twenty-three-year-old assistant librarian at Berkeley, and moved in with her. Such was his force of personality, that he was able to persuade Mary Brunner to allow other women to come and live with them, and he ended up with a harem of eighteen women.

Charles Manson deployed his magnetic personality to establish himself as some sort of guru in the Haight-Ashbury district. During the 'Summer of Love' in 1967, Haight-Ashbury was a key hippie locale, and Charles Manson was right at the centre of things. He expounded a philosophy that contained some of the Scientology teachings he had read in prison. Soon he had a group of willing followers, most of them female. During that summer, Manson and about eight followers boarded an old school bus decked out in hippie style. They took out many of the seats and put in coloured rugs and cushions instead. They took the bus north as far as Washington state, then south through Los Angeles to Mexico.

The events that would reach their climax in the appalling murders were set in train in early 1968.

According to some accounts, Dennis Wilson of the Beach Boys picked up two women hitch-hikers who turned out to be Manson followers. He took them to his house at Pacific Palisades for a few hours, before going off for a night recording session. When he returned home in the small hours, he was met in the driveway (of his own house) by Charles Manson, who had come out of the house. Dennis Wilson was uneasy and more than a little frightened, but Manson assured him that he had no intention of doing him any harm. Manson kissed his feet. Charles Manson aspired to be a success in the music industry, and he must have seen Dennis Wilson as not only an idol and role model but as someone who was in a strong position to help him. One wonders how things would have gone that night if Mr Wilson had been a lawyer or a factory worker.

When they went inside, Wilson met twelve strangers, nearly all women. This was the Family, though over the next few months their number doubled, and the cost to Wilson of having them stay in his house was very high. There was a large bill for the treatment of their sexually transmitted diseases, and another for the destruction of the uninsured car they borrowed. Dennis Wilson and Charles Manson talked together and Wilson sang, while the Family acted as their servants. Wilson was very generous. He paid for studio time so that Manson could record his own songs. He also introduced Manson to various people in the music industry. They included Gregg Jakobson and Terry Melcher. Gregg Jakobson was intrigued by 'the whole Charlie Manson package' and paid to have some of Manson's musical material recorded.

Eventually, Dennis Wilson had had enough of keeping open house for Manson and the Family. In the summer of 1968, Wilson's manager told the Family to move out. Manson established a new base at Spahn's Movie Ranch near Topanga Canyon; the ranch had been a TV and movie set for Westerns, but by the late 1960s it had become almost derelict. Members of the Family acted as a basic maintenance team. Manson also ordered the women to offer occasional sex to the eighty-year-old owner, George Spahn. Spahn in return let the group live there for nothing.

Charles Watson joined the Family at Spahn's ranch. He was a college drop-out who had moved to California, and he had met Manson at Dennis Wilson's house.

In early November 1968, Manson moved the Family at a new base near Death Valley, where they moved into two disused ranches, Myers and Barker.

Myers was owned by the grandmother of one of the women in the Family. Barker was owned by an old woman who had been persuaded that Manson and another man in the family were musicians looking for somewhere congenial to work. She agreed on condition that Manson did some repairs. Manson presented her with one of The Beach Boys' gold discs as a present; he had been given several by Dennis Wilson.

When they had been at the Spahn Ranch, perhaps in October, Manson and Watson visited an acquaintance who played them the Beatles' *White Album*, which had recently been released. Charles Manson was obsessed with the Beatles. While in prison, he had boasted that he could surpass the group in fame. To the Family, he spoke of the Beatles in almost religious awe. Manson had also been developing the idea that the tension between blacks and whites was growing and that there would soon be a black rebellion in US cities. On a cold New Year's Eve at Myers, the Family gathered round a large fire, outdoors, listening to Manson explaining that the social unrest he had been predicting was also being predicted by the Beatles. It was there, in code, in the songs on the *White Album*. Soon he would be maintaining that the message on the *White Album* was directed at the Family, that it was an elect group that had been chosen to save the worthy in the coming maelstrom.

Then the Family moved to a canary-yellow home in Canoga Park, not far from the Spahn Ranch. This location would allow the group to remain invisible, submerged beneath the awareness of the outside world; Manson nicknamed it the Yellow Submarine, a reference to another Beatles song. There they prepared for the apocalypse which Manson had called Helter Skelter, again after a Beatles song.

By February 1969 Manson's vision was complete. The Family would produce an album, like the Beatles', which would set off the apocalypse. Hideous murders of whites by blacks would be answered by retaliatory murders. There would be a split between racist whites and non-racist whites, which would lead to the self-destruction of the whites. The triumph of the blacks would precede their being ruled by the Family, which would ride out the racial conflict in a secret city under Death Valley. The Family planned the desert refuge and worked on the songs that would become part of the world-changing album. They were told Terry

Melcher was coming to hear the musical material, so the women cleaned the place and prepared a meal – but Terry Melcher did not come. Manson went to find him.

On 23 March 1969, Manson arrived at 10050 Cielo Drive, Los Angeles, which he thought was Terry Melcher's home. In fact the property belonged to Rudi Altobelli; Terry Melcher had been the tenant but was not any longer. From February onwards the tenants were Roman Polanski and Sharon Tate. Shahrokh Hatami was in the house, preparing to photograph Sharon Tate before she set off for Rome the following day. Hatami spotted Manson approaching the house and went out to see what he wanted. Manson mentioned a name Hatami did not recognise, presumably Terry Melcher's, and Hatami explained that this was the Polanski residence. Hatami suggested he could try the back alley, meaning the path to the guest house, but he was concerned about this stranger's intrusion. Then Sharon Tate appeared at the front door, behind Hatami, asking who was calling. Manson continued to the guesthouse and then returned and left the property.

That same evening, Manson was back at the Polanski residence, and he went straight to the guesthouse. He entered the enclosed porch and spoke to Rudi Altobelli, who was emerging from the shower. Manson asked for Melcher, but Altobelli sensed that Manson was looking for him. Altobelli told Manson through the screen door that Melcher had moved to Malibu and said he didn't know his new address. Manson asked a question and Altobelli confirmed that he too was in the music business. But Altobelli remembered meeting Manson the previous year at Dennis Wilson's house and knew that Manson must already know that. Altobelli had politely complimented Manson on his music when he listened to some tapes Dennis Wilson played. There was some deception going on. Altobelli told Manson he was leaving the country the next day. Manson said he wanted to meet him on his return. Altobelli's instinct was to fend Manson off; he would be gone for a year, he said, and then asked how Manson had found the guesthouse. Manson said the people in the main house had directed him. Altobelli then made it clear he didn't want Manson disturbing his tenants. Manson left.

Altobelli flew to Rome the following day, with Sharon Tate. She asked him whether 'that creepy-looking guy' had gone back to the guest house.

On 18 May, Terry Melcher went to the Spahn

Ranch to listen to Charles Manson and the Family sing. On another occasion he visited with a mobile recording unit to tape the music.

Shortly after that, Manson said the Family might have to show the blacks how to set Helter Skelter in motion. The revolution would need to be funded and Watson was given the task of raising money. Watson unwisely defrauded a black drug dealer, Bernard Crowe, who threatened to wipe out the community at the Spahn Ranch. Manson's response was to shoot Crowe at his flat in Hollywood on 1 July 1969. This may be seen as the start of the spree of violence that was to culminate in the Tate murders. A news report that the dumped body of a 'Black Panther' had been found in Los Angeles seemed to Manson to be confirmation that Crowe was dead. In fact Manson had not killed Crowe; even so he expected retaliation from the Black Panther group, to which he assumed Crowe had belonged, and surrounded the ranch with armed guards. Tex Watson saw these events as proof that Helter Skelter was coming soon.

Then came the Hinman murder. Manson knew Gary Hinman a little, and thought Hinman had inherited some money. Manson wanted that money. He sent a former Family member, Boby Beausoleil, to Gary Hinman's house with Mary Brunner and Susan Atkins. They tried to persuade Gary Hinman to hand over to them the money Manson thought he had inherited. Hinman would not co-operate, so the three of them held him captive for two days. Manson appeared with a sword and slashed Hinman's ear. Then Beausoliel stabbed Hinman to death, apparently on Manson's instruction. Before they left Hinman's house, one of the killers used Hinman's blood to draw a panther paw on the wall and write the phrase 'political piggy'. The paw was a Black Panther symbol, and the intention was to imply that the Black Panthers were responsible for the killing.

The three killers subsequently gave varying accounts of what happened. Beausoleil gave interviews in 1981 and 1998 in which he said he went to Hinman to take back money from Hinman for drugs that had been bad. He said Brunner and Atkins had been passengers, that they had accompanied him just to see Hinman. But this does not match what Atkins wrote in her 1977 autobiography, in which she says Manson told the three of them to go to Hinman's and collect the inheritance, which Manson believed amounted to 21,000 dollars. Manson had said to her that if she wanted to do something important, she could kill Hinman and collect the money.

On 6 August, Beausoleil was arrested when he was found to be driving Hinman's car. When police looked over the car they found the murder weapon in the boot. Manson announced, 'Now is the time for Helter Skelter'. On 8 August, Manson sent Watson with Atkins, Linda Kasabian and Patricia Krenwinkel to 'that house where Melcher used to live' and 'totally destroy everyone in it, as gruesome as you can.' The women were told to do whatever Watson told them to do.

The four of them arrived at Cielo Drive. Watson climbed a telegraph pole and cut the phone line. Assuming the gate might be alarmed, they climbed up a bank on one side and dropped down into the grounds. Headlights from further into the property came towards them. Watson stepped into the path of the car, stopping it, and shot dead the driver, eighteen-year-old Steven Parent. Watson cut out the screen protecting an open window in the house, went in through the window and let the women in through the front door.

A friend of Roman Polanski, Wojciech Frykowski, was asleep on a couch in the living room. He woke up and Watson kicked him in the head. Frykowski asked who he was and what he was doing there, and Watson said, 'I'm the devil, and I'm here to do the devil's business.'

Atkins was sent by Watson to round up the other occupants of the house. There were three, Sharon Tate, now eight-and-a-half months pregnant, Jay Sebring, a hair stylist and Tate's friend and former lover, and Abigail Folger, who was heiress to the Folger coffee fortune and Frykowski's lover. Roman Polanski, Sharon Tate's husband, was working on a film project in London.

Sharon Tate was a former beauty queen who had become a film actress. Her first big success had been in *The Eye of the Devil* with David Niven and Deborah Kerr. It had been while she was in London in 1966 for the filming of *The Eye of the Devil* that she had met Polanski, and he had then cast her as the lead actress in *The Fearless Vampires* and also in the role of Jennifer in *Valley of the Dolls*. It was only in 1969, the year in which she was to die, that they rented the house in Cielo Drive from Terry Melcher, Doris Day's son.

On the fateful August night, Sharon Tate was entertaining some friends at her home. It was a happy little gathering, with no apprehension, no prior warning that anything unpleasant was going to happen. Winifred Chapman, Tate's housekeeper, noticed some unusual things when she arrived at the house at eight the next morning. A fallen telephone wire was draped across the gate. There was an unfamiliar white Rambler parked in the driveway. The front door was open. Then she saw to her horror that there were splashes of blood everywhere. There was a body on the lawn. She screamed and ran through the house and down the driveway; on the way she noticed there was another body slumped in the car.

When the police arrived, they found two bodies on the lawn, not one. There was a young woman in a nightgown with multiple stab wounds and a man in his thirties whose face had been battered. His body was punctured with dozens of stab wounds. Later they were identified as Folger and Frykowski.

Unnerved, the police approached the house itself cautiously. They saw the word 'PIG' scrawled in blood on the front door. In the living room they found the body of a heavily pregnant young woman lying on the floor, smeared with blood. There was a rope round her neck, which passed up over a rafter; attached to the other end was the body of a man, also drenched in blood. These two were later identified as Sharon Tate and Jay Sebring.

On the same night as Sharon Tate's ill-fated

dinner party, two people arrived home from holiday in another part of Los Angeles. They were Leno and Rosemary LaBianca. Their home was 3301 Waverly Drive, in the Los Feliz district. The Family evidently finished their appalling massacre at Sharon Tate's house, returned to Manson, who sent them out the very next night to the LaBianca home, apparently choosing the house at random. Manson listened to the Family's account of the Tate murders and was displeased by the description of the victims' panic. He decided to go with his group of killers this time, 'to show them how to do it'. He took the group from the previous night, together with Leslie Van Houten and Steve Grogan. They drove around for a while, while Manson considered a number of possibilities. Then he made a decision and gave directions that took them to 3301 Waverly Drive, the home of supermarket executive Leno LaBianca and his wife Rosemary, who co-owned a dress shop. It was probably not a coincidence that the house was next door to a house where Manson and the Family had attended a party some months earlier.

The following day, Leno LaBianca was found dead with a pillowcase over his head, a cord round his neck and a carving fork sticking out of his stomach. The word 'WAR' was cut into his flesh. Los Angeles

Police Department officers found Leno's wife in the master bedroom with a pillowcase over her head, and forty-one stab wounds. The couple had been viciously and repeatedly stabbed with a bayonet. As at the Tate house, there was writing in blood on the walls: 'DEATH TO PIGS', 'RISE', and on the refrigerator door 'HELTER SKELTER'.

Manson wanted to turn the LaBianca murder into a more spectacular setpiece. He wanted to go on to another house and do the same again. He directed Kasabian to drive them to the home of an actor acquaintance. Manson left the second trio of Family members at the actor's apartment block and drove back to the Spahn Ranch. Kasabian had evidently had enough, or simply did not want to see her actor friend killed, so she sabotaged this killing. She deliberately knocked on the door of the wrong apartment, waking up a total stranger. After this setback, the leaderless group abandoned the double murder plan and left.

The police were at a loss to understand what was happening. The murders were obviously following a pattern, but had no obvious meaning or motive.

Then the case took a new turn when a woman awaiting trial for murder in an LA prison made a chilling confession. She was Susan Atkins. She was to be tried for an unrelated murder, but confessed freely to her cellmate her involvement in the Sharon Tate murders. Atkins seemed to be in a state of ecstasy as she told how her lover Charles Manson was Jesus Christ and he was going to lead her to a hole in Death Valley where there was a secret civilisation. Some people will believe anything, it seems. The cellmate must have been even more alarmed when Atkins described the Tate murders. Three girls and a man had done the killings, acting under Manson's orders. She said they had chosen the Tate mansion because it was isolated and because they 'wanted to do a crime that would shock the world would have to stand up and take notice [of].' Atkins' extraordinary confession included the LaBianca killings too.

Atkins said there were several more celebrities on the Family's death list. She had planned to cut the words 'helter skelter' on the face of Elizabeth Taylor with a red-hot knife, and then gouge out her eyes. She planned to cut off Richard Burton's penis and send it in a bottle, along with Elizabeth Taylor's eyes, to Eddie Fisher. Frank Sinatra was to be skinned alive while being made to listen to his own records (the ultimate torture). The Family was going to make purses out of Sinatra's skin and sell them in hippie shops. Tom Jones was to have his throat cut after being forced to have sex with Atkins. It sounded far too crazy to be true, but the Tate murders had been committed; they were all too real. Fortunately, the police had received some clues that the Manson Family might be involved from some other sources, including a member of a motorcycle gang called the Straight Satans, so they were readier to believe Atkins' macabre confessions than they might have been. Even so, it was not until November 1969, three months after the murders, that they got round to interviewing Atkins' cellmate about the confession.

A problem in reconstructing the crimes was and still is that the various Family members developed different versions of what happened, mainly to make it appear that their own roles had been either less or more than they were. Each member of the Family wanted to appear either less culpable or more important. In the LaBianca murders, Manson was keen that every member of the Family should play a part in the killing. Tex Watson found Krenwinkel stabbing Rosemary LaBianca, but he wanted to be sure that Van Houten did some stabbing too. He told Van Houten to stab. She did, plunging a knife into Rosemary LaBianca's back sixteen times. When she was on trial, Van Houten claimed that Mrs LaBianca was already dead when she started stabbing her. This may in fact have been true, as the post mortem evidence suggested, but Van Houten's motive was clearly to try to reduce the criminality of what she had done.

The police investigation into the Hinman and Tate murders was meanwhile under way. It was established that Steven Parent, the young man shot in his car in the Tate driveway, was a friend of William Garretson, who in turn was the young man Rudi Altobelli had hired to house-sit for him while he was away. Steven Parent had visited Garretson and just been unlucky in trying to drive out at the moment when the killers arrived. The police suspected William Garretson of being involved, though he said he had seen and heard nothing on the night of the murders; he passed a lie detector test and the police released him.

The Garretson lead had led nowhere. Then the LA Police Department made another and more serious mistake. On 12 August they announced to the press that any connection between the Tate and LaBianca killings had been ruled out. On 16 August the sheriff raided the Spahn Ranch and arrested twenty-six people including Charles Manson – but as 'suspects in a major auto theft ring'. The law had its eye on Manson, in other words, but for stealing Volkswagens and turning them into dune buggies. The Family was released a few days later. On the whole it was younger officers investigating the LaBianca case, a separate team from the one working on the Tate murders, and they noticed a possible connection between the writings in blood at the LaBianca house and the Beatles' most recent album. The LaBianca team then checked for possible similar crimes, and noted the Hinman case. The detectives working on the Hinman case had interviewed Bobby Beausoleil's girlfriend, Kitty Lutesinger. She, it turned out, had been one of the women arrested a few days before with the Manson Family. The LaBianca detectives decided to talk to Kitty Lutesinger too. She mentioned a motorcycle gang Manson had tried to enlist as bodyguards at the Spahn Ranch. The gang members then provided information that suggested a link between Manson and the murders.

Susan Atkins was arrested following her confession to the sheriff's detectives that she had been involved in the Hinman murder. Atkins was moved to a detention centre in Los Angeles, where she gave accounts of the horrific mass murders she had been involved in – to two cellmates.

After several false starts and false leads, the Los

Angeles Police Department went into action on 1 December 1969, issuing warrants for the arrest of Watson, Krenwinkel and Kasabian in the Tate murders, and their involvement in the LaBianca murders was noted. Charles Manson and Susan Atkins were in custody already, so they were not mentioned. Van Houten's involvement in the LaBianca murders had not yet been recognised. Fingerprint evidence quickly established that the suspects had been at the crime scenes. A ten-year-old boy, Steve Weiss, had found a gun near the Tate residence in September and handed it in to the police. In December, his father made several concerned calls to the police before the LAPD finally located the paperwork relating to the gun in its files, submitted the weapon for ballistics tests and then confirmed that it had been used in the Tate murders.

The trial started in June 1970. The prosecution's principal witness was Kasabian. As she had not directly participated in the killings, she was granted immunity in exchange for her testimony about the events surrounding the crimes. The prosecution developed the idea that Manson was trying to trigger race war. Manson had declared 'now is the time for Helter Skelter'. Linda Kasabian was able her own testimony, that on the night of the

LaBianca murders Manson contemplated dropping Mrs LaBianca's wallet in a black neighbourhood. Manson wanted a black person to pick it up and use the credit cards, so that the establishment would assume it was an organised black activist group that had killed the LaBiancas. Kasabian supported this with various comments Manson had made, such as 'I want to show blackie how to do it.'

The progress of the trial was impeded by members of the Family loitering near the courthouse and trying to dissuade witnesses from testifying. They identified themselves by carrying an X on their foreheads, like Manson. Two prosecution witnesses were threatened, one of them badly burned in a suspicious fire in his own van. A former Family member, Barbara Hoyt, was seen as knowing too much, and she was taken to Hawaii where she was given a hamburger spiked with several doses of LSD. She recovered in hospital, and became determined to give her evidence in court. She had been co-operating with the Family because she was 'trying to keep them from killing my family'. At the time of the trial she was constantly under threat: 'Your family's gonna die.'

Further problems were created by a statement from President Nixon, which was represented in a *Los Angeles Times* headline as 'Manson Guilty, Nixon Declares'. The accused naturally claimed that the outcome of their trial had been prejudiced. In October, Manson leapt over a table and tried to attack the judge; he was manhandled out of the courtroom by bailiffs, while the female defendants stood and chanted in Latin. After that, Judge Older took to carrying a revolver in court.

Manson addressed the court for an hour, saying things like, 'The music is telling the youth to rise up against the establishment. Why blame it on me? I didn't write the music. . . To be honest with you, I don't recall ever saying "Get a knife and a change of clothes and go and do what Tex says".'

Further problems flowed from the evident orchestration of the defendants' testimony. The women of the Family had evidently been trained by Manson to present him as innocent; they claimed to have done it all, even the planning. Judge Older in the end commented that it had become obvious that the defendants were acting in collusion with each other.

On 25 January 1971 the four defendants were found guilty on each of the twenty-seven counts against them. Atkins, Krenwinkel and Van Houten testified that the murders had been designed as copycat versions of the Hinman murder, for which Atkins took credit. This plan, to draw suspicion away from Bobby Beausoleil, by replicating the crime for which he had been jailed, was not Atkins' but Linda Kasabian's. So, this was the Family's attempt to have revenge on Kasabian for her treachery – and exonerate Charles Manson. But none of this scheming worked. On 19 April 1971 Judge Older sentenced the four to death.

A few weeks before this, the decomposed body of Ronald Hughes was found wedged among boulders. It could never be proved, but it was a rumoured that Hughes had been murdered by the Family because he had stood up to Manson and refused to let Van Houten give the evidence that would have absolved Manson of the crimes. Shorty Shea was murdered at the Spahn Ranch by Manson, probably because he found out about the Tate and LaBianca murders; Manson was convicted of that murder too. There seemed to be no end to it. Later, Steve Grogan told the prosecutor in his case exactly where the body of Shea had been buried. The recovery of Shea's body led to a favourable view of Grogan's application for parole. So far, Grogan is the only one of those convicted to have been given parole. Susan Atkins died of a brain tumour in prison in 2009. Manson himself has survived being set on fire by another prisoner. Because Tex Watson was in Texas, he was tried separately, but he too was sentenced to death. In February 1972 all five death sentences were reduced to life imprisonment after California abolished the death penalty.

In 1975, one of the Family members, Squeaky Fromme, tried to assassinate President Ford in Sacramento. Fromme was sentenced to a minimum of fifteen years and a maximum of life in prison; following the death of John F. Kennedy, it became a federal crime to attempt to assassinate the Preident of the United States. She escaped briefly in 1987 and tried unsuccessfully to reach Manson, the moth fluttering again at the flame.

Manson lives on, now a fairly passive and well-behaved prisoner in his mid-seventies. It seems extremely unlikely he will ever be given parole. He may no longer be dangerous in person, though even that could not be guaranteed, but what he represents is extremely dangerous. He is that special someone that so many weak, morally and spiritually disaffected extremists, from Satanists to neo-Nazis, are on the look-out for. He is that special someone to lead them to Heaven or Hell, and it scarcely matters to them which.

PAN AM FLIGHT 103
THE LOCKERBIE BOMBING (1988)

Pan Am Flight 103 was a routine scheduled flight, Pan American World Airways' third daily transatlantic flight from London Heathrow to New York John F Kennedy. The thing that was different about the flight on Wednesday 21 December 1988 was that it ended, with dramatic and unforeseen suddenness, when without warning the plane disintegrated in mid-air, killing everyone on board, as it flew over southern Scotland. The plane was a Boeing 747 commissioned in 1970, carrying 243 passengers and sixteen crew. All of those on board died, as did eleven people on the ground when large sections of the plane fell on the small town of Lockerbie. In all 270 people died.

There was no mystery about the cause of the crash. The plane had broken up because of an explosion on board, caused by a bomb that had been deliberately included in the luggage. What was less clear was where the responsibility lay for planting the bomb, and there is still uncertainty about that.

At 7 pm air traffic controller Alan Topp watched

on his radar screen as Flight 103 crossed the inner end of Solway Firth. The plane was flying north-westwards at 31,000 feet, at a ground speed of 500 mph. A couple of minutes later the signal from the plane disappeared. Alan Topp tried to make contact with Captain MacQuarrie, but got no response. There should have been a single radar echo on the screen, but now there were four. As the seconds passed the echoes began to fan out. Eight seconds after the explosion, the wreckage of the plane had spread across an area a mile in diameter. A British Airways pilot, Robin Chamberlain, was flying another plane, the Glasgow-to-London service, and he could see a huge fire on the ground. Alan Topp could see on his screen the evidence of PA103's continuing disintegration, as a multiplicity of radar echoes moved eastwards with the wind, airborne wreckage drifting away from the site of the explosion.

The explosion had punched a substantial hole in the left side of the fuselage, and after that the plane had rapidly disintegrated. The cockpit was found intact on the crash site. US investigators were lowered into it before it was taken from the crash site and while the bodies of the flight crew were still in it. They came to the conclusion that no emergency procedures had been initiated. Pressure control and fuel switches were both set for 'cruise'; the crew were not wearing oxygen masks, which would have been needed within five seconds of a rapid depressurisation of the plane. The explosion must have happened with absolute suddenness, and this pointed definitively to a bomb. British investigators concluded that the nose of the aircraft, containing the cockpit, separated from the rest of the plane within three seconds of the explosion. The cockpit voice recorder, which was installed in the tail, was found in a field by police officers. The recorder gave no evidence of an emergency call being made. There was only a split-second hissing sound as the explosion destroyed the communciations centre. The lighting system would have failed at the same time, plunging crew and passengers into darkness.

The explosion originated in the hold, but its effect was magnified by the fourfold difference between cabin pressure and the air pressure outside the plane. As the communications system was disrupted, the front section of the fuselage started to roll and twist. Shock waves from the explosion bounced from one side of the plane to the other, splitting the fuselage open. The whole front section of the aircraft, containing the flight deck, crew and first class section, broke away, flying up and to the right, hitting the No 3 engine as it too snapped off. The plane went into a steep dive. With the break-up came depressurisation of the main cabin. The disappearance of the front section exposed passengers to greater-than-hurricane-force winds. The passengers would have been suddenly unable to breathe and death would quickly have followed. Some passengers were hurled to the back of the plane, others blown right out into the night; the temperature outside was -46 degrees Celsius. It may seem unlikely that any passengers survived this ordeal, but one American forensic expert thought that as many as 147 passengers, and the flight crew, may have reached the ground still alive and strapped to their seats; they were uninjured by the explosion and died on impact with the ground. The nose section crashed in a field near a small church in the village of Tundergarth. The crew and several first-class passengers were still strapped to their seats. A flight attendant was still alive when a farmer's wife found her, but she died almost immediately.

After the explosion, the fuselage carried on moving forward and down, but when it reached 19,000 feet it was diving almost vertically. During this dive, it broke up. The section attached to the wings landed first, in Sherwood Crescent, hitting the ground at

500 mph. The impact made a crater fifty metres long. The house that it landed on was atomised, along with its occupants. The fuel ignited, creating a fireball that destroyed several houses and killed eleven people on the ground. The fireball spread, scorching cars as they passed on the southbound carriageway of the A74 Glasgow-Carlisle road. Four people died in one house, 15 Sherwood Crescent, where Jack and Rosalind Somerville lived with their children Paul and Lynsey. Father Patrick Keegans, the Roman Catholic priest at Lockerbie, lived at 1 Sherwood Crescent; his was the only house in the street that was not gutted by fire and not destroyed by the impact.

Of the people on Flight 103, passengers and crew, 190 were American, 43 were British. The rest consisted of very small numbers belonging to nineteen other nationalities. Among the passengers was the UN Commissioner for Namibia, Bernt Carlsson, who was to have attended the signing of the New York Accords later that month. There were also two leading figures in Volkswagen, the Chief Executive Officer James Fuller and Marketing Director Lou Marengo. There were forty-eight American students who were flying home from courses they were pursuing in London. There were at least four US intelligence officers on board, giving rise to a number of conspiracy theories regarding the motive for the bombing. Matthew Gannon was the CIA deputy station chief in Beirut. Major Chuck McKee was working with the Defence Intelligence Agency in Beirut. Ronald Lariviere and Daniel O.Connor were security officers from the US Embassy in Beirut, and they were on the flight to act as bodyguards to Gannon and McKee. A Special Agent from the US Department of Justice, Michael Bernstein, was also on the flight. At the back of the plane was twenty-two-year-old Khalid Nazir Jaafar, who had moved from Lebanon to Detroit with his family. Given his Lebanese background and the fact that he had been visiting relatives in Lebanon, Jaafar was an early suspect in the investigation into the bombing.

Another suspect was an Indian national, forty-seven-year-old car mechanic Jaswant Basuta. He had booked on the flight, intending to return to New York to start a new job there. He arrived at the departure lounge at Heathrow just too late to be allowed onto the plane, after friends and relatives from Southall had delayed him by buying him drinks at the bar. His luggage went on the flight without him, which immediately laid him open to suspicion as the potential bomber. He was interviewed and released without charge. Long afterwards, Jaswant Basuta reflected, 'I should have been the 271st victim. I still feel terrible for all the people who died.'

The surviving residents of Lockerbie had another ordeal to live through. While investigators were trying to work out exactly what had happened as the plane exploded and broke up, the bodies on the ground could not be moved. People had to get used to the idea of having the bodies in the road and in their gardens for days. One resident said:

A boy was lying at the bottom of the steps on to the road. A young laddie with brown socks and blue trousers on. Later that evening my son-in-law asked for a blanket to cover him. I didn't know he was dead. I gave him a lamb's wool travelling rug thinking I'd keep him warm. Two more girls were lying dead across the road, one of them bent over garden railings. It was just as though they were sleeping. The boy lay at the bottom of my stairs for days. Every time I came back to my house for clothes he was still there. 'My boy is still there,' I used to tell the waiting policeman. Eventually on Saturday I couldn't take it no more. 'You got to get my boy lifted,' I told the policeman. That night he was moved.

A number of people had near-misses, in the sense that they narrowly missed being booked onto Pan Am Flight 103. Pik Botha, the South African foreign minister, was supposed to board 103, but managed to take the earlier 101. He and his delegation of twenty-two officials were heading for New York to sign the three-sided agreement which handed control of Namibia to the United Nations. The Four Tops, an R & B group, had been scheduled to take Flight 103 after a European tour, but they had overslept after a late recording session. Johnny Rotten (John Lydon) of the Sex Pistols was also booked on 103 with his wife, but they missed it because of delays.

An anonymous warning was given on 5 December to the US Embassy in Helsinki by a man with an Arabic accent. He said that a Pan Am flight from Frankfurt to America would be blown up by people associated with the Abu Nidal Organisation. The attack would come within two weeks and it would be a Finnish woman who would unwittingly take the bomb on board. This warning was taken seriously by the US government. Pan Am were alerted, but a security team in Frankfurt found the warning the day after the bombing beneath a pile of papers on a desk; the warning had been received but not acted upon. The security screeners at Frankfurt, it turned out, had not all been briefed to identify Semtex, which is the sort of plastic explosive likely to be used by terrorists. On 13 December, the warning was posted in the US Embassy in Moscow and spread from there to American journalists and businessmen. It is said that a number of Americans in Moscow booked with carriers other than Pan Am, which left empty seats on Pan Am 103 that were later sold cheaply through bucket shops.

A few days before Lockerbie, the Palestine Liberation Organisation warned that extremists might mount terrorist attacks in order to undermine the PLO's dialogue with the United States. Britain's security forces took this warning seriously.

Identifying those responsible was made harder because individuals representing several groups phoned the media to claim responsibility, among them the Guardians of the Islamic Revolution, the Islamic Jihad Organisation and the Ulster Defence Association. One thing that had become clear was that the perpetrators intended the plane to crash into the North Atlantic Ocean, destroying most of the evidence. It was only by chance that the plane left Heathrow late and the timing device detonated the bomb while the plane was still over the UK. The investigators were able to piece together far more about the nature of the explosion because all the fragments fell down onto dry land; there was a lot of evidence. The fuselage was reconstructed, revealing a 50cm hole consistent with an explosion in the forward cargo hold. It was possible to calculate the exact location and the quanity of explosive used.

Pieces of a Samsonite suitcase were recovered; this was believed to have contained the bomb. Pieces of a circuit board were found that were part of a Toshiba Bombeat radio cassette player. This was similar to one used to hide a Semtex bomb found two months earlier by German police in the hands of the Palestinian militant group Popular Front for the Liberation of Palestine. Articles of baby clothing, subsequently shown to have been made in Malta, were also believed to have come from the same suitcase. The clothes were traced to a Maltese merchant, Tony Gauci, who became a key witness for the prosecution as he was prepared to testify that he had sold the clothes to a man of Libyan appearance.

Many commentators have remarked that this is all too good to be true, leading as it does to the identification of a particular Libyan suspect. But the key witness was interviewed more than a score of times and he gave conflicting evidence about the the person who had bought the clothing from him, their age, appearance and the date when the purchase was made. Tony Gauci's evidence was a seriously weak link. He eventually identified Abdelbaset Ali al-Megrahi as the purchaser. Megrahi had only been in Malta on 7 December, so it had to be assumed that that was the date of the purchase; it was the only date it could have been – if Megrahi was indeed the person responsible for planting the bomb. Here the forensic reasoning was looping back on itself.

Megrahi was put on trial and found guilty. But a report containing information not available to Megrahi's defence lawyers stated that, four days before he first positively identified Megrahi, Tony Gauci had seen a picture of Megrahi in a magazine article which alleged a connection between Megrahi and the bombing. The Gauci identification was therefore worthless. The date of the purchase is also to be doubted as Gauci said in his statement that the Christmas lights had not been switched on at the time when the clothes were purchased, and it has subsequently been established that the date when Malta's Christmas lights were switched on was 6 December. Given that Megrahi had not by then arrived in Malta, the purchaser of the baby clothes could not have been Megrahi. The Scottish police also failed to tell the defence lawyers that another witness had seen Libyans making a similar purchase on another day.

The circuit board fragment found in the plane wreckage was identified as a piece of an electronic timing device of a kind found on a Libyan agent arrested ten months earlier, when carrying materials for a Semtex bomb. The timer was allegedly traced through a Swiss manufacturer, Mebo, to the Libyan military. A Mebo employee identified the fragment at Megrahi's trial. But this testimony cannot be taken at face value either. Edwin Bollier, the owner of Mebo, has revealed that in 1991 he was offered four million dollars by the FBI to testify that the fragment of timer was part of a Mebo MST-13 timer supplied to Libya. Mr Bollier was scrupulous enough to decline this incentive. More recently, in 2007, Mr Bollier's employee admitted that events were not as he described at Megrahi's trial; he said that, without Mebo's permission, in June 1989 he had given a circuit board from a prototype MST-13 timer to 'an official investigating the Lockerbie case'. It now begins to appear that a timing device of a type known to have been supplied to the Libyan military was deliberately included in the remains of the plane – after the explosion. Dr Hans Kochler, UN observer at the Lockerbie trial, has seen a copy of the Mebo employee's affidavit and says, 'The Scottish authorities are obliged to investigate the situation.' This would seem to be even more pressing, given that technicians at the FBI Laboratory never tested the timer fragment for explosives residue, 'due to budgetary reasons'. Thomas Thurman, who led the forensic investigation and identified the fragments' connection with Libya, admitted that it was the only real piece of evidence they had against Libya. Others have commented that without the timer there probably could not have been a trial at all.

How did the luggage get from Malta to Lockerbie? Investigators discovered that a bag had found its way onto Pan Am 103 by way of the interline baggage handling system at Frankfurt at the approximate time that bags were being unloaded from Flight KM 180 from Malta. This seems very unlikely. The documentation for Flight KM 180 showed that all the bags carried on that flight were accounted for. Yet the court preferred to believe that one of the bags from KM 180 was taken at Frankfurt and put onto Pan Am 103 and it was that bag that contained the bomb. A completely different scenario is suggested by the surprising and highly significant 2009 revelation that the Pan Am baggage area at

Heathrow was broken into seventeen hours before Pan Am 103 took off. Security guard Ray Manley reported the break-in at the time. The police lost his report and it was never brought up at Megrahi's trial. But what it implies is highly significant. It implies that the bomb was actually smuggled into the baggage area at Heathrow, not at Frankfurt, and certainly not at Luqa Airport on Malta either. And this removes Megrahi as a suspect.

The trial of Megrahi was a long time in preparation. Three years of preparation by the FBI and the Dumfries and Galloway Constabulary. 15,000 witness statements were taken. In November 1991 an indictment for murder was issued against Abdelbaset Ali al-Megrahi, who was a Libyan intelligence officer and head of security for Libyan Arab Airlines. A second indictment for murder was issued against Lamin Khalifah Fhimah, who was the Libyan Arab Airlines station manager at Luqa airport in Malta.

A massive amount of pressure was applied to force Libya to hand the two men over for trial. UN sanctions were applied against Libya. There were also protracted negotiations with the Libyan leader, Colonel Gaddafi. Megrahi and Fhimah were handed over on 5 April 1999 – to Scottish police at Camp

Zeist in the Netherlands. It was seen as important to choose a neutral venue for the trial.

Megrahi and Fhimah elected not to give evidence. Probably, if they knew they were innocent, they also knew that all the evidence against them was going to be rigged – and very expensively and expertly rigged, at that. Resistance was futile. On 31 January 2001, Fhimah was acquitted. Megrahi alone was convicted of murder by a panel of three Scottish judges and sentenced to twenty-seven years in prison. The judgement accepted without question the Malta connection and the identification of the electronic timer.

The Lockerbie judgment stated; 'From the evidence which we have discussed so far, we are satisfied that it has been proved that the primary suitcase containing the explosive device was dispatched from Malta, passed through Frankfurt and was loaded onto PA103 at Heathrow. It is, as we have said, clear that with one exception the clothing in the primary suitcase was the clothing purchased in Mr Gauci's shop on 7 December 1988. The purchaser was, on Mr Gauci's evidence, a Libyan. The trigger for the explosion was an MST-13 timer of the single solder mask variety. A substantial quantity of such timers had been supplied to Libya. We cannot say that it is impossible that the clothing might have been taken from Malta, united somewhere with a timer from some source other than Libya and introduced into the airline baggage system at Frankfurt or Heathrow. When, however, the evidence regarding the clothing, the purchaser and the timer is taken with the evidence that an unaccompanied bag was taken from KM180 to PA103, the inference that that was the primary suitcase becomes, in our view, irresistible. As we have also said, the absence of an explanation as to how the suitcase was taken into the system at Luqa is a major difficulty for the Crown case but after taking full account of that difficulty, we remain of the view that the primary suitcase began its journey at Luqa. The clear inference which we draw from this evidence is that the conception, planning and execution of the plot which led to the planting of the explosive device was of Libyan origin.'

Megrahi's appeal against conviction was refused in the spring of 2002. The grounds of the appeal rested on two areas of evidence where the defence claimed the original court was mistaken: the evidence of the Maltese shopkeeper, Tony Gauci, which the judges accepted as sufficient to prove that the 'primary suitcase' started its journey in Malta;

and, disputing the prosecution's case, fresh evidence would be brought by the defence to show that the bomb's journey actually started at Heathrow. That evidence, which was not heard at the trial, showed that at some time in the two hours before 00:35 on 21 December 1988 a padlock had been forced on a secure door giving access airside in Terminal 3 of Heathrow airport, near to the area referred to at the trial as the 'baggage build-up area'. The defence lawyers claimed that the PA 103 bomb could have been planted then.

On 14 March 2002 it took Lord Cullen less than three minutes to deliver the decision of the High Court of Justiciary, three minutes to sweep all that to one side. The five judges rejected the appeal, ruling unanimously that 'none of the grounds of appeal was well-founded', adding perfunctorily, 'this brings proceedings to an end'. The following day, a helicopter took Megrahi from Camp Zeist to continue his life sentence in Glasgow.

Dr Hans Kochler, the international observer appointed by the UN Secretary-General, described the decisions made by the trial and appeal courts as a 'spectacular miscarriage of justice'. He issued a series of statements in 2003, 2005 and 2007, demanding an independent international inquiry into the case.

Megrahi continued to protest his innocence. His appeal to the European Court of Human Rights was declared inadmissible in the summer of 2003. In September 2003 Megrahi applied to the Scottish Criminal Cases Review Commission, again in an appeal against his conviction. In June 2007 the Review Commission announced that it was referring his case to the Court of Criminal Appeal in Edinburgh; it had been found that Megrahi 'may have suffered a miscarriage of justice'. Dr Kochler was again strongly critical. He was contemptuous of the Review Commission's exoneration of police, prosecutors and forensic scientists with regard to Megrahi's alleged wrongful conviction. As he said pithily to the press in June 2007, 'No officials to be blamed, simply a Maltese shopkeeper.'

A second appeal hearing came in the autumn of 2007. Megrahi's defence lawyer raised a number of legal issues with a panel of three judges. One was the existence of several documents that were shown before the trial to the prosecution but not disclosed to the defence. These are believed to be documents relating to the Mebo timing device. The defence lawyer also asked for documents connected with payment of two million dollars made to Tony Gauci for the testimony which led to Megrahi's conviction. By January 2009 it was reported that although Megrahi's second appeal was scheduled to begin in April 2009 the hearing might last as much as twelve months because the case was so complex. It began in April, but was adjourned in May. It reconvened in July only to be told that because one of the judges was ill the final two appeal session would run November-December 2009 and January-February 2010. Megrahi's lawyer was dismayed by the endless delays; she said, 'There is a very serious danger that my client will die before the case is determined.'

Then, it seems, a deal was struck. Megrahi could either continue with the seemingly interminable appeal process or he could apply for release on compassionate grounds. It perhaps suited the authorities to release him without admitting his innocence, because of the explaining that would then have to be done about the handling of his trial – and the subsequent appeals. On 25 July 2009, Megrahi did apply for release on compassionate grounds and shortly after that applied to have his appeal dropped. Megrahi served eight-and-a-half years of his sentence in Greenock Prison, continuously maintaining his innocence. On 20 August he was released and flown home to Libya the same day, to a storm of protest from the families of victims of the Lockerbie bombing. The problem was that he had not been released because of a mistrial, or a miscarriage of justice, but because he was terminally ill. His survival beyond the approximately three months prognosis generated a good deal of controversy.

But, if it was not Megrahi, who was really responsible for the Lockerbie bombing? The fact that the Libyan government has formally admitted responsibility for the incident may seem like strong evidence that it was a Libyan-inspired terrorist act. But it is not conclusive evidence; those close to Gaddafi have said that the admission was only made in order to get trade sanctions lifted. Even if the admission of guilt is true, it does not amount to an admission that Megrahi was the terrorist, and the available evidence points away from him, and away from Malta. The evidence points to a terrorist cell acting in the UK, and planting the bomb at Heathrow.

In the 1980s Libya was involved in a series of military confrontations with the US Navy in the Gulf of Sidra. Two Libyan aircraft were shot down in 1981. Then two Libyan radio ships were sunk in the Gulf of Sidra. Two more Libyan vessels were sunk in March 1986. It seemed likely that the April 1986 bombing of a West Berlin nightclub frequented by

American soldiers was a retaliation to these attacks.

Then, on 15 April 1986, ordered by President Reagan, US Air Force warplanes made direct military strikes against Tripoli and Benghazi. The planes, even more controversially, flew from US air bases in Britain. These airstrikes caused many military and civilian casualties. Among the dead was Hanna, a little girl Gaddafi claimed he had adopted. It may well have been in retaliation for this that Gaddafi sponsored the the September 1986 hi-jacking of Pan Am Flight 73 at Karachi. And the bombing of Pan Am 103 might have been ordered for the same reason. Given that the American President Ronald Reagan and the British Prime Minister Margaret Thatcher had together organised the Benghazi-Tripoli airstrikes, it would have been appropriate to set up the bombing of a Pan Am Boeing 747 loaded with American passengers – and set it up through a terrorist cell in Britain.

For many commentators, like Paul Foot and Dr Kochler, the Lockerbie bombing case was not satisfactorily resolved. The wreckage of the plane was collected from the fields round Lockerbie and painstakingly reassembled near Carlisle as part of the crash investigation. Later the debris was transported to a scrapyard near Tattershall in Lincolnshire where it has been stored ever since. This storage is costing the authorities a significant sum of money, rumoured to be £800 per month; it looks as if they too sense that this case is not yet closed.

9/11

(2001)

The infamous Al Qaeda attack on the World Trade Centre and the Pentagon, now almost universally referred to by its date, 9/11, represents perhaps the most spectacular mass murder of recent decades. It is in many ways unique: uniquely brazen, uniquely public, uniquely prejudiced in the way symbolic places, rather than groups of people, were targeted, and of course unique in the scale of gratuitous human suffering involved and the numbers of lives lost. Those, like me, who saw it unfolding on television, will always remember the shock that it generated, the sheer scale of the violence inflicted.

On 11 September 2001, a coordinated series of terrorist attacks was launched at the United States, and mainly against its civilian population. Nineteen men working for the Al-Qaeda organisation commandeered four commercial passenger jet airliners, abducting their passengers and in effect turning the aircraft into powerful guided missiles. Each group of hijackers included one trained pilot. Two of the pilots succeeded in crashing their planes into the World

Trade Centre in New York City, one plane into each tower. American Airlines Flight 11 crashed into the north side of the North Tower of the World Trade Centre at 8.46 am local time. United Airlines Flight 175 crashed into the South Tower at 9.02 am local time, an event which was captured on live television by reporters from around the world who had their cameras trained on the buildings after the first crash. The crash damage was structurally crippling, causing both towers to collapse completely within two hours.

The pilot of the third team successfully (ie according to the terrorists' plan) crashed a plane into the Pentagon Building in Virginia. American Airlines Flight 77 collided with the Pentagon at 9.37 am local time.

Half an hour later, the passengers and crew members on the fourth hijacked aircraft, United Airlines Flight 93, tried to wrest control of their plane from the hi-jackers. The hi-jackers lost control of it as they fought with the passengers and it crashed in a field just outside Shanksville in southwest Pennsylvania, at 10.03 am local time. Debris from the plane was found up to eight miles away. No-one survived in any of the hijacked aircraft and altogether about 3,000 people died in these attacks.

The fatalities were nevertheless lower than at first thought. At the time of the attacks about 16,000 people were below the levels where the planes hit the World Trade Center complex. Of these, nearly everyone escaped by evacuating the towers before they collapsed.

Even so, most of the deaths were in and round the World Trade Centre, where 2605 civilians and firefighters were killed. For a long time there was great uncertainty about the number of dead, partly because the collapsing buildings tore and shredded the victims' bodies into tiny and often unrecognisable fragments. Bone fragments were still being found as late as 2006 when the Deutsche Bank Building was demolished.

As well as the 110-floor Twin Towers, five other buildings at the World Trade Centre site and four subway stations were either destroyed or severely damaged. All seven buildings in the World Trade Centre Complex had to be demolished. The Deutsche Bank Building across the street from the World Trade Centre eventually had to be demolished as well, due to the toxic conditions inside it, which rendered it unusable. Part of the Pentagon was severely damaged by fire and collapsed.

Passengers and crew members were able to use

their mobile phones to make calls from the stricken planes. They reported that several hi-jackers were on board, and the FBI later confirmed that there were four on United 93 and five each on the other three flights. It seems that to gain control in each plane they used box-cutter knives to kill stewards and at least one passenger. They also used bomb threats and tear gas to keep passengers at bay.

In the fourth plane, the passengers discovered on their phones that other planes had been hi-jacked and deliberately crashed into buildings and realised that that was the fate intended for them too. They knew the only way to prevent it was to regain control of the plane or force it down prematurely in a rural area where as little damage would be done as possible. One of the passengers, Todd Beamer, rallied the passengers in an onslaught on the hi-jackers, with the phrase, 'Let's roll.' Later it would become the war cry for American soldiers fighting Al-Qaeda in Afghanistan. Shortly afterwards, the aircraft crashed into a field, killing everyone on board.

Conditions inside the World Trade Centre were appalling, as floors filled with flames and smoke. Two hundred desperate people jumped to their death from the burning towers onto the streets and rooftops of adjacent buildings far below – just to escape a worse death inside the building. Those on the levels above the point of the plane's impact were trapped; some made their way up towards the roof in the hope that they would be rescued there by helicopter, but no such rescue could be attempted as the towers were like huge chimneys belching out great plumes of thick billowing smoke, making it impossible for helicopters to land. The occupants in any case found that they were unable to get out because the doors to the roof were locked. Much would be said later in the 9/11 inquiry about the unsatisfactory emergency exit routes within the buildings.

It must have seemed as if the only worse thing that could happen next was that the fire and smoke would gradually spread upwards through both towers, engulfing the whole of the top of each building. But far worse than that was to follow. The impact of the planes flying into them had seriously weakened the structure and the buildings totally collapsed. The south tower (WTC 2) fell at about 10.05 am, after burning for almost an hour. The north tower (WTC 1) fell at 10.28 am, after burning for an hour and 43 minutes. A third building, 7 World Trade Centre (WTC 7) also collapsed, but later in the day at 5.30 pm, after being heavily damaged by debris from the collapse of the Twin Towers a short distance away.

The fires had weakened the trusses supporting the floors, so the floors sagged. The sagging floors pulled on the exterior steel columns to the point where the columns bowed inwards. With the core columns damaged, the buckling exterior columns could no longer support the buildings, so the towers collapsed, floor upon floor, folding up like a telescope.

The explosive and spectacular collapse of the Twin Towers released thousands of tons of toxic debris, including asbestos, lead, mercury and very high levels of dioxin from the fires. The fires went on burning for three months in a scene of appalling and unearthly desolation that became known as Ground Zero. The discharge of toxins led to debilitating illnesses among rescue workers and the residents, students and office workers of Lower Manhattan and Chinatown.

Virtually every country in Europe has experienced invasions, sometimes repeated invasions, but the United States has had no experience of invasion or co-ordinated terrorist attacks. As a result, the attacks created large-scale confusion and disbelief. It was a major culture shock, a national rite of passage far more momentous than Pearl Harbour.

The 9/11 attacks were the result of a well-organised conspiracy. According to the 9/11 Commission Report, Khalid Sheikh Mohammed was the mastermind behind the attacks, though apparently in some matters he was guided or overruled by Osama bin Laden, who therefore must take his share of responsibility for the events. Originally, twenty-seven members of Al-Qaeda were supposed to enter the United States to take part, but in the end only nineteen participated. Ramzi Binalshibh and Mohamed al-Kahtani, who were both thought to have been intending to join the team, were denied entry into the US. Al-Kahtani was later captured in Afghanistan and imprisoned at Guantanamo Bay.

It was alleged that Zacarias Moussaoui was considered as a replacement for Ziad Jarrah, one of the conspirators who at one point threatened to drop out because of tensions amongst the plotters. The plan to draft Moussaoui onto the team was not in the end put into effect, allegedly because the Al-Qaeda hierarchy doubted his reliability. Moussaoui was arrested in America on 16 August 2001, four weeks before the attacks, on a token charge of violating immigration laws, but the real reason was that FBI agents suspected him, after he had taken flying lessons earlier that year, of having plans to commit an act of terrorism. In April 2005, Moussaoui pleaded guilty to conspiring to hi-jack planes, and to involvement with Al-Qaeda. He nevertheless denied that he knew beforehand about the 9/11 attacks. At his sentencing hearing in March 2006, Moussaoui claimed that, on Osama bin Laden's instructions, he and Richard Reid were due to hi-jack a fifth plane and fly it into the White House. Moussaoui's own defence lawyers did not believe this; they dismissed it as fantasy, saying that he was only peripheral to Al-Qaeda, a 'hanger-on'. On 3 May 2006, Moussaoui was sentenced to six life terms in prison without parole. At least two FBI agents suspected beforehand what it was Moussaoui was involved in, but failed to get permission from their superiors, even after repeated requests, to obtain a warrant to search Moussaoui's computer.

Moussaoui's claim that at one stage the plan was larger in scale and included flying a plane into the White House seems to have some truth in it. According to another 'insider', there was even a plan to mount a simultaneous attack on London; the Palace of Westminster and Tower Bridge were the targets. The attack on London was allegedly aborted at the last minute when the would-be hi-jackers, who were actually waiting to board the planes they were going to hi-jack and destroy, saw the colossal scale of the damage that had been done in America, which was far greater than they had expected. They panicked and fled. Presumably, the hi-jackers had no idea that the Twin Towers were going to collapse completely.

In February 2006, President Bush revealed that Al-Qaeda had also initially planned to crash a plane into the tallest building in the western United States, the Library Tower in Los Angeles, on the same day. This attack was postponed by Osama bin Laden, and subsequently foiled as security intensified. The American government also claimed early on that the White House and Air Force One (the President's plane) had been targets, although the source of these threats was not disclosed.

The 9/11 attacks, as carried out, were incredibly ambitious. If the additional attacks just discussed had also been carried out the effect on the West would have been paralyzing. In scale they might be thought of as major military attacks, the equivalent to an invasion without a prior declaration of war. They might be thought of as war crimes, except that no state of war existed. They are referred to as terrorist attacks, in spite of their huge scale. Because they were attacks on unprepared and innocent civilians, they might also be regarded as crimes against humanity.

The American government came to the conclusion that Osama bin Laden and Al-Qaeda were responsible for the attacks. Five days after the attacks Osama bin Laden denied responsibility; 'I stress that I have not carried out this act, which appears to have been carried out by individuals with their own motivation.' Later he admitted responsibility. In November 2001, American soldiers found a videotape in the ruins of a house in Jalalabad in Afghanistan, and on the tape Osama bin Laden admits to Khaled al-Harbi that he knew beforehand about the attacks. The following month bin Laden released another video praising the act of terrorism against America; 'It was a response to injustice, aimed at forcing America to stop its support for Israel, which kills our people.' Then in 2004 bin Laden publicly acknowledged his organisation's responsibility for the 9/11 attacks and admitted his own involvement. His justification for the carnage was that 'we are a free people who do not accept injustice, and we want to regain the freedom of our nation.' The motives underlying the Al-Qaeda campaign were listed in a 1998 fatwa issued by Osama bin Laden and others; America's support of Israel, its occupation of the Arabian Peninsula and its aggression against the Iraqi people. America stands condemned because it plunders the resources of the Middle East, dictates policy to the governments of those countries, has military bases in the Middle East in order to threaten Muslim states and seeks to divide and politically weaken Muslim states. It was exactly as might have been predicted with the improving education and the rise of nationalism in the Middle East – that the West's expectation that it could continue to exert imperialist control over the area was unrealistic; it could only provoke increasing resentment and frustration.

Finally, in a sound tape that was broadcast by Al Jazeera in May 2006, bin Laden owned up; he personally had given the nineteen hi-jackers their orders. It appears, according to some commentators, that he wanted to provoke a very strong anti-Muslim response in America in the hope that this would ensure that Muslims in the Middle East would react as violently as possible to any stepping-up of American involvement in their region. And the reaction was indeed strong and provocative. Following the attacks, 80,000 Arab and Muslim immigrants were fingerprinted and registered under the US Alien Registration Act of 1940. There were some hate crimes in America directed against people who were Middle Eastern in appearance. At least nine people were murdered within the United States as part of the retaliation. Balbir Singh Sodhi, one of the first victims of this demonisation phenomenon, was shot dead on 15 September. The poor man was a Sikh, not a Muslim; an unenlightened American shot him for wearing a turban.

Most governments and newspapers round the world condemned the terrorist attacks. Only a month after the attacks, America was able to lead a broad coalition of international forces into Afghanistan in pursuit of Al-Qaeda forces. The intention was to topple the Taliban government for harbouring a terrorist organisation, and there was the faint hope that they might find and capture or kill bin Laden himself. Pakistan decisively aligned itself with the United States in the war against Osama bin Laden and Al-Qaeda. Many countries introduced anti-terrorism legislation, freezing bank accounts of businesses and individuals suspected of having Al-Qaeda links. Civil rights protections were also circumvented. The American military set up its highly controversial detention centre at Guantanamo Bay in Cuba, and the legality of these protracted detentions without trial has been questioned by member states of the European Union, the Organisation of American States and Amnesty International.

Several conspiracy theories have emerged, including the speculation that the US government knew of the impending attacks and failed to act on that knowledge, or even planned the attacks. Some people question the accepted account of 9/11, speculating that the collapse of the World Trade Centre was caused by explosives. The idea of involving the American establishment in setting up the catastrophe is that it would have been a way of justifying invading Afghanistan and any other countries of the American administration's choice. Some argue that a commercial airliner did not crash into the Pentagon, and that United Airlines Flight 93 was shot down by the US military to prevent it from reaching its target. Doubtless new conspiracy theories will appear in future years.

The attacks prompted the Bush administration to declare a 'war on terrorism', to bring Osama bin Laden and Al-Qaeda to justice and stop new terrorist networks emerging. It launched an invasion of Afghanistan which was the main refuge of Al Qaeda. Other countries, such as the Philippines and Indonesia, also increased their military readiness to deal with conflicts with Islamic extremist terrorism. Bush also had his sights on Iraq, which he portrayed as a hotbed of terror, so the origin of the later invasion of Iraq is clearly traceable back to 9/11. There was no evidence that the Iraqi dictator, Saddam Hussein, was involved in any way in the 9/11 atrocity, but polls showed that enough Americans thought he might be to justify an invasion. The conspiracy that led to the 9/11 attacks was very effective. It was a spectacular blow to American national pride and complacency, and it produced vivid images – notably the photographs of the Twin Towers with flames and smoke pouring from their upper floors – that have become iconic. The ramifications and implications of the 9/11 attacks have been enormous, prompting the West into invasions which have been very costly to America and its allies and which the West may well come to regret.

911 DAYS AFTER 9/11
THE MADRID TRAIN BOMBINGS (2004)

The Madrid train bombings were a series of co-ordinated attacks on commuter trains in the Spanish capital. They happened in the morning of 11 March 2004, a few days before the Spanish general election. The human casualties were high, compared with those resulting from the rather similar attack on the London commuter system the following year.

The official Spanish judicial investigation concluded that the attacks had been carried out by a terrorist cell inspired by Al-Qaeda. On the other hand, no evidence has come to light of any direct Al-Qaeda involvement. The way the bombings were represented by the two main political parties was criticised for its bias. The bombings had an effect on the outcome of the election. The incumbent Popular Party led by José Maria Aznar had been showing a small but narrowing lead in opinion polls. But immediately after the bombings the PP leaders claimed they had evidence pointing to the guilt of the Basque separatist organisation ETA; this outcome would have helped the PP to win the election, while finding that an Islamist group was to blame might not, as it could have been argued that the attack was a consequence of Spain's involvement in the Iraq War, a decision made by the Popular Party government, and an unpopular one among the Spanish electorate. In the end the PP government lost the election because of the way it tried to manipulate the situation to its own political advantage.

The explosions, ten of them, happened on board four commuter trains, all travelling in the same direction and on the same railway line between Alcala de Henares and Atocha station in Madrid. Later it was discovered that thirteen explosive devices had been planted, but three had not gone off. Bomb disposal teams detonated two in controlled explosions, but the third was not discovered until the evening, after it was stored (by mistake) with luggage taken from one of the trains.

The four trains had set off from the Alcala de Henares station between 7.01 and 7.40 am. All of the explosive devices are believed to have been hidden inside rucksacks. There were witness reports of three people in ski masks getting on and off the trains several times at Alcala de Henares between 7.00 and 7.10 am. These were presumably the bombers loading their bombs onto the trains. A Renault van was found parked outside the station at Alcala de Henares, containing detonators, audio tapes with verses from the Koran, and mobile phones.

The explosions took place between 7.37 and 7.40. At Atocha Station, three bombs exploded on train number 21431. Video recording from the station's security CCTV system showed that the first bomb exploded at 7.37, and the second and third bombs exploded within four seconds of each other at 7.38. At El Pozo del Tio Raimundo Station, two bombs exploded in different carriages just as the train was starting to leave the station at 7.38. At Santa Eugenia Station, one bomb exploded on train number 21713 at 7.38. At Calle Tellez, about 800 metres from Atocha Station, four bombs exploded in different carriages of train number 17305 at 7.39. It was clear that the bombs were intended to detonate simultaneously, blowing up four trains at different points along a busy commuter route.

At 8 am emergency relief workers started to arrive at the scenes of the bombings – a slow response time, given that this was a major emergency happening in a capital city in a Western country where terrorist attacks had been anticipated. By 8.30 the emergency ambulance service, SAMUR, had set up a field hospital at a nearby sports facility. Residents and bystanders did what they could to help the relief workers.

The Madrid bombs killed 191 people, of whom 142 were Spanish, and wounded 1,800. The number of victims was higher than in any previous terrorist attack in Spain, far exceeding the 1987 bombing of a Barcelona supermarket in 1987, which had killed 21 and wounded 40. The Barcelona attack was claimed by ETA. Madrid was the worst incident of its kind in Europe since Lockerbie in 1988.

Shortly after the Madrid bombings a strange device was found on the rail track of a high-speed train (AVE). This consisted of twelve kilogrammes of Goma-2 explosive with a detonator and 136 metres of wire, though the wire was not connected to anything. The device lacked an initiation system and was therefore not capable of exploding. The Spanish authorities chose not to investigate this 2 April incident.

Shortly after the AVE incident, or non-incident, the police identified a flat in Leganés, south of Madrid, as the place used as a base for the bombings. Seven suspects, including the alleged ringleaders, were inside the flat when it was surrounded during a raid on the evening of 3 April. Just after 9 pm the police started to attack the premises, and the three men inside set off explosives, killing themselves. One police officer was killed and eleven were injured in the explosion. Among the dead suspected ringleaders was Serhane Ben Abdelmaji, who was known as The Tunisian and is thought to have masterminded the plot. Another suspect who died in the suicide explosion was Jamal Ahmidan, a hashish trafficker who had turned Islamic extremist, and who was nicknamed The Chinese. At least four suspects, including two who may have been central to the attack, vanished. Abdelmajid Bouchar, who is believed to have planted the bombs, seems to have fled from the flat just before the alleged ringleaders killed themselves.

The assumption was made that the group of militants who died at Leganés were the people responsible for the Madrid train bombings. The investigators moved on to try to find out where the 200 kg of explosives used in the bombings had come from. They discovered that they had been purchased from a retired miner who still had access to mining and blasting materials. It is thought that as many as eight other suspects involved in the bombing attacks succeeded in escaping on the day of the suicide bomb.

The fall-out from the Madrid bombings was considerable. If Al-Qaeda was prepared to carry out this kind of attack in Madrid, then it could well be prepared to carry out similar attacks in other West European capital cities. If Madrid, then why not Paris and London? In fact, London was to follow in July 2005. High levels of security alert were declared in France and Italy.

After a long investigation, Judge Juan del Olmo altogether ruled out ETA involvement in the Madrid bombings. The link to Al-Qaeda remained unknown. In August, Al-Qaeda stated that it was 'proud' of the Madrid bombings, but we know from other terrorist attacks that false claims to responsibility are commonly made. Nor was it established who had masterminded the attacks. One theory is that the Algerian Daoud Ouhnane was the mastermind behind the Madrid bombings. In January 2007, the press reported that Ouhnane was trying to find ways of returning to Spain in order to launch fresh attacks, though this report lacked confirmation. The Spanish judiciary formed the view that the terrorist cell was a loose association of Moroccan, Syrian and Algerian Muslims, and that they were the suspects in the Madrid bombings; Judge Juan del Olmo charged twenty-nine suspects for their involvement. Five of the suspects were later released. British journalists commented that, 'Those who invented the new kind of rucksack bomb used in the attacks are said to have been taught in training camps in Jalalabad in Afghanistan, under instruction from members of Morocco's radical Islamist Combat Group.'

This Combat Group has a developmental history that is closely tied to the rise of Al-Qaeda in Afghanistan. It was formed at the end of the 1990s and its early role was to give logistical support to Al-Qaeda in Morocco, finding its members places to live, providing them with papers, opportunities to marry Moroccans, and false identities that would allow them to travel to Europe. After 9/11, which made the Moroccan government decide to fight terrorism, the Combat Group opted to organise terrorist attacks within Morocco itself. It is assumed that the Moroccan Jamal Zougam was connected with the Combat Group. Many of these associative connections are little more than assumptions and some commentators are uneasy about the uncorroborated assumption that Al-Qaeda is behind the bombings. On the other hand the later evidence emerging pointed towards the involvement of extremist Islamist groups, and the Moroccan Islamic Combat Group was named as a focus of investigation.

Prosecutor Olga Sanchez made the interesting point in March 2005 that the bombings had happened 911 days after 9/11; in other words a symbolic date had been chosen for the attacks, though one that would have been very hard to predict. The way that the date was arrived at would have had a kabbalistic charge for the local Al-Qaeda groups. In fact 2004 was a leap year, so 912 days had passed between 11 September 2001 and 11 March 2004; on the other hand, it could still be argued that there are 911 days between the two dates. Another way of looking at it was that exactly two-and-a-half years had elapsed since the 9/11 attacks in America.

The explosives used in the Madrid bombings were not dynamite but a military type. The device found in an unexploded backpack several hours after the explosions was Spanish-made Goma-2 ECO. It consisted of 10 kg of explosive with 1 kg of nails and screws packed round it as shrapnel. But this bomb may not be representative of the others. The coroner commented that no shrapnel was found in any of the victims' bodies. Goma-2 ECO had not been used by Al-Qaeda before. The thirteenth bomb used a mobile phone as a timer. This required a SIM card to activate the alarm and so cause the detonation. The SIM card in this unexploded device was extremely useful in leading the police directly to one of the suspects. On 13 March, three Moroccans and two Pakistani Muslims were arrested for involvement in the bombings. It was confirmed that the attacks had been made by an Islamic group. Only one out of the five detained that day was actually charged, and that was Jamal Zougam.

The trial of twenty-nine alleged bombers started on 15 February 2007. The court dismantled all the conspiracy theories one by one, including the alleged involvement of ETA. At the trial the defendants withdrew their earlier statements and denied involvement. The Spanish press commented that the trial was unsatisfactory because it was evident that the organisers and planners of the attack were not in the dock. There was also dissatisfaction about the poor forensic science regarding the explosives, and about the failure of the court to establish a firm link with Al-Qaeda.

On 31 October 2007 the trial verdicts were given. Of (now) twenty-eight defendants, twenty-one were found guilty on charges ranging from forgery to murder. Nine of the twenty-eight defendants were Spanish people charged with supplying the stolen explosives used in the bombings. All twenty-eight had pleaded not guilty. Two of the defendants were each sentenced to over 40,000 years in prison, although Spanish law limits the actual time served in prison to forty years. The prosecutors were trying to construct symbolic sentences for the eight leading defendants: thirty years for each of the people they killed in the attacks, eighteen years for each of the people they wounded and other lengths of time for the other terrorism charges. Spain has no death sentences or life sentences available.

7/7
THE LONDON BOMBINGS (2005)

The London bombings of 7 July 2005 are often
referred by their date, 7/7, American-style, to express
their kinship with 9/11 in America. Both attacks
were masterminded by Al-Qaeda. Both had several
geographical targets. The difference between them
is that the 9/11 attacks used commercial aircraft
deliberately flown into high-profile buildings, while
the 7/7 attacks used bombs carried onto the London
public transport system. The result was similar:
indiscriminate killing and maiming of an innocent
civilian population, a reaction of shock and disbelief,
and a determination by the victim community not
to be intimidated by the atrocity.

The attacks came during the morning rush hour,
when militants associated with Al-Qaeda exploded
four bombs. Three of them went off on London
Underground trains in quick succession. A fourth
went off an hour later on a double-decker bus in
Tavistock Square. All four of the suicide bombers
died as they killed fifty-two innocent rush hour
travellers. About 700 people were injured as well.

This incident was the worst and deadliest act of terrorism to take place in the United Kingdom since the bombing of Pan Am Flight 103 over Lockerbie in 1988. It was the worst bombing in London since the Second World War. The motive of the bombers was opposition to the British government's support of Saudi Arabia and to its involvement in the Iraq War. The suicide bombers were prompted in their actions by the teachings of Osama bin Laden.

At 8.50 am, the three bombs being carried on the London Underground exploded within fifty seconds of each other. The first bomb went off on an eastbound Circle Line train travelling between Liverpool Street and Aldgate. The train had left King's Cross St Pancras eight minutes earlier. At the moment of the explosion, the train's third carriage was 90 metres into the tunnel from Liverpool Street. The second bomb exploded in the second carriage of a westbound Circle Line train which had just left Edgware Road and was heading towards Paddington. This train too had left King's Cross about eight minutes earlier. The third bomb exploded on a southbound Piccadilly Line train, travelling between King's Cross St Pancras and Russell Square. The bomb went of about a minute after the train left King's Cross, and it had only travelled 450 metres.

In the initial chaos, it was unclear what had happened, not least because the explosions had happened in tunnels and therefore were difficult to reach. But it was also because survivors emerged at the stations on each side of the explosion, giving an impression that there was an incident at each station. At first it was thought that there had been six explosions; the later bomb on the bus brought the reported total to seven. The Circle Line is a cut-and-cover tunnel, only seven metres below the surface; it has two tracks and so is fairly wide. The force of the explosions on this line was able to spread, reducing their destructive effect. But the Piccadilly Line is a deep, bored tunnel up to thirty metres underground, with narrow, single-track tubes only 3.6m wide. This confined space reflected and concentrated the force of the blast.

The final bomb went off at 9.47 am, on a No 30 bus in Tavistock Square, on its way from Marble Arch to Hackney Wick. The bus had travelled through the King's Cross area. It left Marble Arch at 9 am and arrived at Euston station at 9.35, where crowds of people had been evacuated from the tube and were boarding buses instead. The explosion tore the roof off the bus and destroyed the back of the bus. Most of the people at the front of the upper deck survived. By chance the explosion happened close to the British Medical Association building in Upper Woburn Place and several doctors in the building were able to provide emergency medical aid. Two injured passengers were able to report seeing a man explode in the bus and that man was later identified as Hasib Hussain. He was later identified on CCTV footage as leaving Boots on King's Cross station at 9 am. So, the common factor in all the bombings was King's Cross. The logical explanation is that the bombers set off as a group, travelled to King's Cross and then boarded their different trains from there; the one puzzle is why one member of the suicide team boarded a bus, not a train, and why his detonation was half an hour later than everyone else's. The terrible damage caused to the victims' bodies led to a long delay in reporting the death toll from the bombing. Because of the fragmentation, it was not immediately obvious how many bodies there were.

The suicide bombers were picked up by CCTV at 7.21 am, approaching and entering Luton station. The four bombers were together as a group: Hasib Hussain, Germaine Lindsay, Mohammed Sidique Khan and Shehzad Tanweer. Mohammed Sidique Khan was thirty years old and of Pakistani descent. He lived at Beeston in Leeds with his wife and child, and worked as a learning mentor at a primary school. It was ironic that he should have worked in a caring profession and yet travelled to London to kill seven total strangers. Shehzad Tanweer was twenty-two years old and also of Pakistani descent. He lived in Leeds, was single, living with his parents; he worked in a fish-and-chip shop. He was responsible for killing eight people.

Germaine Lindsay was nineteen years old and had been born in Jamaica. He lived in Aylesbury with his young son and his pregnant wife. He killed twenty-seven people, including himself. Hasib Hussain was eighteen years old and of Pakistani descent. He lived in Leeds with his brother and sister-in-law. He killed fourteen people including himself.

The Home Secretary, Charles Clarke, explained that the four men had no previous record, were unknown to the authorities. Three of them had come from Leeds. On the day of the attacks, all four of them had travelled to Luton by car, and then to London by train. They were picked up CCTV at Luton at 7.21, and then arriving at King's Cross station at 8.30.

Two of the bombers made statements on videotape describing their motives in becoming what they called 'soldiers' and what everyone else called 'terrorists'. A videotape broadcast by Al

Jazeera on 1 September 2005 showed Mohammed
Sidique Khan. He said:

> *I and thousands like me are forsaking everything for*
> *what we believe. Our drive and motivation doesn't*
> *come from tangible commodities that this world has to*
> *offer. Our religion is Islam, obedience to the one true*
> *God and following the footsteps of the final prophet*
> *messenger. Your democratically elected governments*
> *continuously perpetuate atrocities against my people all*
> *over the world. And your support of them makes you*
> *directly responsible, just as I am directly responsible*
> *for protecting and avenging my Muslim brothers and*
> *sisters. Until we feel security you will be our targets and*
> *until you stop the bombing, gassing, imprisonment and*
> *torture of my people we will not stop this fight. We are*
> *at war and I am a soldier. Now you too will taste the*
> *reality of this situation…*

On 6 July 2006, Al Jazeera broadcast a videotape
made by Shehzad Tanweer. According to him, the
non-Muslims of Britain deserve such attacks because
they voted for a government that continued 'to
oppress our mothers, children, brothers and sisters
in Palestine, Afghanistan, Iraq and Chechnya.' The
addition of Chechnya to this list was odd, in that

that territory was being oppressed by Russia, not by the West. It also implies that the bombs were somehow designed to distinguish between Muslims and non-Muslims, and also to distinguish between those who voted for the current government and those who voted against it. Not all British voters vote for the government of the day, so not all should be held accountable for the government's actions. The political rationale Tanweer offered, no doubt dictated by Al-Qaeda advisers, was entirely bogus; the attacks were indiscriminate, which is what made them so particularly abhorrent and meaningless.

Among other things that were confused at the onset of the bombings was the nature of the bombs themselves. Forensic experts initially thought military grade plastic explosives had been used. As the explosions, on the trains at least, were more or less simultaneous, it was assumed synchronised timed detonators were used. But these assumptions changed as more information became available. The bombs were not plastic explosives at all but home-made organic peroxide-based devices. And there were no timing devices. Presumably the bombers synchronised their watches and agreed beforehand when they would detonate. The later bomb on the bus required some other explanation.

These were the first suicide bombings in Western Europe. The French Interior Minister, Nicolas Sarkozy (later to become French President), astonished the British Home Office when he said at a press briefing that one of the named bombers had been described the previous year at an Anglo-French security meeting as an asset of British intelligence. The Home Secretary, Charles Clarke, commented that this was 'not my recollection, to say the least'. Another strange claim came from the one-time head of the CIA's anti-terrorism centre. He told a Guardian journalist that two unexploded bombs had been recovered as well as mechanical timing devices; this claim was rejected by the British police.

The original intention of the bombers appears to have been to have four simultaneous explosions on the Underground, forming a cross of fire to north, south, east and west of King's Cross. One of the bombers, perhaps setting off a little later, was turned away from the Underground because explosions had already begun. Unable to take the Undergound, he got on a bus instead. Probably he intended originally to take the Northern Line. The Underground bombs exploded when trains were passing, so that two trains would be affected, rather than just one. It was this feature of the explosions that led to the first thought that suicide bombers were involved, rather than parcel bombs left under seats with timing devices.

In the wake of the bombings, the police raided six properties in Leeds on 12 July. They also raided a property in Aylesbury. A significant amount of explosive material was found during the Leeds raids and in Shehzad Tanweer's car, left at Luton station; these explosives were detonated in controlled explosions. There was speculation that the bombers had links with an Islamist cell in Luton that was broken up in August 2004. The discovery of that cell followed the arrest of Muhammed Naeem Noor Khan in Lahore, Pakistan. His computer was said to contain plans for attacks on Underground trains in London, as well as for attacks on financial buildings in New York and Washington. The cell was under surveillance, but the surveillance operation was spoilt by an American newspaper publishing his name on 2 August 2004. This forced British police to make arrests before they had finished their investigation. The US Homeland Security Secretary, Tom Ridge, later apologised for giving the name to the US press. When the Luton cell was broken up, one member, Mohammad Sidique Khan, was scrutinised by MI5, and they decided he posed no significant threat.

In March 2007, three people were arrested in connection with the 7/7 bombings. Two were at Manchester Airport attempting to board a plane for Pakistan. The third was arrested in the Beeston area of Leeds, at a house where one of the suicide bombers had lived. Two months later the police arrested four more people, on charges of commissioning, preparing or instigating acts of terrorism. One of them was Hasina Patel, the widow of the 7/7 ringleader Mohammed Sidique Khan. Three of those arrested were released, but one was charged with possessing an Al-Qaeda training manual. Possession of a document containing information likely to be useful to a person committing or preparing an act of terrorism is a serious offence, carrying a maximum sentence of ten years in prison.

In May 2006, Sheikh Abdullah el-Faisal was deported to Jamaica, his country of origin, from Britain. He had reached the parole date of his prison sentence. He had been found guilty three years before of inciting people to murder Jews, Americans and Hindus, and of using threatening words to stir up racial hatred. In 2006, John Reid MP alleged in the Commons that Sheikh Abdullah el-Faisal had been a significant influence on the Jamaican-born Briton Germaine Lindsay, one of the 7/7 bombers.

The Guardian reported that the police had investigated Mohammed Sidique Khan as a potential terrorist suspect twice in 2005. This is somewhat at variance with the official line that there was no warning or prior intelligence regarding the bombings, and so is some of the foreign press coverage of the situation developing in Britain. In the wake of the 2004 Madrid train bombings, the Syrian-born cleric Sheik Omar Bakri Muhammad gave a warning that 'a very well-organised' group based in London, which he referred to as 'Al-Qaeda Europe', was 'on the verge of launching a big operation'. In December 2004, Bakri warned that if Western governments did not change their policies, Muslims would give them 'a 9/11, day after day after day'. In November 2004 there was a posting on the Newsweek website revealing that US authorities had evidence that terrorists were planning an attack in London. The article explicitly said that 'fears of terror attacks have prompted FBI agents based in the US Embassy in London to avoid travelling on London's popular underground railway or tube system.' Did the British authorities really have no idea that there was going to be an Islamist attack on the London tube system?

Somebody Yelled 'Get the Gun!'
THE TUCSON ASSASSINATION ATTEMPT (2011)

US Congresswoman Gabrielle Giffords, one of the rising stars of the Democratic Party, was the target in an assassination attempt on 8 January 2011. She was in Tucson, Arizona, meeting the electorate at a Safeway supermarket in her usual informal way, without any security.

A young white man opened fire, shooting her at point blank range. He fired just one shot at her, hitting her in the temple. It must have looked like a fatal shot. The gunman then turned and shot anyone and everyone near him. He shot twenty people, of whom six were killed outright. Among the dead were a nine-year-old girl, Christina Green, a judge and one of Miss Giffords' aides.

The gunman, alleged to be twenty-two-year-old Jared Loughner, ran out of ammunition and paused to reload. A woman bystander heroically snatched the new magazine as he tried to reload. She was sixty-one-year-old Patricia Maisch. She said later,

'The woman next to me was shot and I was expecting to be next. Then two men knocked him over and somebody yelled "Get the gun!" so I knelt up. He reached into his pocket and brought out a magazine. A third man came up and grabbed him. He dropped the magazine and I was able to pick it up and secure it. The three men were on him but his legs were flailing, so I knelt on his ankles. He didn't look angry, just a dead face – nothing.' One of those three men holding Loughner down was seventy-four-year-old Colonel Bill Badger. He was slightly injured by a bullet grazing the back of his head. 'I grabbed him round the throat,' the colonel said.

Then law enforcement officers reached him and took the suspect into custody.

Gabrielle Giffords was rushed to hospital for surgery to remove bone fragments from her brain and relieve any pressure to the brain. The surgeons were relieved to find that the bullet had passed through only one hemisphere of the brain, not both. This greatly improved Miss Giffords' chances of recovery with minimal brain damage. In fact within a few hours of surgery she was responding to simple commands and the surgeons were cautiously optimistic about her chances of recovery.

Initially the police suspected a second man of

involvement, perhaps of driving him to the scene of the shootings. But within twenty-four hours the man was cleared of suspicion. Jared Loughner, the man accused of the multiple murders, appeared in court charged with the attempted assassination of Gabrielle Giffords. He wore a khaki uniform and a white T-shirt; his hands and waist were tied by a chain. He had a bruise to his left eye and a lump on the top of his shaven head. Prosecutors described him as 'a danger to the community'. Jared Loughner smiled nervously as he was told he could face multiple death sentences for the murders. The magistrate, Lawrence Anderson, told him he had been charged with five felonies, the attempted assassination of Gabrielle Giffords, the first degree murders of John Roll, a sixty-three-year-old Arizona judge, and Gabriel Zimmerman, a thirty-year-old aide of Miss Gifford, and the attempted murders of two other congressional aides. The two alleged murders could carry the death penalty as a maximum sentence. Mr Loughner agreed that he understood the proceedings.

Mr Loughner was supported by Judy Clarke, a lawyer appointed for him and who specialises in cases that may carry the death sentence. Miss Clarke previously defended the Oklahoma bomber, Timothy McVeigh.

The FBI discovered a signed note in a safe in Mr Loughner's home. It read 'I planned ahead', and referred specifically to Giffords. In filing the document with the court, the FBI alleged that the shootings were premeditated.

The prosecutor, Wallace Kleindiest, argued that Mr Loughner was a danger to the community and that there was a risk of flight, given the severe penalties he might face if convicted. The magistrate accepted this argument, ruling that Mr Loughner should be detained until further order. A preliminary hearing was set for 24 January, but further charges may be brought from the state of Arizona; the suspect could also be charged with domestic terrorism.

Meanwhile, investigators continued to explore what may have been in the suspect's mind in the weeks leading up to the attack. In messages left on the Internet, Jared Loughner presented himself as a social outcast with nihilistic beliefs and a fixation with grammar. At a public meeting with Gabrielle Giffords three years before the shooting, he put the question to her, 'What is government if words have no meaning?' Miss Giffords was stuck for an answer. One commentator observed that Mr Loughner's language and mindset resemble those of David Wynn Miller, a retired welder and political activist who believes that the US government uses grammar to control people's minds. David Miller has invented his own form of grammar called 'truth language' which he alleges sets people free of government. Mr Miller dissociated himself from the shootings, which appalled him, but agreed with Loughner's pre-shooting statement that 'the government is implying mind control and brainwash[ing] on the people by controlling grammar'. Mr Miller thought Mr Loughner might have visited his website, but considered him disturbed.

FBI agents explored other aspects of Mr Loughner's mindset. He apparently believed that the NASA space shuttle missions were faked. Possibly this is connected with the fact that Miss Giffords' husband, Mark Kelly, was a pilot on some of these missions.

The attempted assassination of Gabrielle Giffords, a moderate Democrat, sparked a bitter nationwide debate about the increasingly violent tone of political discourse since Mr Obama's election. In the aftermath of the shootings, there was a great deal of soul-searching about the inflammatory and combative tone of much of American political debate. Ironically, given Jared Loughner's obsession, the focus has been on the kind of language, the kind of political rhetoric and imagery used by politicians, which might be raising the risk of violence of this kind.

There was a particular focus on the style of some recent Republican rhetoric coming from the direction of Sarah Palin. Her mid-term campaign included a graphic that showed a map of America with the crosshairs of a gunsight marking the Democratic congressional district seats that Republicans should target. The visual language of gunfire used here has been criticised. Republicans have been incensed at what they see as an unfair attempt to blame Sarah Palin for the assassination attempt on a Democratic politician. Miss Palin herself was quick to retaliate. 'Acts of monstrous criminality stand on their own, not with maps of swing districts used by both sides of the aisle.' She attacked the journalists and commentators who had criticised her, using the phrase 'blood libel'.

But those drawing attention to the graphic did so not because it came from the Republicans but because it is symptomatic of the over-colourful and over-heated rhetoric of political debate in America at the moment. There has been a call for more restrained and moderate language in American politics in the future, on all sides.

In the wake of the shootings, President Obama

visited Tucson to pay tribute to the victims and in doing so made an emotional appeal for restraint.

At a time when our discourse has become so sharply polarised – at a time when we are far too eager to lay the blame for all that ails the world at the feet of those who think differently than we do – it is important to make sure that we are talking to each other in a way that heals, not a way that wounds. What we can't do is use this tragedy as one more occasion to turn on one another. Let us use this occasion to expand our moral imaginations, to listen to each other more carefully, to sharpen our instincts for empathy and remind ourselves of all the ways our hopes and dreams are bound together.

President Obama went on to pay tribute individually to each of the civic-minded people of Tucson who were killed. They had been 'fulfilling a central tenet of our democracy envisioned by our founders – representatives of the people answering to their constituents. Our hearts are broken by their sudden passing. Our hearts are full of hope and thanks for the thirteen Americans who survived the shooting.'

The President spoke about Gabrielle Giffords, the indomitable forty-year-old Democratic congresswoman who had been holding a meet-and-greet event with constituents when she was shot. Before the ceremony Mr and Mrs Obama had visited the nearby hospital where she was recovering. The crowd at the McKale Centre arena gave Mr Obama a standing ovation when he revealed that Ms Giffords had opened her eyes for the first time since undergoing brain surgery.